GREAT DECISIONS

Editorial Advisory Committee

CHAIRMAN

David B.H. Denoon
Professor of Politics and Economics
New York University

Barbara Crossette
Specialist on the UN
and South-Southeast Asia

Michael Doyle
Harold Brown Professor
of International Affairs,
Law and Political Science;
University Professor
Columbia University

Christine E. Lucas
Chief of Operations
Leadership Florida, Tallahassee

Ponchitta A. Pierce
Magazine Writer, Television Host
and Producer, FPA Director

Lawrence G. Potter
Director of Research and Publications of
The Gulf/2000 Project
Adjunct Associate Professor of
International Affairs, Columbia University

Thomas G. Weiss
Presidential Professor
of Political Science
The CUNY Graduate Center

Karen M. Rohan
FPA Editor in Chief,
Ex officio

Foreign Policy Association

Dame Jillian Sackler
Chairman of the Board of Directors

Noel V. Lateef
President and CEO

EDITOR IN CHIEF
Karen M. Rohan

ASSISTANT EDITOR
Matthew Barbari

EDITORIAL CONSULTANTS
Ann R. Monjo
Lillian Marx

PHOTO EDITOR
Cynthia Carris Alonso

MAPS
Robert Cronan
Lucidity Information Design, LLC

EDITORIAL INTERN
Madeline C. Hone

A Centennial Message

Accepting the Nobel Peace Prize for his mediation of the Russo-Japanese War, Theodore Roosevelt issued a magisterial challenge to "those great powers honestly bent on peace." He urged them to accede to a League of Peace, which would "keep the peace among themselves and prevent, by force if necessary, its being broken by others."

In the ensuing decade, Woodrow Wilson would imagine a world in which "conquest and aggrandizement" were relegated to the dustbin of history. Wilson advocated for a "great association of nations" that would offer "mutual guarantees of political independence and territorial integrity to great and small states alike."

The founders of the Foreign Policy Association resolved on Armistice Day 1918 to do their part to help shape a new world order—one in which the scourge of war would be banished from the face of the earth. Speaking to the Foreign Policy Association in 1944, President Franklin Delano Roosevelt would set out his vision for the United Nations:

> *Peace, like war, can succeed only where there is a will to enforce it and where there is available power to enforce it. The Council of the United Nations must have the power to act quickly and decisively to keep the peace, by force if necessary. A policeman would not be a very effective policeman if, when he saw a felon break into a house, he had to go the town hall and call a town meeting to issue a warrant before the felon could be arrested....Now, it's obvious that we cannot attain our great objectives by ourselves. Never again, after cooperating with other nations in a world war to save our way of life, can we wash our hands of maintaining the peace for which we fought.*

Waging peace requires unprecedented strength and a big heart. Listen to this exhortation:

> *It's impossible,* said Pride.
> *It's risky,* said Experience.
> *It's pointless,* said Reason.
> *Give it a try,* whispered the Heart.

Give it a try we must. Andrew Carnegie implored: "Whoso wants to share the heroism of battle, let him join the fight against ignorance and disease and the mad idea that war is necessary." Preventing deadly conflict is one of the overarching challenges of our times. Yet, in an extraordinary keynote address at the centennial celebration of the Foreign Policy Association in New York City, Ambassador William J. vanden Heuvel observed:

> *There is so little talk of peace in our society today. Even at the United Nations, where the prevention of war is a primary mission, there is a sense of fatalism as valiant efforts are reduced to failure. The Syrian civil war is an example. The Great Powers could stop it, but they do not.*

Ancient countries are destroyed. Any pretense of civilization is ravaged. Six hundred thousand people have been killed—600,000 people have been killed—and there is hardly anyone who can tell us what the war is about. It has produced refugees and displaced populations that are numbered in the millions, and whose attempted migration to Western Europe undermines the governments of nations that have been our principal allies.

For Ambassador vanden Heuvel, endless war presents the greatest threat to democracy.

The United Nations estimates that 80 percent of its humanitarian funding needs are currently driven by conflict. The United Nations World Food Program has concluded that conflict causes 60 percent of life-threatening hunger. The number of displaced persons due to conflict or natural disaster is estimated at 65 million according to the International Rescue Committee, half of whom are children. Indeed, 24 people are forced from their homes by conflict or natural disaster every minute.

The genesis of the United Nations and its continuing vital role gives credence to what the anthropologist, Robert Boyd, describes as "cumulative cultural evolution." Boyd argues: "We humans would not be an exceptional species if we did not adapt culturally." Among our most important cultural traits is the ability to cooperate across diverse backgrounds. From what we know of human fallibility, there has never been a greater need for intensive cooperation than in the nuclear age. An inadvertent, unforced error, could set off a train of events that could destroy civilization as we know it. A culture of global cooperation for peace and conflict prevention is our best hope.

The triumph of hope over history? Perhaps. But progress is rooted in idealism as well as in realism. The genius of the leaders who sought to overcome the recurring folly of war was their peculiarly American, some might say messianic, boldness. Indeed, from a geopolitical perspective, Wilson and the Roosevelts are authentically revolutionary figures. Their willingness to transcend nationalism was steeped in the benefits they rightly perceived from disseminating democratic values and from preserving world peace.

Dr. David A. Hamburg, who chaired the landmark Carnegie Commission on the Prevention of Deadly Conflict, has observed:

The remarkable improvements in the human condition that have occurred during our lifetime suggest that prevention of mass violence is also within reach in this century. *We recognize that our species is a dangerous one, in all likelihood inheriting behavioral inclinations that predispose it to damaging others. Yet we have also seen the evolution of capacities for conflict resolution; for mutual accommodation; and for cooperation beyond prior experience in seeking peace, shared prosperity, and recognition of our common humanity.*

On this the hundredth anniversary of the end of the Great War and of the founding of our old and honorable Association, we not only cling to hope but we rededicate ourselves to education for peace.

Noel V. Lateef

Noel V. Lateef
President and Chief Executive Officer
Foreign Policy Association

GREAT DECISIONS 2019

About the cover

An aerial photo shows a boat carrying migrants stranded in the Strait of Gibraltar before being rescued by the Spanish Guardia Civil and the Salvamento Maritimo sea search and rescue agency. That day, September 8, 2018, 157 migrants were rescued.

Marcos Moreno/AFP/Getty Images

GREAT DECISIONS IS A TRADEMARK OF THE FOREIGN POLICY ASSOCIATION.

© COPYRIGHT 2019 BY FOREIGN POLICY ASSOCIATION, INC., 470 PARK AVENUE SOUTH, NEW YORK, NEW YORK 10016.

All rights reserved.

No part of this book may be reproduced in any form, or by any means, without permission in writing from the publisher.

PRINTED IN THE UNITED STATES OF AMERICA BY DARTMOUTH PRINTING COMPANY, HANOVER, NH.

LIBRARY OF CONGRESS CONTROL NUMBER:
2018965242

ISBN: 978-0-87124-264-8

Researched as of November 26, 2018.

The authors are responsible for factual accuracy and for the views expressed.

FPA itself takes no position on issues of U.S. foreign policy.

The Eni supercomputer: a combination of expertise and computing power.

At Eni's Green Data Center, HPC4 is fully operational. It is one of the world's most powerful supercomputers, capable of performing up to 22.4 million billion mathematical operations per second when combined with existing operational systems. Thanks to the skills of our people and Eni's proprietary algorithms, it makes our day-to-day activities safer, faster and more efficient.

The energy to see
and the energy to do.

American foreign policy in 2019: a framework for analysis

by Robert P. Haffa, Jr.

Each year, our Great Decisions group meeting in Naples, Florida, anxiously awaits the list of topics selected by the Foreign Policy Association (FPA) for discussion. Those subjects structure our deliberations for the next several weeks, and participants are always looking ahead to see where—or to what part of the world—this year's book will take us. Because our seminar rotates discussion leaders each week, several members will quickly volunteer to introduce some of the topics perceived by them to be the most interesting—often owing to personal business, government or travel experience. That's all to the good, and individual insights always add value to our roundtable discussions, along with the recommended readings and attendant videos.

However, though this topic-by-topic approach frequently concentrates on the "leaves" of the subject, it illuminates to a lesser degree the "trees" surrounding the issues, while the "forest" representing the policy environment remains shrouded in shadow. In a way, I am reminded of the times I spent teaching political science at the Air Force Academy. Cadets were so concentrated on the course requirements at hand (i.e., those affecting their grades), they were astonished to discover a relationship among their political science classes in terms of theories of international politics, case studies in American foreign policy decisionmaking, area studies and defense policy. Therefore, as our Great Decisions group delves into specific issues, we often try to step back to consider what American foreign policymakers might do to achieve objectives in a certain issue area, and to deliberate on how policies in a region or on a subject of importance might prompt unforeseen or undesirable consequences elsewhere.

Therefore, to assist our discussions this year, I am proposing a "framework for analysis" within which to reference the topics presented by the FPA for 2019. The purpose of this framework is to offer a larger context for discussion, while providing some benchmarks, or guideposts, suggesting emerging or future paths of American foreign policy. Strategic and long-range planners in business and government are familiar with building hypothetical scenarios designed to reveal commonalities across an array of possible outcomes. Here, we want to use this framework to rise above focusing on a single state, region or issue, and to consider instead how larger or less evident forces in the international political system may affect more narrow foreign policy choices and outputs.

A framework for analysis is an oft-used tool in political science to simplify what is a chaotic and anarchic international environment. The *level* of analysis is an important entering argument. Should we attempt to examine the issue at hand based on the actions and attitudes of *individual* policymakers? If we focus on "summit" diplomacy, for instance the recent meetings between U.S. President Donald Trump (2017–present) and North Korean leader Kim Jong Un (2011–present), Russian President Vladimir Putin (2000–08, 2012–present) and Chinese President Xi Jinping (2013–present), the personal views and agendas of those principals become very important. But describing and explaining North Korean-U.S. or Russian-U.S. foreign relations also profits from understanding historical behavior at the *state* level. How have these (or other) states interacted previously when confronted with similar situations? Finally, insight into interaction on the level of the *system* is useful, as foreign policies chosen by individuals or states may be a reaction to an external environment in which multilateral interests and balance-of-power politics come into play. As we approach these 2019 topics, we want to be mindful of the influence of individual, state (and non-state) and system interactions on our great decisionmaking.

What might be a good organizing device to frame our Great Decisions discussions? There are plenty from which to choose. In his classic 1967 textbook *International Politics,* K.J. Holsti proposed some key concepts: the *system* in which state action occurs, the foreign policy *outputs* or outcomes, factors *explaining* those decisions, and resulting *patterns* of conflict and cooperation of actors. Such a conceptual framework enables a political scientist to set about the tasks of description, explanation and prescription in an orderly and productive manner.

In his work examining American foreign policy, Wil-

ROBERT P. HAFFA, JR., *is a member of the Board of Directors of the Naples Council on World Affairs. He also works as an adjunct faculty member of the government department of Johns Hopkins University in Washington, DC. Dr. Haffa holds a B.S. in international affairs from the U.S. Air Force Academy, an M.A. in political science from Georgetown University, and a Ph.D. in political science from the Massachusetts Institute of Technology.*

liam O. Chittick suggests a set of foreign policy values—community, security and economic—as a framework for analysis. This organizing device, based primarily on survey responses to questions about ranking American foreign policy objectives, suggests that these three "bins" provide a value-oriented guide to U.S. priorities overseas. To apply this framework to some contemporary foreign policy issues: Strengthening international institutions or improving the global climate are *community* objectives; maintaining U.S. military primacy and combatting international terrorism are *security* goals; and controlling and reducing illegal immigration and reducing the U.S. trade deficit with foreign countries are principally *prosperity* values. How should we prioritize these objectives in specific cases? That there is some overlap among issues within these categories emphasizes the importance of integrating the framework so that a singly targeted objective is not allowed to override considerations of the other two. Applying each of the components to a foreign policy issue area allows the decisionmaker to weigh the effects of a declared or actionable policy across a range of plausible outcomes.

Another framework to help us think about contemporary issues in foreign policy asks, "Which world are we living in?" The July/August 2018 issue of *Foreign Affairs* suggested a half-dozen answers to this question. Historians and political scientists often employ a similar device by asking, "What year is it?" Is the present economic situation similar to that of 1929, 1980 or 2008? Does the geopolitical balance of power resemble 1940? 1919? 1848? *New York Times* columnist Thomas Friedman thinks we are in a time unlike any other. He contends we are transitioning from an *interconnected* to an *interdependent* world—and political parties across the globe are finding it hard to keep up. The *Foreign Affairs* authors develop contrasting narratives of six different worlds, characterized by: great power rivalry; a resilient liberal international order; tribalism and nationalism; class struggle; the digital revolution; and climate change. Combining the ingredients of these different worlds could serve as a useful recipe for analyzing contemporary American foreign policy.

Building on these varied approaches, here's what I suggest might act as a useful framework for analysis as we approach this year's Great Decisions topics. First, I'll list and describe each component of the framework. At the end of this introductory piece, I'll briefly suggest how some of them might be applied to the issues you will discover as you turn the pages of ***GREAT DECISIONS 2019.***

- The return of great power confrontation
- The choice of foreign policy instruments in the U.S.'s grand strategy
- The state of the liberal international order
- The process of making American foreign policy
- The return of great power competition

The U.S. does not issue a single, formal document outlining its foreign policy, but each new administration does publish an unclassified National Security Strategy and a National Defense Strategy. These documents tend to enumerate objectives, rather than describe the means or strategies to achieve these ends with specific resources. Nevertheless, they offer us a reasonable portrayal of the international environment as viewed from the perspective of U.S. national security. Both of the documents recently issued under the Trump administration are good references for the first component in our framework for analysis: the rise of great power competition.

As appraisals of the threats to the U.S.'s global interests go, these documents are straightforward. "The central challenge to U.S. prosperity and security," according to the National Defense Strategy, "is the *reemergence of long-term, strategic competition*" (emphasis in original) with the would-be great powers of Russia and China. The National Security Strategy asserts that Russia and China seek to challenge U.S. power, influence and interests by making economies "less free and less fair," and by expanding their military capabilities. Concurrently, they strive to "control information and data to repress their societies and expand their influence." The Defense Strategy expresses concern that China seeks to achieve "Indo-Pacific regional hegemony in the near-term" and to replace the U.S. as the guarantor of the international order in the future. Russia, according to this assessment, wishes to restore the regional hegemony it achieved during the Cold War (1947–91) days within its former empire. Russia is attempting to do this by weakening the North Atlantic Treaty Organization (NATO), and by using emerging technologies to "discredit and subvert democratic processes in Georgia, Crimea and eastern Ukraine." These goals are buttressed by irregular warfare troops and tactics on the ground, and underwritten by an expanding nuclear force and doctrine.

A strategic competition among great powers is not a new element in American foreign policy. Indeed, there are well-supported arguments that it was the "unipolar moment"—the post-Cold War period in which the U.S. appeared without equal—that was the anomaly in international relations. Challenges to a Pax Americana were sure to rise. Now, analysts of the contemporary international scene are troubled by the thought that American foreign policy may have become

! Before you read, download the companion **Glossary** that includes definitions, a guide to acronyms and abbreviations used in the article, and other material. Go to **www.greatdecisions.org** and select a topic in the Resources section on the right-hand side of the page.

complacent in the interim, as the U.S. appears to have retreated from overseas diplomatic and defense commitments. Declaratory documents such as those referenced here, and policies implemented in support of them, seek to allay those concerns.

This great power competition, as in the Cold War, is not purely military. Foreign policy scholars and practitioners point to the use by Russia and China of "political warfare"—the coercive use of mainly nonmilitary instruments to alter adversary behavior. In a 2018 monograph issued by the Center for Strategic and Budgetary Assessments, the authors posit that Russia and China see political warfare as a "standard instrument of statecraft," having spent years refining this instrument not only to preserve domestic control but also to challenge their foreign rivals. This approach is attractive to these revisionist actors from several perspectives: It is less costly and less likely to escalate; it is only moderately ambitious in that its methods involve sowing doubt, creating confusion, undermining trust and imposing costs; and it leverages the digital revolution to flood audiences, foreign and domestic, with false information. As in the case of countering opposing military buildups, the first task for the American foreign policy establishment regarding political warfare is to recognize the problem. Only then can remedial action, such as focusing intelligence collection and streamlining organizational responses to these information attacks, be taken.

Finally, as we consider great power competition as an important element of our framework for analysis, we should also be mindful of the proposition that authoritarian governments may not be as disruptive as we fear. They may be destabilized internally by the rise of an influential middle class or other economic or political forces. Robert Kaplan suggests that Russian and Chinese domestic stability cannot be taken for granted, and may force these actors to place more of their emphasis on quashing internal dissent rather than expanding their regional influence. Perhaps that will occur. For now, however, the U.S. must prepare for a long-term strategic competition.

The choice of foreign policy instruments in U.S. grand strategy

As we face myriad foreign policy challenges in 2019, what should the U.S.' "grand strategy" be? The academic dean of the subject, John Lewis Gaddis, defines grand strategy as aligning "potentially unlimited aspirations with necessarily limited capabilities"—the ultimate matching of objectives and resources. But Gaddis also argues that, as perceptions of resources change, strategies may be altered while the objective remains constant. For example, during the Cold War, the goal of containing the Soviet Union was adopted by succeeding administrations, but the means to this end—the wielding of the instruments of foreign policy—varied considerably.

The consensus on containment as an objective vanished with victory in the Cold War, and academics and politicians deliberated on the meaning of the unipolar moment, the "end of history" and the new world order. This strategic debate was characterized by disagreement over which grand strategy could most effectively guide post-Cold War American foreign policy. Since that time, given the declaratory and practiced policies of all subsequent administrations, the choices appear to have narrowed to three: Liberal internationalism, coupled with cooperative security, is defined as *primacy*; neo-isolationism, combined with offshore balancing, is characterized as *restraint;* and *selective engagement* occupies a middle ground between these two, allowing its practitioners to be more flexible and pragmatic in exercising U.S. power.

Most students of U.S. grand strategy conclude that the objective of *primacy*—maintaining leadership of the liberal international order—has guided foreign policy for the last two decades. But, like containment during the Cold War, the goal of primacy has been characterized by both continuity and change, with newly elected administrations emphasizing different elements of national power in its pursuit. Hal Brands, a professor at the Johns Hopkins School of Advanced International Studies, notes that successive administrations have declared the purpose of maintaining U.S. leadership, but switched courses of action "in light of changing global circumstances and the painful lessons of the previous administration." Emphasis is placed on differing instruments of power depending on the perceived ability of the U.S. to marshal needed resources in pursuit of objectives. Each new administration chooses from a menu of military, economic, diplomatic and information capabilities, and invests in those instruments accordingly.

What are the arguments for continuing the grand strategy of primacy, and what are the implications of such a strategy? Those supporting a policy of primacy are particularly concerned with great power rivalry and see the military instrument as central to victory in this long-term competition. They focus on the rise of Chinese conventional power along the Pacific Rim, Russia's encroachment into the former Soviet states in Eastern Europe, and the nuclear potential of Iran in the Middle East and of North Korea in Northeast Asia. Proponents of primacy call for the U.S. to develop new military competitive advantages, and to do so more quickly than our emerging adversaries. They also champion the forceful use of the other instruments of foreign policy: economic sanctions, information warfare and aggressive diplomacy in international fora.

Critics of primacy as a grand strategy fear that it will lead the U.S. into costly and unnecessary wars. They describe seeking primacy as costly, wasteful and self-defeating, as it leads to countervailing behavior by competitors, free riding by allies and widespread anti-Americanism. Rather than a status quo policy aimed at preserving U.S. leadership in the international political system, primacy appears to its domestic opponents as a strategy that leads to unnecessarily high defense spending and counterproductive foreign wars.

Opponents of a primacy-oriented grand strategy often advocate for one of *restraint*, or neo-isolationism. According to this view, the U.S. can no longer afford to maintain world order, and instead should devote its attention and scarce resources to nation-building at home. They would agree with public opinion polls ranking "defending our allies' security" near the bottom of U.S. foreign policy priorities. Their principal lament is that American foreign policy has become too militarized, and they maintain that the U.S. can achieve most of its goals abroad by emphasizing other instruments of national power.

Those who oppose a grand strategy of restraint see it as a recipe for the loss of U.S. influence abroad and, with it, diminished U.S. security and prosperity. In their view, an isolated U.S. will embolden our competition, spawn anti-American resentment, weaken U.S. economic leadership, and encourage destabilizing nuclear weapons proliferation. Any savings in the defense budget resulting from restraint will be offset by a loss of economic, diplomatic and informational power.

Building on the concerns of emerging great power competition, a grand strategy of *selective engagement*, or "offshore balancing," narrows the U.S. world view. It calls for military engagement abroad, but only when that military power can be useful in deterring great power conflict. Thus, selective engagement seeks a middle course between an isolated, retrenching U.S. and one with the power and motivation to act as the world's sheriff. Selectively engaging preserves the status quo, withdraws U.S. military commitments from regions likely to spiral out of control and emphasizes diplomatic overtures, economic benefits and information campaigns to encourage U.S. allies to bear a greater share of the burden in areas of non-vital interest.

Critics of selective engagement attack the grand strategy from both sides. Champions of primacy fear that such a strategic choice lacks the commitment to principles and values that characterizes American foreign policy, and that it fails to differentiate between good and evil. By ignoring less-than-vital interests, we encourage regional mischief-making, tolerate peripheral wars detrimental to the international order and "green light" authoritarian violations of human rights. From the restraint perspective, neo-isolationists argue that too much emphasis on the military instrument in great power relations risks future great power wars.

Past U.S. administrations have blended their grand strategies to fit the international circumstances as they saw them—and adjusted accordingly. Yet, as Hal Brands suggests, every presidential administration since 1989 has incorporated a bipartisan commitment to "sustaining U.S. leadership and primacy, and the liberal international order that American power underpins." Yes, there were changes in emphasis, particularly regarding the use of the military. The Bill Clinton administration (1993–2001) attempted to use economic incentives to encourage democratic reforms overseas, and hesitantly considered the use of force. President George W. Bush (2001–09) advocated coercive democratization as a solution to Middle Eastern terrorism. President Barack Obama (2009–17), elected in part to conclude U.S. wars in the Middle East, sought to retrench forces from large-scale engagement and adopt a more targeted approach to counterterrorism. Thus far, despite tweets to the contrary, the Trump administration has mainly followed the Obama military doctrine where U.S. forces are engaged in the Middle East. On the other hand, it has disregarded multilateral diplomatic forums, invoked economic sanctions, threatened trade wars and boosted the defense budget.

Each of these post-Cold War administrations, in hindsight, would likely agree that formulating a grand strategy for a country as large and powerful as the U.S. is not an easy proposition. With a stake in so many foreign policy issues, facing a range of capable competitors, and with a wide variety of effective instruments from which to choose, a grand strategy may prove elusive. But weighing the U.S.' role in the international political system, and choosing the right instruments to underwrite that role, are essential to a coherent and effective foreign policy.

The state of the liberal international order

A year ago, in *Great Decisions*, we discussed "the waning of Pax Americana." The issue at hand was whether the "liberal international order"—the rules-based system of stable and peaceful interstate relations, open markets, individual freedoms and international institutions—could long endure. Since that time, the debate has deepened, and both champions and critics of such an order have moved to the fore. As we examine this year's set of topics, it is worth considering the health of that international order as the U.S. pursues varying foreign policy objectives with allies, friends and potential adversaries. The order is under strain, and its resilience is being questioned.

Robert Kagan, a senior fellow at the Brookings Institution in Washington, DC, fears that the liberal world order, now roughly 70 years old, is collapsing. In one respect this is not surprising; seven decades without great power conflict might seem an anomaly when compared with the state-based, balance-of-power system of previous eras. Moreover, there is some disagreement among political scientists on exactly how important this international order was to a lengthy period of peace and prosperity. Those fearful of the order's decline point to a shared international interest, strengthened over decades, that fostered economic growth, democratic norms, institutional rules and political stability. Those who doubt the centrality of the liberal international order in solidifying these gains point to inherent weaknesses and inconsistencies within the order, and to its ultimate reliance on the willingness of the U.S. to use its instruments of national power to keep the system intact.

Thus, a central question concerning the health of the liberal international order today references our thoughts about grand strategy. If we agree that this post-World War II (WWII), post-Cold War system is worth preserving to avoid conflict, set rules and establish institutions, do we also believe that it requires U.S. primacy to impose that structure and enforce its rules? Or can the U.S. retreat, retrench, selectively engage and count on others to invest in that order? Just how resilient is it?

To assess the state of the liberal international order, we can take its temperature as it encounters various challenges. The reemergence of illiberalism, autocracy, nationalism, protectionism, spheres of influence and territorial revisionism call the stability of the international political system into question. Consider these challenges to the international liberal order as we explore the Great Decisions topics presented to us:

THE DEMANDS OF STATE SOVEREIGNTY. The liberal international order is being buffeted by resurgent state sovereignty, reminiscent of the Westphalian order centered on nation-states and balance-of-power politics. The contemporary tension is between a global system with international obligations and a state system that emphasizes national interests. China is challenging U.S. power along the Pacific Rim, and although its intentions are unclear, its military and economic moves are worrisome. Russia's foreign policy of confrontation and revanchism is equally problematic, as it shores up dictators, expands Russian influence in the Middle East, and seeks alliances with the U.S.' friends and foes. Rogue states with nuclear power and nuclear potential threaten the non-proliferation regime, and combatting terrorism and dealing with climate change require international cooperation.

THE RESURGENCE OF NATIONALISM. Hand in hand with newly empowered state sovereignty is a rebirth of nationalism that is threatening the international consensus needed for collective action. In Europe, particularly, this consensus appears under attack where the UK, Italy, Poland and Hungary have evidenced their distrust of the European Union (EU). The UK's decision to withdraw from the bloc ("Brexit") is the most dramatic example of this new nationalism. Under a liberal international order, states need not compete for military superiority, but can form strategic alliances to balance the power of a potential aggressor, or seek spheres of influence as a buffer zone to protect national borders. Nationalistic behavior, by contrast, is reminiscent of the 1930s, the result of which was world war.

THE PULL OF POPULISM. The liberal international order can be threatened by domestic challenges as well as foreign ones. This has been manifested recently by a populist wave undermining faith in international institutions that support the international order. Populism, in this unfavorable light, sees these institutions as interfering with the will of a homogeneous majority. At the same time, it resists the actions of what it perceives as an elite-led government aiding and protecting ethnic and religious minorities. These populist movements have been stoked by concerns that migration is threatening national culture, and by anti-Muslim attitudes that are shaped by fears about terrorism. Again, Europe displays troubling signs of this trend, with the rise of the far-right Alternative for Germany party, the increasing popularity of Austria's Freedom Party, and the anti-internationalist views being expressed by political parties in Italy, the Czech Republic and Slovakia. At their best, these movements will remain on the fringe and contribute to the debate over economic equality. At their worst, they encourage autocratic leaders and promote illiberal governments.

THE FRAYING OF ALLIANCES. Alliances cut across the international order to facilitate cohesion and cooperation. They can be diplomatic, military, economic, informational or some combination of all of these. And unlike those formed to balance the power of competing nation-states, alliances in the liberal international order offer a value proposition of shared interest. The 36 members of the Organization for Economic Cooperation and Development, for example, form a core of countries promising the economic benefits of joining the alliance and adhering to its rules. Nevertheless, two key European institutions, NATO and the EU, are under political and economic strain. They face pressures that include growing trade disputes between the U.S. and its European allies, and accusations by the U.S. that its NATO allies are "free riding" rather than shouldering a fair share of the financial burden for collective defense. Both NATO and the EU, of course, have been regarded as troubled partnerships in the past. But further tears in the fabric of unity might prompt what some describe as a "new world disorder."

The process of making American foreign policy

Who makes American foreign policy, anyway? Often, our Great Decisions seminar discussions come down to this question. The answer, of course, is that foreign policy decisionmaking is a complex process conducted by humans and, thus, is imperfect. Understanding the people and positions responsible, and the processes involved, is a final component of our analytical framework.

As political scientist Roger Hilsman wrote, we, as Americans, like to think of the decisionmaking process as a dignified, rational progression, one of analyzing problems and systematically evaluating varied courses of action. Then, after all responsible parties are heard from, a prudent policy is declared and implemented. The reality, as he admitted, is quite different. Very often, policies evolve in a series of incremental steps, as varied stakeholders wield their influence. The actors in this process are many, with different attitudes and agendas. The president, granted the constitutional authority for the conduct of foreign affairs, certainly is the lead actor. But the president is aided by the National Security Council (NSC) and the cabinet secretaries that find foreign relations in their bailiwick. Congress also has a constitutional role in making foreign policy. The weight of the electorate, public opinion, interest groups and the media will be felt in varying degrees, depending on the issue and its domestic effects. Understanding who makes foreign policy demands an understanding of the politics of policymaking.

The president

In our introduction to the 2017 edition of *Great Decisions*, we noted that the principal factor moving American foreign policy in the direction of either continuity or change would be the election of Donald Trump. In many cases, that has been true. That's because, as political scientist Morton Halperin put it, "the president stands at the center of the foreign policy process." According to this perspective, the president is the principal figure in determining the general direction of policy. As he or she does so, the president serves as the surrogate for the national interest and holds sway over the influence wielded by the other contributors to the decisionmaking process.

Just how influential is the president in the making of American foreign policy? *Presidential Power*, the classic book by Richard Neustadt, may have been overcome by events. Neustadt's thesis, in his original 1960 work and his 1980 update, was that the office of the president was characterized by weakness, not strength. Rather than a policy leader, the president was ultimately a policy clerk. The power of the office was inherently the power to persuade through vested authority, professional reputation and prestige. From the end of WWII to the end of the Cold War, the president's foreign policy was constrained by precedent, treaties, allies and institutions designed to contain the Soviet Union. Instruments changed in their emphasis, but the objective remained constant. Since the end of the Cold War, these constraints have gradually been removed, granting the president greater flexibility and decisionmaking power. These days, academics write about an "unconstrained presidency."

The executive branch

Within the executive branch, the president has plenty of help to strengthen his hand. The NSC has gradually increased its policymaking power as a series of presidents have gathered close to them the increased numbers needed to put a White House stamp on American foreign policy. Now, as the NSC staff has grown from just 50 under President George H.W. Bush (1989–93) to more than 400 under Presidents Obama and Trump, there is a concern that the Council is implementing foreign policy rather than coordinating it, thereby diminishing the role of the State and Defense Departments, and other departments with foreign policy equities. Such an organization, dedicated to the political success of the president and serving at his pleasure, can foreclose plausible options advanced by other bureaucratic organizations charged with foreign policy decisionmaking.

We wrote earlier of using a levels-of-analysis framework to assist in the understanding of American foreign policy, and such an approach is also useful for examining foreign policy decisionmaking. Since Graham Allison's seminal study of the 1962 Cuban Missile Crisis, scholars have utilized a framework of the rational individual decisionmaker, the outputs and routines of a major organization such as the State Department, or the outcomes of the work of many actors in the bureaucracy, to describe and explain foreign policy decisions. Those all apply. But when considering the power of the president and his closest advisers, group dynamics also come into play. In his book *Groupthink*, research psychologist Irving Janis warned of the internal workings of a cohesive group where "the members' strivings for unanimity override their motivation to realistically appraise alternative courses of action." The result can be fiascos in foreign policy, owing to a single mindset of concurrence-seeking rather than a collective approach to action. To ward off such intelligence failures, Janus advocates casting a wide net to include varied stakeholders, and ensuring that differing views are considered and evaluated prior to embarking on a course of action.

The most recent National Security Strategy makes a strong case for upgrading U.S. diplomacy to compete in the current international environment, and students of American foreign policy traditionally look to the Department of State for formulation and implementation of that policy. Unfortunately, in this era of the 24-hour news cycle and the demand for a rapid U.S. response to myriad international crises and events, the State Department has appeared unwilling or unable to respond quickly to meet that need. Some argue that to regain influence, the State Department should concentrate its limited resources and staff on area expertise, high-level representation and public diplomacy. But others lament the decline in qualified professionals within the department. They point to the

"Mahogany Row Massacre"—in which senior, experienced diplomats were asked to resign by the Trump administration's transition team—and to the additional staff reductions that continued under Secretary of State Rex Tillerson (2017–18). In late 2018, nearly 60 senior State Department posts, including 49 to replace ambassadors, awaited Senate confirmation. One way of getting around this problem is the use of "special envoys," an approach now embraced by Secretary of State Mike Pompeo (2018–present). While these appointed diplomats (currently tasked with Iran, North Korea, Syria and Afghanistan) may be more responsive to diplomatic needs, they further undercut the policymaking influence of the State Department as a whole.

Congress

What about the role of the U.S. Congress in making foreign policy? The Constitution awards Congress oversight of key political appointments, and gives it powers over trade agreements and the use of force. But the age of politics "stopping at the water's edge"—a plea for bipartisanship during the earliest days of the Cold War—is long gone. The rise of partisanship on foreign policy issues allows the president to ignore Congress rather than to persuade it. Moreover, Congress has appeared increasingly reluctant to take a stand on tough policy issues—particularly regarding the authorization of the use of military force and the status of trade agreements. The decline in foreign policy expertise within the Congress also limits its influence, with increased turnover, less seniority and fewer members regarded as foreign policy specialists. However, the number of congressmen with military experience now appears on the rise, as veterans of the wars since 9/11 seek and win office. And, clearly, with the Democrats poised to become the majority party in the House, this will weaken the president's foreign policy hand.

Public opinion

Congress is responsible to the electorate, but judgment varies on just how influential public opinion is on foreign policymaking. Political scientists traditionally have seen public opinion as a minor player in policymaking—as placing limits on the scope or duration of a course of action, such as a military intervention, and establishing a mood, rather than a mandate. This view was derived from the belief that all politics are local, and that the average American knows little and cares less about foreign affairs. Often, opinion polls bear this out by documenting huge gaps in knowledge (who did the U.S. fight in WWII?) or erroneous beliefs (the amounts the U.S. grants in foreign aid).

More recently public opinion has been given greater weight in shaping and constraining foreign policy. According to one study, "Researchers have found that the public is generally well informed about, and interested in, international affairs, that foreign policy affects vote choice, and that public opinion affects policy output." Yet disagreement remains about how public opinion might affect foreign policy decisions. In one view, leaders can be swayed by the public mood out of fear of political repercussions. In another, selection matters. Citizens will vote for candidates campaigning on appealing foreign policy platforms, and politicians largely adhere to those platforms after taking office.

Recent public opinion polls document that most of the public takes the view that the U.S. does too much to try to solve the world's problems and offers too much aid to foreign countries. This, of course, was a major theme in President Trump's "America first" campaign and has led to the withdrawal from treaties and institutions, the renegotiation of trade agreements, and the questioning of allies' commitments and contributions.

Great Decisions 2019: a framework for analysis

As we deliberate the topics that lie ahead, we may find it useful to step back from the relatively narrow subject at hand and speculate a bit more broadly on that topic's implications for some larger issues. Are these areas subject to great power competition? Is a grand strategy evident in pursuing American foreign policy objectives, and are the instruments of national power being employed effectively? Are rules of a stable international order being followed or violated by actors seeking to change that order and their influence within it? How are these American foreign policy decisions being formulated and implemented? This year's readings give us not only a rich menu of deep dives, but also a structured recipe for policy analysis.

REFUGEES AND GLOBAL MIGRATION. Migration and immigration have become contentious issues in many countries, particularly after 2015, when more than 1 million immigrants and refugees, largely Muslim, entered Europe. Immigration tends to divide globalists supportive of cross-border migration, from nationalists protective of their boundaries and culture. That divide can threaten the rules-based liberal international order. U.S. immigration policy specifically banning immigrants and refugees from certain countries and lowering the number of refugees allowed to enter the country, is an example of how domestic policy can influence foreign policy decisionmaking. Might action taken by the U.S.' great power competitors, through manipulation of social media, exacerbate these cleavages?

THE MIDDLE EAST: REGIONAL DISORDER. Which part

of our framework might we consider applying here? Great power competition is stirring in the region, most notably as Russia tries to keep a foothold in Syria. The international order is being threatened by state and non-state actors alike. In Syria, U.S. diplomatic efforts have failed to broker a compromise among competing groups, while the U.S. has announced the intention to leave some military forces there—if Iran does. Regarding Iran, the U.S. withdrawal from the 2015 nuclear agreement has caused fissures with our allies, raised the chances of near-term military conflict, imposed economic sanctions and continued the need for increased arms sales to the U.S.' Middle East allies. Conflicting messages from different parts of the U.S. foreign policy decisionmaking apparatus further confuse the region and add to its disorder. U.S. commitments to Israel and Saudi Arabia may not have restored the order the U.S. sought in the region.

NUCLEAR NEGOTIATIONS: BACK TO THE FUTURE? In terms of great power competition, might there be room for an extension of the New Strategic Arms Reduction Treaty in 2021? The U.S. and the Soviet Union were successful in negotiating limits to nuclear weapons at the height of the Cold War, so the frosty relations that exist between the two nuclear superpowers today should not deter such an agreement. Nor should a new treaty prohibit the nuclear modernization plans on either side, although fewer weapons systems might be acquired. Considerations of grand strategy apply here as well: Does primacy reign supreme? And what other factors regarding Russia (economic sanctions, human rights concerns, Intermediate-Range Nuclear Forces Treaty violations, vote meddling and cyberattacks) might influence U.S. foreign policy decisionmakers to trust, but verify?

THE RISE OF POPULISM IN EUROPE. Populism is a force in nearly every Western country today, as anti-establishment political candidates have won significant domestic followings by promising to defend "the people" from the influx of foreigners and the neglect of a ruling elite. Denmark, France, the Netherlands and Germany have seen the rise of right-wing populism. Taken to extremes, these populist movements could threaten the liberal democracies that form the basis of the international order. As that order is in the U.S.' interest, Washington may try to apply diplomatic and information instruments to help reach reasonable compromises among competing European interest groups.

DECODING U.S.- CHINA TRADE. Here we are back to great power competition, although this battlefield is an economic one. The U.S.' strategic intentions regarding its interests and influence in the Pacific Rim are important, as are the instruments of national power it chooses to influence Chinese behavior regionally and globally. American foreign policy in the past urged China to follow the rules-based international order. But recent U.S. abandonment of the 2015 Paris climate accords and the Trans-Pacific Partnership trade deal might lead the Chinese to wonder what rules apply to the U.S., and which to them. The current U.S. view of China as a strategic competitor will likely continue to spill over into trade negotiations and tariffs—if not trade wars.

CYBER CONFLICTS AND GEOPOLITICS. In cyber conflicts, great power competition has found a new domain, referred to earlier as a form of political warfare. As such, it raises the information instrument of national power to new levels and suggests a grand strategy of selective engagement on a cyber battlefield. The principal challenge facing American foreign policy decisionmakers in the cyber world is uncertainty. Who is the attacker? How should we respond? How do we know we have the right target? Can deterrence be applied to cyberwarfare? In addition, China and Russia are not the only cyber players, as Iran and North Korea have also attacked U.S. information systems. Does the "hacked world order"—using social media to pursue political ends—undermine the liberal one?

THE U.S. AND MEXICO: PARTNERSHIP TESTED. In terms of instruments of national power, diplomatic and economic agreements dominate American foreign policy with Mexico. The recent renegotiation of the North American Free Trade Agreement seems to have satisfied both parties, but the outcome will be subject to review under Mexico's new president, López Obrador. U.S.-Mexican diplomatic relations may depend on whether Obrador conducts reforms to strengthen democratic processes, or if he centralizes power and moves Mexico in a direction emulating an authoritarian Venezuela. The liberal international order, at least as it exists south of the U.S. border, is at some risk.

STATE OF THE STATE DEPARTMENT AND DIPLOMACY. This topic goes to the heart of our discussion of the American foreign policy decisionmaking process. The traditional State Department might be described as the last bastion of the liberal international order, promoting democracy, human rights and the rule of law abroad. The rise of great powers has lessened the ability of the State Department to extend the reach of these values and, with that, to extend U.S. primacy. The State Department also loses influence if its diplomats are bypassed in the policymaking arena, and if the instruments of military, economic and cyber power are turned to more frequently than diplomacy. Secretary of State Pompeo has pledged to return "swagger" to the State Department. We'll see.

Refugees and global migration

by Karen Jacobsen

A desperate crowd of asylum seekers from the three accepted nationalities queue to enter Macedonia from Greece on December 4, 2015. Macedonia enacted new border restrictions that limits accepted asylum seekers to Syrians, Iraqis and Afghanis. (NURPHOTO/GETTY IMAGES)

Each year millions of people leave their homes, either because they are forcibly displaced or because they are seeking ways to improve their lives. Millions more return to their homes, either because they are required (say, if they are deported) or by choice. Most of these migrants and returnees remain within their own countries, and are known as "internal migrants." Their number is much larger than international migrants, but we have no real way of estimating that number. International migrants (also referred to as "foreign-born population") are defined as those who leave their home countries and take up residence in another country for more than one year. Only a small proportion of the world's population—about 3%—are international migrants. (This population excludes short-term visitors, tourists, business travel, etc., but includes refugees.) Thus, most of the world's population, both those who migrate and those who stay home, remain within the countries of their birth.

We think of migration, both internal and international, in terms of those who have been forcibly displaced as a result of conflict, violence and persecution, and those who have migrated for other reasons. At the end of 2017, there were more than 64.5 million displaced people worldwide, of whom some 40 million remained within their home countries (internally displaced persons or IDPs), and another 24.5 million people left their countries to become refugees. Much larger numbers of people, some 233 million, migrated for reasons such as finding work, education, health care or simply to join their families who have already moved.

Notably, many people move for both reasons and can be both internal and external migrants. For example, a person

KAREN JACOBSEN *is the Henry J. Leir Professor of Global Migration at the Fletcher School of Law & Diplomacy, Tufts University. Her work explores the lives of refugees and migrants and how governments and host societies respond to them.*

Families move out of their homes and wheel away their possessions as the town of Sandouping is reduced to rubble. It will be flooded when China's Three Gorges Dam project is complete. In all, up to 1.3m people will be displaced by the project.(DERMOT TATLOW/PANOS PICTURES/REDUX)

might initially be displaced by conflict within her own country, becoming an IDP; then if her persecution or the violence continues, she might flee again across the border and become a refugee. Years later, she might decide to migrate elsewhere, perhaps to join her family or to find work. Because it is difficult to separate out reasons for migration we tend to think in terms of "mixed migration flows," a term that recognizes how migrants move for many different reasons.

In 2017, the number of international migrants was some 258 million, an increase of 49% from the year 2000. However, as a percentage of the global population (7.6 billion in 2017), the number has not changed much. In 2000, just 2.8% of the world's population were international migrants, and by 2017, this proportion had increased only to 3.3%. In other words, 97% of the global population stays in their home countries. Of these international migrants, some 25.4 million were displaced across a border and include 19.9 million refugees under the mandate of the United Nations' refugee agency known as UNHCR and another 5 million Palestinian refugees under the mandate of UNRWA. (See box below.)

Who are the migrants?

Within these categories of international and internal migration, there are many types of migrants, conventionally divided into "forced" and "voluntary" migrants. However, rather than thinking in terms of this binary, it is more useful to think of migration occurring along a *choice* spectrum.

On the one end, are those who have no choice, who are physically forced to move, often by the threat of violence or physical destruction to them or their families. These people include slaves and trafficking victims who are kidnapped, and disaster victims whose homes are destroyed in a natural disaster (such as an earthquake, tsunami or volcano eruption) or a 'man-made' environmental disaster (such as the nuclear meltdown at Chernobyl), or because of national development projects such as the building of a dam (such as the Three Gorges Dam in China) that destroys their homes and livelihoods. For these people, there is little choice but to move or die. On the other end of the spectrum are those who want to move for lifestyle reasons – for pleasure or adventure or who want to return to their homes to retire or because they feel happier there or miss their family. The two ends of the spectrum clearly represent different approaches to migration. What about those who fall between those two ends—people who are neither

UNHCR and UNRWA

The Office of the United Nations High Commissioner for Refugees (UNHCR) was created in 1950 after World War II and is headquartered in Geneva, Switzerland. The agency is mandated by the UN primarily to protect the rights and well-being of refugees, forcibly displaced communities and stateless people, and to assist in their voluntary repatriation, local integration or resettlement to a third country. Over time, UNHCR's mandate has expanded to include protection and assistance to other persons "of concern," including internally displaced persons (IDPs). The agency leads and coordinates international action to resolve the problems of refugees and other people of concern worldwide.

UNRWA, which stands for the United Nations Relief and Works Agency for Palestine Refugees in the Near East, was set up as a relief and development agency for Palestinian refugees in 1948 (before the creation of UNHCR). Today UNRWA supports more than five million registered Palestinian refugees and their descendants who fled or were expelled from their homes during the 1948 Palestine war and the 1967 Six Day war. UNRWA provides education, health care, and social services in Jordan, Lebanon, Syria, the Gaza Strip and the West Bank, including East Jerusalem. Outside these five areas Palestinian refugees are assisted by UNHCR.

! Before you read, download the companion **Glossary** that includes definitions, a guide to acronyms and abbreviations used in the article, and other material. Go to **www.greatdecisions.org** and select a topic in the Resources section on the right-hand side of the page.

physically forced to move nor making a "lifestyle choice"?

Most types of migration lie between the two ends of the spectrum i.e. not either physically forced to move or making lifestyle changes. Migrants with somewhat more choice move:

- for work, or economic reasons,
- to seek education or health resources not available in their home areas
- for family reasons (to get married, or join their children or community)
- Because they want to leave their homes to seek a better, more exciting life—the "bright lights, big city" (this is often the reason young people leave their homes, especially those who live in rural areas)

People with less choice move:

- because they are being persecuted for their ethnic, religious or other identity or for political activities (According to the 1951 Refugees Convention, these people are defined as "refugees" in legal parlance)
- to escape war or conflict (War victims are not always legally defined as refugees, it depends which international laws and treaties a country has signed onto)
- because their livelihoods can no longer support them or their families. (These people comprise by far the largest proportion of migrants, although there is no real way to count them. They include those who are experiencing the impact of climate change and cannot feed their families because drought or water levels have rendered their farmland no longer viable, and those who have no livelihood because of insufficient land or because there are no jobs.

These are underlying or proximate causes that provide the wider context for migration. Given this context, households and individuals engage in a wide range of decision-making about who should migrate, where, when and how.

Migration decisionmaking

The decision made by households and individuals about when, how and where to migrate is different from the underlying structural causes of migration. Household decisionmaking is influenced by many subjective factors, including emotions and aspirations. Here we focus on two areas of decision-making: where to go, and how to go.

Like all migrants, refugees usually have a preferred destination country, and often a particular city or area within that country. This preference is usually because refugees have family or community there, or they might have heard of the place from others (often through social media). However, migrants' choices about where to go are heavily constrained by states' control of their borders and admission of immigrants. The next section outlines how states control borders and admission of immigrants, and how refugees and asylum seekers fit into this system.

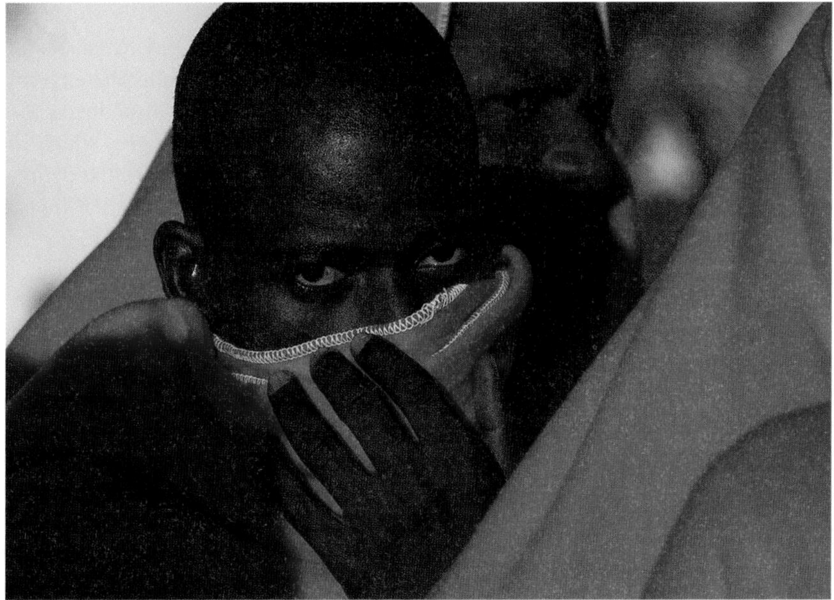

A migrant seen looking on as he waits to be assisted during his arrival at Malaga, Spain, after being rescued by the Spanish Maritime Rescue service in October 2018.
(JESUS MERIDA/LIGHTROCKET/GETTY IMAGES)

Legal migration

Today, no countries have open borders. (This may seem an obvious statement, but passports only became widespread after World War I; in 1900 most of the world's 56 countries were divided into empires with largely open borders between them.) Every state in today's global system has its own laws and policies about who is permitted to cross its borders, and how they will do so. This means migrants must either have a visa (of which there are many types), or seek asylum at the border. Some states have regional border treaties that exempt citizens from passport control; the most well-known is the European Union, but other regions of the world do too, such as South America and West Africa.

Most of the world's 248 million international migrants travel to their destination countries on visas issued by individual states (or sometimes by regional bodies, such as the EU's Schengen visa that allows visitors to travel within the EU). These visas permit them to work, study, visit family, invest, seek medical care and engage in myriad other activities. For our purposes, let U.S. focus on one category of these migrants: refugees and asylum seekers.

Refugees and asylum seekers

At the end of 2017 there were 25.4 million refugees and 3.1 million asylum seekers worldwide, (about 10% of international migrants). States define these two groups, refugees and asy-

Soldiers checking the papers of Czechoslovakian refugees crossing the border into Germany in January, 1948. (WALTER SANDERS/THE LIFE PICTURE COLLECTION/GETTY IMAGES)

lum seekers, in highly specific ways. For the state, a refugee begins as an asylum seeker—a person who seeks asylum on the basis of having fled her own country because of having been persecuted for reasons of race, religion, membership in a particular social or political group. The asylum seeker must formally apply to the government of the destination country and then go through a process known as "refugee status determination." This process differs in every country and can take many months or even years before a decision is made. The state deems the asylum seeker to be "genuine" if she meets the legal definition of a refugee, which in most countries is similar to the definition set out in the international treaty known as the 1951 Refugee Convention. According to the convention, a refugee is "a person who is outside his or her country of nationality or habitual residence; has a well-founded fear of being persecuted because of his or her race, religion, nationality, membership of a particular social group or political opinion; and is unable or unwilling to avail him- or herself of the protection of that country, or to return there, for fear of persecution."

A Palestinian carries United Nations Relief and Works Agency for Palestine Refugees (UNWRA) aid sacks on his shoulders in Rafah, Gaza on September 27, 2018. A U.S. decision to cut UNWRA funding is expected to affect the lives of Palestinians in Gaza. (ABED RAHIM KHATIB/ANADOLU AGENCY/GETTY IMAGES)

Most member states of the United Nations (148 out of 191) are party to the two major international instruments (treaties) concerning refugees: the 1951 Refugee Convention and its 1967 Protocol. However, 43 member-states have not signed or ratified these treaties. Some of these non-party states host significant refugee populations, and their not being a party can influence UNHCR's ability to work with the host state to help refugees, and can also mean the host state is less willing to comply with international humanitarian standards. Because the 1951 Convention and its Protocol are international treaties, states that have ratified them have obligations. One is that a state is required to create and implement domestic legislation and policy concerning its response to refugees. This means most states have specific domestic laws that set out how refugees and asylum seekers are defined, what the state's duties toward them are and what the refugees' responsibilities are.

If an asylum seeker meets the state's definition of a refugee, she receives asylum and is formally considered to have refugee status. If she does not meet the state's definition, her case is rejected, she will not receive refugee status, and her immigration status in the country will need to be "adjusted." Depending on the country, she will either have to leave the country, or she can appeal, or try to qualify to remain under some alternative immigration status. When we talk about asylum seekers, therefore, we are talking about people who are still caught up in the process of having their legal status determined. At the end of 2017, there were more than 3.09 million asylum seekers worldwide, mostly in Europe. In contrast, the world's refugees have been granted some form of asylum, either because they have successfully navigated the asylum process and are formally defined as

"Convention refugees," or because the state has recognized them as "prima facie" refugees (often applied to large groups of people fleeing generalized violence). Some 5.86 million are Palestinian refugees who live in Jordan, Lebanon and Syria and the Territories of the West Bank and Gaza Strip. They fall under the mandate of UNRWA, a refugee agency set up in 1948 (before the creation of UNHCR) that continues to provide assistance to them.

Destination states match strict definition of refugees, asylum seekers and legal migrants with close control of their borders. Only those migrants who have the appropriate visa or who have been qualified as "genuine" refugees are permitted entry. This means the number of legally admitted migrants each year is vastly exceeded by those who would like to leave their countries. Many more people say they want to migrate than who actually do so. One estimate is that 14% of the world's adults—nearly 710 million people—want to permanently migrate to another country. Some proportion of this number chooses or becomes caught up in irregular migration i.e. without state approval and the proper documents, or "illegally."

Where do refugees live?

One of the global consequences of state control of borders is the distribution of refugees worldwide. Some 85% of the world's refugees live in host countries neighboring the home country from which they fled. The majority were in Sub-Saharan Africa, followed by Asia, Turkey (alone hosting more than 3 million mainly Syrian refugees), then Europe and the Americas *(Table 1)*.

Syrian students arrive at a school built for Syrian refugees, at a refugee camp in Kilis, Turkey. on September 30, 2015. In 2015, approximately 230,000 Syrian refugee children received education in Turkey. (KEREM KOCALAR/ANADOLU AGENCY/GETTY IMAGES)

Most will remain in these neighboring countries until either they return to their home countries, or they are permitted to become integrated into the host country. A very small number (less than 1% of all refugees) will qualify to be resettled to other (third) countries. They undergo the resettlement process, which includes substantial layers of screening, while still in their host country.

Very few countries resettle refugees. In 2017, just 102,800 refugees were resettled in 35 countries (less than 1% of global total, and down 46% from 2016.) Just three countries (U.S., Canada, Australia) resettled more than 75,000 refugees. Until 2017, the U.S. was resettling some 70,000 refugees each year, making it by far the largest resettlement country. In 2017, the Trump administration reduced the resettlement quota and the United States accepted 65% fewer than in 2016. However, the U.S. still took the highest number: 33,400, or 33% of total resettled. Canada took 26,600 and Australia (15,100). In 2018, the resettlement quota for the U.S. is expected to be further reduced.

Table 1. Refugees, asylum-seekers, internally displaced persons (IDPs), returnees (refugees and IDPs), by region of asylum

Country/territory of asylum	Refugees	People in refugee-like situations	Total refugees and people in refugee-situations	*Of whom assisted by UNHCR*	Asylum-seekers (pending cases)	Returned refugees
Sub-Saharan Africa	6,236,495	31,709	6,268,204	*5,479,759*	508,794	526,521
Asia and Pacific	4,153,991	55,740	4,209,731	*2,650,568*	159,919	62,157
Turkey	3,480,348	-	3,480,348	*1,194,381*	308,855	-
Mid East + North Africa	2,653,717	51,226	2,704,943	*2,460,619*	234,834	78,086
Europe	2,608,270	25,656	2,633,926	*57,606*	999,773	412
Americas	484,261	159,934	644,195	*50,568*	878,723	205
Total	**19,617,082**	**324,265**	**19,941,347**	***11,893,501***	**3,090,898**	**667,381**

(Source: Author's adaptation of UNHCR 2017 Statistical Annex, Table 1)

** According to UNHCR, this category includes persons who outside their country or territory of origin who face protection risks similar to those of refugees, but for whom refugee status has, for practical or other reasons, not been ascertained.*

Undocumented (irregular) migration

Many migrants and refugees who would like to migrate to other countries are not able to do so legally because of state control of borders. For example, in 2017 Turkey hosted the largest population of refugees in the world (more than 3.4 million), and it is likely that many of the refugees there who have the means, would like to migrate to other countries, especially Europe. However, many European countries have blocked their borders, or have signed agreements with Turkey to prevent out-migration, and options for onward migration from Turkey are very limited, as they are with many other transit countries where migrants and refugees are "stuck."

For those who are stuck, and assuming they have the means to pay a smuggler, one option is to use illegal means to travel to destination countries. It is important to note that even when people do have the option of illegal migration, many refuse to do so, both for moral reasons (not wanting to act in an unlawful manner) and because they are afraid to take the risks involved with smugglers. However, there are also many desperate people who do take the smuggler option—we have no data to indicate what proportion of all those who could migrate illegally this might be.

New approaches have been developed in recent years that seek to make better estimates of how many people are smuggled each year. The global picture of irregular migration is highly complex and largely incomplete, in part because undocumented migrants do not want to appear on the official radar, and also because the status of migrants can change during their journey to and through countries of transit and destination. In some cases, changes in national laws and policies can turn regular migration into irregular migration, and vice-versa. There is no valid way to estimate the number of migrants who travel undocumented, but there are various indicators, often developed in different regions or by different countries. For example, 2016 the EU established has a special European Border and Coast Guard Agency known as Frontex for the purpose of monitoring its sea borders. Among the data Frontex collects is the number of attempted border crossings.

Implications of global migration

The current migration crisis in Europe began in 2015, peaked in 2016, and is now ebbing. EU countries received over 1.2 million first-time asylum applications in 2015, more than double that of 2014. Asylum applications were heavily concentrated in four states (Germany, Hungary, Sweden and Austria), which received two-thirds of EU asylum applications in 2015. As a result, Hungary closed its borders and refused to accept any more migrants. In 2016 the number of migrants crossing the Mediterranean dropped to 364,000. It fell again in 2017 with fewer than half as many migrants reaching Europe by sea, and the number is down to pre-2015 levels halfway through 2018. The main arrival states (as opposed to states with high asylum applications) were the states with long sea borders: Greece, Italy and Spain.

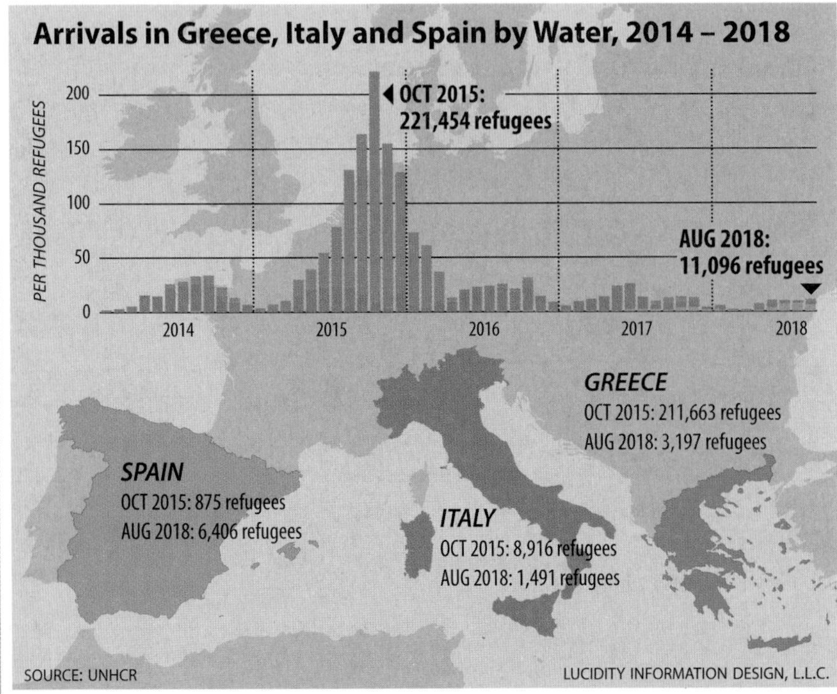

The dramatic surge in migrant arrivals in the Eastern Mediterranean beginning in August 2015 occurred for several reasons. The main cause, responsible for about half of the migrants trying to cross the Mediterranean, was the war in Syria, which by 2015 had already displaced some 11.6 million Syrians, more than 4 million out of the country, since the war began in 2011. But Syria was by no means the only country from which thousands of refugees and other migrants were fleeing. Countries such as Eritrea, Afghanistan, Kosovo, Iraq and Nigeria, all also afflicted by violence, persecution and instability, had created massive displacement both within and across borders. For both Syrians and other refugees return was not a prospect any time soon. This ongoing displacement was compounded by the fact that by 2015, many neighboring countries of first asylum, such as Jordan and Lebanon, had tightened or closed their borders. These neighboring countries already hosted hundreds of thousands of refugees and by 2015 conditions were deteriorating, as the host population and their governments became increasingly resentful of the ongoing presence of so many refugees. Finding work and enrolling children in school were becoming more difficult for refugees, and in some countries, such as Libya, there was growing conflict and instability. By 2015, all these factors, already in place for several years, had intensified, and at the same time, the smuggling industry was facilitating the journey by bribing coast guards and making the whole process of being smuggled easier. When the weather conditions for crossing the Mediterranean were right in the late summer of 2015, the migration—already in course for the past few years—intensified.

The numbers associated with the 2015 migration crisis are high, but Europe has seen much higher flows. Since the end of World War II, Europe has experienced multiple waves of displacement. In the aftermath of World War II, there were at least two million displaced persons in Europe. In the late 1940s, twelve million Germans were expelled from the Soviet Union, and in 1956, more than 200,000 refugees fled Hungary after the Soviets crushed the revolution (most went to Austria). After European decolonization in the 1960s and 1970s, some five to seven million people, most former settlers, came to Europe from the collapsing colonies. With the end of the Cold War came the war in former Yugoslavia in the early 1990s. An estimated 650,000 Bosnian war refugees fled to European countries and became the first group to acquire "temporary protection" in EU states. The Yugoslav wars, especially the Bosnian conflict, confronted European states with the largest refugee crisis since WWII, and forced them to revise their asylum policies, specify their vague regulations on refugees and attempt to develop a unified policy in response to the pressing issue.

Europe had a long history of migration both within and from outside its borders. However, the 2015 crisis differed from earlier migration movements in ways discussed below.

EU crisis?

Given that migrant arrivals have fallen dramatically since 2015, the nature of the "crisis" has changed. Two political issues face Europe now related to the 1.8 million migrants and refugees who have arrived since 2014.

The first issue is how to absorb or integrate those who have refugee status. What services to provide, where refugees should live, whether and how their movements are controlled, are all issues that EU countries have dealt with differently – and not always in ways that suit either the refugees or the native population. Public anxiety about crime and insecurity has risen in countries like Germany after high-profile assaults involving migrants, including the killing of a 19-year-old German student and the terrorist attack on a Christmas market that killed 12 people. The vast majority of migrants and asylum-seekers since 2015 are Muslim, and this has stirred concerns about their cultural and religious impact. Some governments, like Hungary's, have specifically refused to

The EU-Turkey refugee agreement

The EU's refugee agreement with Turkey, in which Syrian refugees are exchanged between Turkey and EU countries, was signed on March 18, 2016. Under the agreement the EU sends all Syrians who reached the Greek islands illegally back to Turkey. In return, legal Syrian refugees are accepted into the EU. Under the agreement, Turkey was promised €6 billion in financial aid, to be used by the Turkish government to finance projects for Syrian refugees.

As of March 2018, according to the EU Commission, €3 billion has already flowed into Turkey to cover the costs of educating half a million Syrian children. Because return procedures in Greece are slow, only 1,564 Syrians were sent back to Turkey between 2016 - 2018. In addition, a further 600 Syrians were sent back to Turkey under the agreement between Turkey and Greece. In exchange, 12,489 Syrians from Turkey were resettled in EU countries. Germany took in 4,313, the Netherlands 2,608, France 1,401 and Finland 1,002 Syrian refugees. The EU member states Hungary, Poland, the Czech Republic, Bulgaria and Denmark did not accept any refugees at all.

Turkey has repeatedly threatened to terminate the agreement because the EU has not paid the stipulated amount, and because the visa freedom for Turkish citizens provided for under the agreement has not been implemented.

Elderly women, men, children and wounded evacuees sit in a bus on July 26, 1995, as they are driven by Bosnian Serbs from the fallen enclave of Zepa to the frontline crossing point close to the government-held town of Klandanj. (JOEL ROBINE/AFP/GETTY IMAGES)

take in refugees because they are Muslim. Other governments, like Italy's coalition (formed after the election in March 2018), are more circumspect about their Muslim concerns, but are still strongly anti-immigrant and refuse to take in more migrants. Politicians and other political actors have used their citizens' concerns—and the growing anti-immigrant political backlash—to promote anti-immigrant agendas. One consequence has been the rise of right-wing radical groups who have used public concerns about immigration and cultural purity to increase their membership and boost their political and ideological agendas. These agendas include a growing role for independence and separatist movements within the EU's member states.

The second problem concerns threats to the solidarity of the EU as a whole, rather than individual countries, and stems from the lack of agreement about EU-wide "burden-sharing," i.e. who should take responsibility for the newcomers. Under EU law, asylum seekers must lodge their applications in the first EU country they enter. This means border "frontline" states like Greece and Italy, where most migrants enter Europe, receive the bulk of migrants. The EU member states, already divided on the reform of the Common European Asylum System before 2015, have been unable to come to agreement about how to distribute the migrants more evenly across the EU. Frontline countries are increasingly frustrated by the unwillingness of other EU countries to take in refugees. Some like Hungary and Macedonia have closed their borders—often with walls and fences—leaving the border states to deal with the refugees.

Wealthier countries like Germany, which opened its borders in 2015 and received more than a million migrants and refugees, are pulling back on their willingness to take migrants. One outcome of Germany's generous reception was a political crisis for its leader, Angela Merkel, and she is still struggling to recover politically. As border states are being stuck with refugees and migrants their citizens become increasingly resentful and elect anti-immigrant or hardline politicians. In June 2018, the new elected Prime Minster of Italy refused to allow a boat laden with African migrants to dock in Sicily, and the boat drifted at sea until Spain agreed to let the migrants land.

Some observers see this struggle over burden-sharing as a threat to the solidarity of the EU as states like Hungary refuse to fall in line and even threaten to pull out of the EU, the United Kingdom does pull out of the EU and other states adopt bilateral arrangements, like that between Italy and Libya. Everyone agrees Europe needs to urgently overhaul its asylum and immigration rules. However, no one can agree how to do it: some countries are pushing for tougher external border controls, others for fairer distribution of new arrivals. Any solution will have to somehow balance the concerns of the "frontline" southern states with those of the wealthier northern "destination" states, but also deal with the flat refusal of hardline central and eastern European governments such as Hungary and Poland to be pushed into accepting any migrants at all.

While the number of new arrivals had dropped as of mid-2018, the frontline states are still receiving many "irregular" migrants: UNHCR says Spain has received 9,500 by mid-2018, Greece 12,000 and Italy 15,300. The underlying factors that led to the migration surge of 2015 have not gone away; most observers believe it is only a matter of time before the number of arrivals picks up again.

What about the U.S.?

The U.S. has not faced an influx of asylum seekers at its borders of the magnitude Europe faced in 2015, or faced by many other host countries in Africa and the Middle East. There are, however, two major sources of refugees within the region. One is the result of the violence in the Northern Triangle (El Salvador, Honduras and Guatemala), which has resulted in a massive displacement both internally and with external outflows including to the U.S. The other is a beginning migration crisis, resulting from the violence and instability in Venezuela.

Asylum applications from the Northern Triangle region have risen globally over the past few years. Some of these migrants head for the U.S., and come up against the southern border, where they are apprehended by the U.S. Border Patrol. in July 2018, the overall number of apprehensions at the southern border was up nearly 57% from July 2017, with the largest increase in "family units" which increased more than 142% year over year. However, as the Migration Policy Institute points out, the number of apprehensions in 2017 was atypically low because of the "Trump effect", and the number of apprehensions at this writing (August 2018) is not much different from earlier years.

The arrival of Central Americans, including many families and children, at the U.S.'s southern border precipitated a major political crisis in 2018, especially after the Trump administration elected to separate children from

Southwest Border Apprehensions, 2000-2018

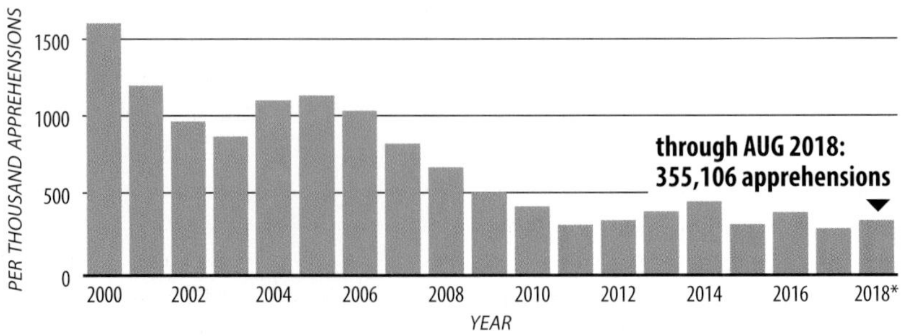

SOURCE: U.S. Border Patrol, "U.S. Border Patrol Monthly Apprehensions (FY 2000 - FY 2017)"
Note: Fiscal years run from Oct. 31st through Sept. 30th of the following calendar year. *Total as of 8/31/2018.

LUCIDITY INFORMATION DESIGN, L.L.C.

their parents and put them in different detention centers.

A second current humanitarian crisis with potential consequences for the U.S. is in Venezuela. Until 2016, Venezuela was a middle-income country with a strong oil-based economy. Under the authoritarian rule of President Nicolás Maduro, the economy has collapsed, there are increasing levels of violence especially in poor areas, and food and medicine is largely unavailable – again especially for the poor. As a result, Venezuelans are fleeing their country. Estimates are imprecise, but range from 1.6 million to 4 million people abroad as of early 2018. UNHCR reports that there were almost 148,000 Venezuelan applications for asylum globally at the end of 2017. Other estimates are that since 2017 more than a million Venezuelans have fled to neighboring Colombia where many lack legal status, and another 52,000 have gone to Brazil. The number of Venezuelans seeking asylum in the United States reached 57,000 by the end of 2107—an increase of nearly 2,500% since 2012. Venezuelans are now the fastest-growing nationality seeking asylum in United States. This does not yet constitute a "migration crisis" for the U.S., and it is unlikely to as the U.S. is not a bordering country with Venezuela. At least in the early years of the Venezuelan crisis the Venezuelans reaching the U.S. will be those who have resources (money and networks). The vast majority, the poor, will continue flee to neighboring countries like Colombia, and it those countries that will—and already do—face a migration crisis. The U.S. will face knock-on implications of such a serious humanitarian crisis in the Americas.

Why 'migration crises'?

There are two sides to the economic impact of migrants—and a lot of evidence can be marshalled to support both sides. One view is that migrants contribute to the economy by bringing their skills, entrepreneurship, initiative and creativity. They also of course accept jobs that locals don't want, and they accept lower wages. The other side is that migrants take local jobs, accept lower wages and worse working conditions, and use government services like schools, health care and in some countries, welfare. Then there are cultural or nativist arguments – which are often used in Europe, but also in other countries – that immigrants are diluting the country's "culture" or weakening the social fabric, or creating other cultural or social problems. Immigrants are the first to be blamed for both economic and social problems, and also for increased crime, although there is much evidence globally and in the U.S. to show that migrants are more likely to be victims than perpetrators.

Depending on your view, arguments can be made for or against the economic impact of migrants. And this position is easily converted by politicians into political support. Add to that the security concerns of natives, and the fact that many immigrants are of a different races, and religion, and you have plenty of fuel for Islamophobia – all fueling the political fight surrounding migrants in both Europe and the U.S. – and in many other countries.

A group of Central American migrants gather in the central park of Ciudad Hidlago, Mexico, October 20, 2018. Mexican authorities for a second straight day refused mass entry to a caravan of Central American migrants held up at the border with Guatemala, but began accepting small groups for asylum processing and gave out some 45-day visitor permits that would theoretically allow recipients time to reach the U.S. (OLIVER DE ROS/AP PHOTO)

'Solving' migration

Migration (mobility) is part of life and history and is a positive force—if everyone had stayed in the same place our species would probably never have survived, and this is very much the case for people in troubled countries today. However, many of the world's destination countries, governments and public alike, see immigration (into their own countries) as a problem that needs to be solved. This "solution" takes two main forms: actively preventing people from migrating or returning them when they get there; and incentivizing people to stay in their own countries or in transit countries.

Policies that incentivize people not to migrate

The "prevention is better than cure" approach takes the form of development policies and programs in the origin country funded by Europe or America, based on the assumption that improving the situation of people in their home countries will make them less likely to want to leave. Development policies aimed at preventing migration can take the form of bilateral policies between sending and re-

A vehicle transporting Syrian refugees from Lebanon is seen at the Zamrani crossing in the countryside of Damascus, Syria, on October 1, 2018. Hundreds of Syrian refugees returned to Syria from Lebanon in response to renewed calls by the Syrian government for refugees to return, state news agency SANA reported. (AMMAR SAFARJALANI XINHUA/EYEVI/REDUX)

ceiving countries, or multilateral arrangements such as the EU's crisis response in 2015 which was to develop three new funding instruments in line with the EU's external priorities. These were the Facility for Refugees in Turkey (2016–17): €1 billion from the EU budget + €2 billion from the member states; the EU Regional Trust Fund in Response to the Syrian Crisis (2015–19): €500 million from the EU budget + €500 million from the member states or other donors; and the EU Emergency Trust Fund for stability and addressing the root causes of irregular migration and displaced persons in Africa (2015–20); €1.8 billion from the EU budget + €1.8 billion from the member states. However, partnerships between the EU and third countries often neglect the perspective and rights of migrants, which is both a problem in itself and is likely to undermine the success of these agreements.

These development policies also targeted the large number of migrants and refugees in transit countries (particularly countries of first asylum), seeking to encourage them not to continue their journeys by helping them integrate more permanently into those countries. The reintegration of returnees is also a policy initiative to encourage people not to migrate again.

Preventing people from leaving or returning them after arrival

Fortress Europe and Fortress America are metaphors for simply preventing people from gaining access to destination countries, either by blocking borders and erecting walls and fences as has been done by countries like Hungary and Macedonia to block migrants coming from Greece, or by making bilateral or multilateral arrangements with transit countries. The most widely known multilateral agreement to stop migration through a transit country is the EU-Turkey refugee agreement. Bilateral deals with sending countries are exemplified by such as the agreements between Italy and Libya, in which Italy agreed to train, equip and finance the Libyan coastguard as part of its effort to stop and turn back migrant boats and force thousands of people to return to Libya against their will.

If prevention fails, destination countries use repatriation, either forced (deportation) or voluntary (with incentives). To this end, countries like Italy have signed repatriation agreements with origin countries. Repatriation is often enabled by the International Organization for Migration (IOM), which is the UN migration agency responsible for migrants (as opposed to UNHCR which is responsible for refugees). IOM has several programs encouraging voluntary repatriation.

Global Compacts

Many of the solutions discussed above are addressed in two new Global Compacts developed over the past two years. Both came out of the 2016 High Level Meeting on Large Movements of Refugees and Migrants and its resulting New York Declaration. The two Compacts are the latest in multilateral efforts to address global migration.

On repatriation

The International Organization for Migration (IOM) is the UN migration agency responsible for migrants (as opposed to UNHCR which is responsible for refugees). IOM and the European Union have a 25-million euro program called the EU-IOM Joint Initiative on Migrant Protection and Reintegration, which is active in 26 countries in the Horn of Africa, the Sahel and Lake Chad region, and North Africa. The initiative supports 'economic reintegration' for returnees in countries of origin. These returnees are often young men in their 20s and 30s, who choose to return to their home countries instead of continuing their journeys to Europe. For example, irregular migration, known as tahriib, has been a popular route out of poverty and unemployment for many Somalilanders. In response, IOM and the EU are training over 60 migrants who opted to return to Somaliland from Libya. The returnees have access to "Start Your Business" training which provides business planning, procurement, marketing and financial planning skills. The goal is to enable returnees to open and grow their own businesses or to make them more employable. After the migrants complete the training, their business plans are vetted, start-up supplies are procured for them and they receive further monitoring and mentoring to ensure the sustainability of their businesses.

The Global Compact on Refugees (GCR) was drafted by UNHCR in consultation with states, and focuses exclusively on refugees (cross-border movements in context of persecution and conflict) and asylum seekers. Its goals are to ease pressures on host countries, by enhancing refugee self-reliance, expanding access to third country solutions (such as resettlement), and supporting conditions for repatriation. However, the GCR does not address internally displaced persons (IDPs—the largest global population of forced migrants), nor those displaced by environmental drivers, or those fleeing life-threatening situations but who do not qualify for refugee status.

The Global Compact for Safe, Orderly and Regular Migration (GCM) is the latest and most ambitious of recent global initiatives and is slated for adoption in December 2018. The GCM focuses on migrants who do not qualify as refugees, including those who are displaced by environmental change, natural disasters and the slow onset effects of climate change. The Compact identifies specific policy goals and best practices to which UN member states can commit in promoting safe and legal alternatives to irregular migration. It seeks to assist and protect the rights of migrants, particularly migrants in transit, and to assist origin countries by providing support for early warning, disaster risk reduction and climate change adaptation programs, emergency preparedness and prevention efforts. It also provides for humanitarian admissions and non-return policies for those in need of international protection who do not qualify as refugees. The GCM is not legally binding, but emphasizes the importance of international cooperation while reinforcing sovereignty. It was drafted through a state-led process (Mexico + Switzerland) and the final draft (expected to be approved at a conference in December 2018 in Morocco) is subject to negotiations but likely to be formally adopted with a few opt-outs, including the U.S. If so, political leadership will be needed to ensure implementation.

Whether these two Global Compacts will make much difference either to the migration policies of states or the decision making or the plight of migrants, is unclear. Some observers say the Compact is a last hope (for a long time) and an important opportunity for states to turn the vision of shared responsibility and cooperation on migration into a concrete plan, by working with each other and with other stakeholders on practical issues that need joint action. However several challenges remain, including how to find an acceptable balance between international cooperation and national sovereignty and decisionmaking, and what if any the significance will be of the U.S. decision not to participate in the process.

One of the biggest challenges to migration, however, does not come from the policy positions of UN member states, but rather from the changing global migration industry. Prior to 2015, regular migration access to Europe was already constrained, but after 2015 as borders slammed shut, regular access whether for asylum seekers or economic migrants became much more difficult. As a result, the smuggling industry grew massively, its agents ranging from local moneymaking schemes to global networks, and its activities increased too: widespread advertising (particularly in social media), "door-to-door" journeys that included multi-city stops with frequent changes of fake documents, passports and visas obtained from corrupted officials in various consulates. The power, sophistication and reach of this industry is unlikely to be stopped by Global Compacts, but the latter is another step in a long history of cooperative efforts to help migrants and address migration problems.

Conclusion

This article has touched on only a few of the many issues raised by global migration, and has not had the space to address many more: how to ensure the smooth, regular and safe movement of people, how to facilitate the integration of migrants and their conversion into citizens, how to secure migration so that it is not a pathway for crime, terrorism and money laundering—among many others. Nor are there easy or obvious answers to the many policy and protection questions raised in this article. We have not attempted to provide answers, nor suggest what it is that citizens like you can do to advocate for the best outcomes. Our hope is that the article will provoke discussion and further reading to promote deeper understanding. One thing only is certain, global migration cannot be ended, and it is trying to stop it is like building a sand castle on the beach.

Members of the Spanish NGO Proactiva Open Arms place a lifejacket on the statue of Christopher Columbus in Barcelona on July 4, 2018, on the day that the NGO Proactiva Open Arms ship arrived with 60 migrants on board rescued as they tried to cross the Mediterranean from Libya after Italy and Malta refused access. (LLUIS GENE/AFP/GETTY IMAGES)

discussion questions

1. How does migration into a certain area or region of the world become a global concern? What issues arise from high rates of migration that affect global foreign policy?

2. What are the most pressing reasons that migration occurs today? What will migration and its causes look like in the future, especially in regards to climate change?

3. How does intervention by international organizations such as the UN ameliorate issues that migration causes? How could agreements such as the Global Compact on Refugees or the Global Compact on Migration benefit both host countries and the migrants? Do you think that the Compacts will have any effect?

4. Although Europe faced a high volume of migration in 2015, the author pointed out that historically it was not a record. What differentiated the 2015 migration "crisis" from Europe's previous periods of high migration?

5. How do the economic and political issues surrounding migration affect the way host countries are able to assimilate migrants? Are these issues a valid argument against migration? Why or why not?

6. Several European countries have had incidents of terrorism perpetrated by migrants. Is migration itself inherently a security issue? How does migration lead to issues such as terrorism? How can political leaders and countries prevent terrorism from migrants?

suggested readings

Agier, Michel. **Borderlands: Towards an Anthropology of the Cosmopolitan Condition**. 208 pp. Cambridge, UK: Polity Press, 2016. Anthropologist Michel Agier draws on his ethnography of "border dwellers" living in migrant camps to address uncertainty and danger around crossing borders.

Bhaba, Jacqueline. **Can We Solve the Migration Crisis?** 140 pp. Cambridge, UK: Polity Press, 2018. Bhaba explains why forced migration demands compassion, generosity, and a more vigorous acknowledgement of our shared dependence on human mobility as a key element of global collaboration.

Feldman-Savelsberg, Pamela. **Mothers on the Move: Reproducing Belonging Between Africa and Europe**. 280 pp. Chicago, IL: University of Chicago Press, 2016. In this book, Pamela Feldman-Savelsberg takes readers back and forth between Cameroon and Germany to explore how migrant mothers—through the careful and at times difficult management of relationships—juggle belonging in multiple places at once: their new country, their old country, and the diasporic community that bridges them.

Don't forget: Ballots start on page 103!

King, Natasha. **No Borders: The Politics of Immigration Control and Resistance**. 216 pp. Chicago, IL: University of Chicago Press, 2016. In No Borders, Natasha King draws on more than a decade of experience as a migrant rights activist as well as extensive research in Greece and Calais in order to explore the dilemmas and challenges involved in translating the "No Borders" slogan into practice.

Kingsley, Patrick. **The New Odyssey: The Story of Europe's Refugee Crisis**. 384 pp. New York, NY: W.W. Norton & Company, Inc., 2017. Journalist Patrick Kingsley investigates the European migration crisis through traveling the migration trail and telling the story of all, from smugglers to politicians.

Rawlence, Ben. **City of Thorns: Nine Lives in the World's Largest Refugee Camp**. 400 pp. New York, NY: Picador, 2017. The stories of nine individuals are intertwined to depict life in the notorious Dadaab refugee camp in Kenya.

Shukla, Nikesh. **The Good Immigrant**. 272 pp. London, UK: Unbound, 2017. A collection of essays by minority immigrants in the United Kingdom, the essays examine what it means to be the "other" in society today.

To access web links to these readings, as well as links to additional, shorter readings and suggested web sites,

GO TO www.greatdecisions.org

and click on the topic under Resources, on the right-hand side of the page.

The Middle East: regional disorder

by Lawrence G. Potter

U.S. President Donald Trump, First lady Melania Trump (2nd from R), Saudi Arabia's King Salman bin Abdulaziz al-Saud (2nd from L) and Egyptian President Abdel Fattah el-Sisi (L) put their hands on an illuminated globe during the inauguration ceremony of the Global Center for Combating Extremist Ideology in Riyadh, Saudi Arabia on May 21, 2017. (BANDAR ALGALOUD / SAUDI ROYAL COUNCIL /ANADOLU AGENCY/GETTY IMAGES)

As the first term of President Donald J. Trump passes the halfway point, the Middle East remains a region in turmoil. A century after the map of the region was decided by colonial powers, states that never achieved coherence or legitimacy are failing. There is a crisis in leadership, with autocrats condemned for incompetence, corruption and greed. The future of borders and the nation state itself has been increasingly called into question as non-state actors such as Islamic State (ISIS) and Al Qaeda carve out roles for themselves. Hope for democracy and change had been high as popular uprisings broke out in the Arab Spring revolts of 2011. Although the leadership was overturned in Tunisia, Libya, Egypt and Yemen, the uprisings failed. Since then, there has been a feeling of hopelessness and apprehension about the future throughout the region.

The wars in Afghanistan and Iraq initiated by the administration of George W. Bush (2001–09) have never really ended, and political stability in both remains precarious. The

LAWRENCE G. POTTER *teaches in the School of International and Public Affairs at Columbia University and was deputy director of Gulf/2000, a major research and documentation project on the Persian Gulf states based there, from 1994 to 2016. He is a longtime contributor to* GREAT DECISIONS *and published "The Persian Gulf: Tradition and Transformation" in FPA's* Headline Series *Nos. 333–334 (Fall 2011).*

People wave Turkish national flags as they stand near the "July 15 Martyrs Bridge" (Bosphorus Bridge) in Istanbul on July 15, 2018. Turkey commemorated the second anniversary of a bloody coup attempt, which was followed by a series of purges in the public sector and changes to boost President Recep Tayyip Erdoğan's powers. (OZAN KOSE/AFP/GETTY IMAGES)

civil war raging in Syria since 2011 has practically destroyed that country, with half a million civilians killed and over ten million displaced. In Yemen, recent estimates indicate 56,000 civilian and combatant deaths between January 2016 and October 2018 in the war which commenced in 2014. In one of the worst humanitarian catastrophes in the world, over 14 million people face starvation.

The three most populous states in the Middle East, Egypt (97.0 million), Iran (81.6 million), and Turkey (81.3 million) are all undergoing serious internal challenges. The younger generation that drove the Arab Spring protests has been bitterly disappointed that its aims of democracy and better governance have not been met. This is especially evident in Egypt where President Abdel Fattah el-Sisi, in office since 2014, imposed a new authoritarianism after ousting the democratically elected Mohammad al-Morsi a year earlier. The Green Movement in Iran mobilized millions in anti-government protests in 2009 before being crushed by security forces. In Turkey, major anti-government protests in Istanbul were put down violently in 2013 and there have been widespread arrests and purges since a failed coup in the summer of 2016. In the Persian Gulf, rulers alarmed by demands for political reform responded by blaming Iran, seeking to buy off political opposition and stepping up internal repression. A blame game is taking place among governments that, terrified of people power, are acting defensively.

Why is this collapse happening now? According to Lebanese journalist Rami G. Khouri, there is a decline of sovereignty in the Arab world that has led to or exacerbated many current problems. He notes that the continuous development of Arab nations that took place from the 1920s to the 1970s has broken down. "We are now living through a gradual series of simultaneous adjustments at national, regional and global levels that have been taking place across the region since the end of the Cold War in 1990 or so. The Saudi-Yemen situation is important because it captures developments at all three levels at the same time, and possibly marks a historic turning point at which regional powers mature in their self-confidence and capabilities, and step up and take greater charge of political dynamics across the region." Proxy wars have broken out in Libya and Syria as neighboring states seek to impose military solutions for regional instability.

In the Arab world, Khouri believes this crisis is the result of failed statehood, including "stunted citizenship, a non-existent social contract, a lack of meaningful citizen participation in national policymaking, and zero real accountability mechanisms to check the excesses or failures of the state." José Antonio Sabadell, a Spanish diplomat who studies "the politics of frustration in the Arab world," found that it "is in the middle of a process of deep social and political change. It has the potential to alter domestic politics and the regional strategic balance and to re-define political ideologies and identities. The emergence of Arab peoples as key political actors, in combination with widespread, profound and mounting popular frustration, is a game changer."

Iran and Turkey, major non-Arab states, are under duress due to autocratic leadership, corruption, economic collapse, media suppression and human rights abuses. Forty years after the revolution, Iranians are fed up with an intrusive and inefficient state, which has led to an outbreak of anti-government protests throughout the country since the winter of 2017–18. Sadegh Zibakalam, a professor of politics at Tehran University interviewed by *The Guardian,* says the situation has become so bad that "people see no light at the end of the tunnel. In no period of time before this, we've had so much anguish, so much anxiety, so much despair about the future of the country." In Turkey, strongman rule by President Recep Tayyip Erdoğan, re-elected in June 2018, has sought to increase the role of religion and roll back many reforms and rights previously taken for granted. By the fall of 2018, the collapse of the value of the Turkish currency caused by misguided economic policies imposed by Erdoğan led to a major loss of confidence in the government.

A new political dynamic is at work, where "the proliferation of failed and weakened states has created new opportunities for competition and intervention, favoring new actors and new capabili-

! Before you read, download the companion **Glossary** that includes definitions, a guide to acronyms and abbreviations used in the article, and other material. Go to **www.greatdecisions.org** and select a topic in the Resources section on the right-hand side of the page.

ties," according to Marc Lynch of George Washington University. "Regional dynamics are no longer determined by formal alliances and conventional conflicts between major states. Instead, power operates through influence peddling and proxy warfare." The interlocking regional crises and terrorist groups that respect no borders are making clear the inability of states to impose order.

Although states remain the primary actors, according to Kristian Coates Ulrichsen, a scholar at Rice University, "they now confront an array of non-state actors and processes, following programmes that do not reflect a coherent 'national' vision, including multinational corporations, trans-national networks and diaspora ethnic and religious groups. Hence, in the era of globalisation and trans-nationalism, states no longer are the sole actors and shapers of policy."

A general view shows the "Si-o-Se Pol" bridge (33 Arches bridge) over the Zayandeh Rud river in Isfahan, which now runs dry due to water extraction before it reaches the city, April 11, 2018. (ATTA KENARE/AFP/GETTY IMAGES)

Aside from dysfunctional politics, societies throughout the Middle East are under great stress due to environmental reasons such as climate change, drought, overpumping of ground water, deforestation and higher temperatures. These have barely been addressed by governments. Eastern Syria suffered a major drought from 2007 to 2010, forcing one and a half million people to flee to the cities and contributing to the current anti-state revolts. In Iran, drought has forced many farmers to abandon their villages and end up, disgruntled and unemployed, in the cities. Lake Urumieh in Iran's northwest shares the fate of the Aral Sea and has shrunk to a fraction of its original size. Iranians are shocked that the Zayandeh Rud, a major river running through their storied city of Isfahan where people used to swim and fish, has now been reduced to a dust bowl.

Throughout the Middle East, the changing media and information environment, including the rise of satellite tv channels and widespread use of social media, have led to a much better-informed populace and broken the state's historic monopoly on information. Al Jazeera, opened in Qatar in 1996, has fearlessly aired regional problems and criticized most regional leaders. It played a major role in covering the unrest in Tunisia, Egypt and Libya, although it was faulted for holding back when it came to protests in Bahrain, Oman and Saudi Arabia, not to mention the internal situation in Qatar. In 2003 Saudi Arabi launched its own network, Al Arabiya, in Dubai as a counter to Al Jazeera and is now setting up media to target the non-Arab Middle East. In his final column in the Washington Post last October 17, murdered Saudi dissident Jamal Khashoggi appealed for a free press in the Arab world, saying it is "facing its own version of an Iron Curtain, imposed not by external actors but through domestic forces vying for power."

Governments are on notice that they must take public opinion into account with their policies. In the backlash to fraudulent elections in Iran in the summer of 2009, a "Twitter Revolution" attracted worldwide support for the protesters, with over two million tweets by half a million users (many from outside Iran). In the Egyptian Revolution of 2011 Twitter was used to communicate, and helped draw 80,000 protestors to Tahrir Square and the streets of Cairo on January 25. The first thing governments do when faced with protests is disable the internet. States now heavily invest in media wars and propaganda to promote their viewpoint and mold public opinion. In Washington, the battle of the consultants and think tanks rages: wealthy Gulf states such as Saudi Arabia, Qatar and the United Arab Emirates (UAE) have poured millions into trying to mold American opinion in their favor.

The U.S. does not have solutions to these problems and there has been an exodus of experienced hands from the Foreign Service under the Trump administration. Nearly two years into his term, the U.S. still does not have ambassadors in Turkey and Saudi Arabia, although a nomination was recently proposed for the latter. The president has proclaimed his wish to reduce American engagement in the region but, as in the case of President Obama's intention to "pivot to Asia," this has proved to be impossible. "Ultimately, the U.S.' position in the Middle East reflects its broader retreat from global leadership," according to Vali Nasr, Dean of the Johns Hopkins School of Advanced International Studies in Washington, D.C.

The process of making policy toward the Middle East as it has been practiced in Washington for decades has clearly broken down and policymaking has become more politicized than ever before. "The U.S. no longer has the power or the standing to impose a regional order on its own terms," according to Professor Lynch. "In all likelihood, U.S. hegemony in the Middle East will never be restored because the region has fundamentally changed....The damage is too deep."

Many have suggested that it is a good time to take stock of U.S. policies toward the region. Robert E. Hunter, former U.S. ambassador to NATO, notes that "despite intense rhetoric about threats to the U.S. homeland from the Middle East, there are in fact few....continuing U.S. security requirements in the Middle East derive almost entirely from partners' concerns and U.S. responses." James Russell of the Naval Postgraduate School suggests "the Middle East has lost its strategic significance for the U.S., and the landscape is littered with America's many failed attempts to save the region from itself."

A region in turmoil

How did the Middle East reach the crossroads it is at today? The roots of the current regional disorder are usually traced to the aftermath of World War I, when the core of the Ottoman Empire was carved up into six new states: Turkey, Syria, Lebanon, Palestine, Iraq and Transjordan, with the later addition of Saudi Arabia and Yemen. Many Arabs resented the arbitrary nature of the borders they were allotted. The Qajar Empire which ruled Persia for the long 19th century was replaced in 1925 by the modern state of Iran, ruled by the Pahlavi dynasty. Major groups such as the Palestinians and the Kurds were bitterly disappointed that they did not achieve statehood at this time, which has led to recurrent political tensions.

With the fall of empires in the wake of war, the nation-state became the most common political unit. However, as Prof. Lisa Anderson of Columbia University notes, "the interwar efforts to fasten the institutions of European-style states to the populations of the region introduced several deeply dysfunctional dynamics into modern political life. They established expectations for government that would prove impossible to meet while imposing a system of rule that, far from creating citizens, often reinforced nonstate identities and created deep communal resentment and anger."

Because many people found themselves minorities in newly created states, laws were introduced to protect "minority rights." In a study of French Mandate Syria (1923–43), Benjamin Thomas White concludes that "in many ways, the history of the nation-state is the history of minorities: that is, the history of the processes that lead certain groups to be defined as 'minorities'." Concern for minority rights has been a thread running throughout the 20th century.

A Turkish Youth Corps with a flag marches through the streets of Aleppo, which was part of the Ottoman Empire until the end of WWI. The Sinai and Palestine Campaign was a secondary theater of war between the Ottoman Empire and Great Britain during World War I (1915–18). (BERLINER VERLAG/ARCHIV/PICTURE-ALLIANCE/DPA/AP IMAGES)

Egypt, Iran, and to some extent Turkey, retain well-established historic identities on a par with a few other countries like China, Russia, India and Japan. However, in many Arab states carved out of the multinational and multiethnic Ottoman Empire, identity and loyalty were not so simple. New states tried to invent traditions to lend themselves legitimacy, with the objective of cultivating a sense of nationalism that aimed to subsume differences of religion, tribe and ethnicity. Thus, the political priority for Iraqi governments from 1920 to 1990 was to create an Iraqi national identity that would supersede sub-identities such as Sunni, Shi'a and Kurd. To some extent this was successful: in Baghdad many Sunnis married Shi'as and joked they were "Sushis." Likewise, in Iran, starting in the 1920s the Pahlavi dynasty sought to create a secular national state, led by Shi'i Persians, with little recognition accorded to minority ethnic, tribal, religious or linguistic groups.

The six-day war in June 1967 was a political turning point for the Middle East. Israel delivered a humiliating blow to the Egyptian, Jordanian and Syrian armies and tripled the size of its territory. It took the West Bank (including East Jerusalem) from Jordan; the Gaza Strip and Sinai from Egypt; and the Golan Heights from Syria. Over 200,000 refugees, including many Palestinians who had taken refuge on the West Bank in 1948, fled to Jordan. The sense of frustration and despair that was widespread among Arabs was particularly acute among Palestinians.

Pan-Arabism, a movement promoting Arab unity, was popular in Egypt in the 1950s and 1960s, but was reckoned to have failed. After another war with Israel in 1973, President Anwar Sadat turned to "Egypt first" patriotism. Many increasingly turned to Islam as an authentic indigenous ideology. "The ubiquity of Islamism is a thoroughly modern phenomenon and represents a major shift in the political landscape of the Arab world," according to Michael Wahid Hanna, Senior Fellow at The Century Foundation. "Significantly, this rising Islamic religiosity also occurred alongside the withering of liberal political thought in Egypt...."

Religious revival led to the rise of charismatic religious and political figures such as Ayatollah Khomeini in Iran. The Islamic revival alarmed the U.S. and other Western countries, which previously associated Islam with stagnation and regarded it as a fatalistic faith that impeded economic and political progress. For the West, the new "political Islam" was associated instead with revolutionary activity and violence, and became a rationale for terrorist groups such as Al Qaeda and ISIS.

This young Iranian soldier shouts "Allahu Akhbar," God is Great, from the trenches during the Iran-Iraq War, in Ein Khosh, Iran, November 1982. (RON EDMONDS/AP PHOTO)

Rise of sectarianism

Three major conflicts in the Persian Gulf—the Iran-Iraq War (1980–88), the Gulf War (1990–91) and the Iraq War (2003–11)—were immensely destructive in terms of lives and infrastructure and raised the level of distrust among people in the littoral states. The Iran–Iraq War for the first time introduced a sectarian dimension to regional conflicts. In both countries, but especially the latter, the demonization of the opponent led to a stronger sense of national identity. Both waged a fierce struggle on the ideological and propaganda fronts. They invoked several broad themes: Arab against Persian, Sunni against Shi'a, and pan-Arabism against pan-Islam. Such discourse served to reinforce mutual hostility even after a cease-fire was finally agreed on.

In the wake of the Gulf War in the spring of 1991, violent uprisings of Iraq's Shi'i Arabs (about 55% of the population) and Kurds (around 20%) broke out and were brutally put down. Saddam Hussein's government, in an attempt to divide opponents, then instituted a process of "retribalization" in which subnational identities were emphasized and Sunni Arabs (about 18%) were firmly in control. This policy went against everything Ba'athism, the state ideology, stood for and has contributed to the unraveling of Iraq in the post-Saddam era.

The fall of the Saddam government in 2003 after another war led to a major change in the status of Shi'as throughout the region and enhanced the power of Iran. For the first time, Iraq had a Shi'a-led government, and Sunnis in Iraq, as well as the Persian Gulf monarchies, were on the defensive. In many states the Shi'as were now perceived as a security problem, not just a religious group. Vali Nasr wrote in 2006, "by liberating and empowering Iraq's Shi'ite majority, the Bush administration helped launch a broad Shi'ite revival that will upset the sectarian balance in Iraq and the Middle East for years to come." This warning proved prescient.

The rise of the Shi'a throughout the Arab world coincided with the rise of the Sunni-led Arab monarchies of the Gulf. Long on the periphery of empires, today the Gulf with its mega oil cities like Dubai, Abu Dhabi and Doha is increasingly regarded as the center of the Middle East, displacing historic cities such as Cairo, Damascus and Baghdad. These centers of Islamic civilization and culture are now impoverished and overwhelmed with domestic problems. The globalization of the Gulf has transformed it at a rapid rate, and people throughout the region have flocked there to work and play.

Arab Spring: a 'false dawn'

The most significant event precipitating the current turmoil in the Middle East was the widespread uprisings of 2010–11, dubbed the Arab Spring.

People demonstrate during a rally in Tahrir Square on February 18, 2011, in Cairo, Egypt. Thousands of people rallied in Tahrir Square calling on Egypt's military to quicken reforms and to celebrate the one week anniversary of Egypt's President Hosni Mubarak being forced from power by mass protests. (CARSTEN KOALL/GETTY IMAGES)

One after the other, rulers were overthrown in Tunisia, Egypt, Libya and Yemen, there were major protests in Bahrain, and a popular uprising began in Syria which continues to the present day. These were "the most dramatic sign of mass discontent in modern Arab history," according to Khouri. "Millions of citizens who had reached a breaking point spontaneously rebelled against their ruling elites; yet those elites today with their foreign supporters continue to ignore most of the uprisings' underlying drivers of discontent and disparity."

The uprisings failed due to brutal crackdowns by the security forces, the lack of effective leadership and a realistic program for alternative rule. Steven A. Cook of the Council on Foreign Relations has characterized the Arab Spring as a "false dawn," and found that Egypt's authoritarianism was only reinforced: "the profoundly repressive state of Egypt's politics exceeded anything under Mubarak, but the underlying patterns of politics and the means of establishing control were largely the same." Hanna finds that "amid this current resurgence of Arab authoritarianism and Islamist militancy, both liberalism and secularism have had little traction....The notion of open and pluralistic societies in the Arab world is more distant than ever."

The popular anger reflected by the Arab Spring and in the wake of the 2009 election in Iran was also reflected in Turkey. Major anti-government protests broke out in Gezi Park in Istanbul and throughout Turkey in the summer of 2013. The original demands were to prevent the destruction of the park, in the heart of Istanbul, and replace it with a shopping mall and restored Ottoman military barracks. They later focused on opposition to President Erdoğan's policies, notably promotion of an Islamist agenda, restrictions on freedom of speech and his increasing autocracy. The occupation of the park by thousands of people was put down violently by Turkish forces. As the official media downplayed the protests, demonstrators turned to social media to communicate with supporters. Like Tahrir Square in Cairo and the Pearl Roundabout in Manama (Bahrain), Gezi park became a large protest camp with thousands of supporters of different political inclinations, all determined to stand up to the state. Clearly, the display of people power at these major protests in Iran, the Arab world and Turkey presage a new kind of politics in the Middle East and the demands of a new generation to be heard.

The feeling of pan-Arab solidarity, thought to be in decline, was clearly a motivating factor in the Arab Spring. It was also a reminder of the artificial boundaries of states. The sanctity of borders had already been breached in 1990 when Iraq sought to take over Kuwait. ISIS, a terrorist group that sought to found a territorial "caliphate," occupied and governed much of Iraq and Syria between 2014 and 2017, making the border irrelevant. This was a powerful challenge to the existing state system, as was the attempt by Kurds in northern Iraq to take advantage of widespread disorder by forming their own state. They held a referendum in September 2017 that endorsed independence, but with no outside support they were soon pushed back on the ground by Iraqi forces. Disregard for Yemen's sovereignty has led to a carving up of the state into spheres of influence controlled by outsiders and terrorist groups. This calling into question of regional borders is a new and unsettling feature of modern politics.

Regional roundup

Saudi Arabia in transition

In June 2017 the new Saudi king appointed his son, Mohammad bin Salman (known as MbS) as crown prince. With a reputation for acting impetuously and brooking no criticism, MbS quickly amassed great power. He downplayed the role of consensus and consultation that has always been the trademark of the Al Saud in favor of more autocratic rule. He sees himself as the voice of the younger generation and the reformer that his country needs. Changes such as reining in the religious police, allowing women to drive and opening movie theaters are unprecedented. However, he has struck back harshly at critics, religious or secular, at home or abroad. Mild criticism by Canada of Saudi treatment of two human rights activists led in August to a break in relations. The most egregious example so far was MbS's role, confirmed by the CIA, in the murder Saudi journalist Jamal Khashoggi in Istanbul last October.

In the face of a serious drop in oil revenues that started in mid-2014, the Saudis have been draining their financial reserves at a rate that cannot be sustained. According to the IMF, by the end of 2018 they will have run through 40% of their massive foreign exchange reserves, worth over $700 billion in 2014. In response, the future crown prince introduced a plan, Vision 2030, in the spring of 2016. This is a major set of reforms that aim to reduce government subsidies, cut dependency on oil, provide jobs for the younger generation, and empower the private sector. The announced intention was to sell off 5% of the shares of Saudi Aramco, the state oil company, which was expected to be valued at $2 trillion and raise $100 million to finance the plan. However, by the fall of 2018 Vision 2030 was in jeopardy and the IPO indefinitely postponed. Many wealthy Saudis are reluctant to invest domestically, fearing the government will confiscate their assets. Although it needed their cooperation to implement Vision 2030, the government sequestered 300 royals and businessmen in the Ritz Carlton Hotel in Riyadh from November 2017 to February 2018 and subjected them to an unprecedented financial shakedown. Foreign investors are hesitating to invest in a country with so little transparency and protections under the law.

MbS has been particularly active in foreign policy. The new, more muscular approach is inspired by a desire to take advantage of the regional turmoil and confidence that he has the support of Washington. The Gulf monarchies are challenged by Iranian-supported Shi'i militias in Iraq, Syria, Lebanon and Yemen, and fear new demands for political and social recognition on the part of their own Shi'i minorities.

For some time, both Saudi Arabia and Iran have engaged in heated rhetoric couched in sectarian terms. How serious is this war of words? Although Saudi Arabia is obsessed with the Iranian threat, the Iranians do not seem too worried about Saudi but keep their focus on relations with major states such as the U.S., Russia and China, as well as Europe. Such rhetoric, however, plays a role in poisoning public opinion and is a factor used to justify the "proxy wars" around the region. According to Professor Lynch, "although Arab fears of Iranian expansionism are grounded in reality, those anxieties have always been far out of proportion to actual Iranian power. Perversely, however, the more that Arab states do to confront Iran, the stronger it becomes."

Crown Prince of Saudi Arabia Mohammed bin Salman Al Saud (L) is welcomed by the U.S. Secretary of Defense, James Mattis (R) during his official visit in Washington, D.C., on March 21, 2018. (BANDAR ALGALOUD/SAUDI ROYALCOUNCIL/ANADOLU AGENCY/GETTY IMAGES)

Game of thrones

The dispute that broke out in June 2017 between Qatar and a quartet of adversaries—Saudi Arabia, the UAE, Bahrain, and Egypt—has shuffled regional alliances, benefited Iran, and caused a serious policy dilemma for the U.S. Although ostensibly about Qatari perfidy, it is a continuation of intermittent Saudi attempts over a long period of time to expand their power throughout the Arabian peninsula.

Statements attributed to Sheikh Tamim bin Hamad Al Thani, the amir of Qatar, on May 23, 2017, allegedly expressed support for Iran, Hamas, Hezbollah and Israel. The Qatari government denied such remarks had been made, and claimed, evidently correctly, that hackers were spreading false rumors. Shortly thereafter, their adversaries withdrew their ambassadors from Doha and expelled Qatari diplomats, closed their airspace to Qatar Airways, the national carrier, and sealed the land border between Saudi Arabia and Qatar, denying vital food imports to Qatar. The campaign against Qatar was remarkably mean-spirited: Qataris were even prevented from performing the Hajj, a religious obligation, to Mecca last fall.

The conflict forms part of the fallout of the Arab Spring, in which states took different approaches toward political Islam and the role of elections. Although both Saudi Arabia and Qatar follow the austere Wahhabi school of Islam, the Qataris observe a more moderate version. Like the Turks, the Qataris support the Muslim Brotherhood, an Islamist democratic movement which is abhorred by the Saudis, who have long promoted the ultra-conservative Wahhabi strain of the faith. The quarrel is not about sectarian issues: for example, Shi'i Iran came to the rescue of Sunni Qatar while Saudi Arabia has taken steps to reconcile with Shi'i leaders in Iraq. The competing versions of Islam promoted by Turkey and Saudi Arabia amount to a struggle for the allegiance of all Muslims.

This attempt to pressure Qatar has now backfired and put Saudi Arabia and the UAE on the back foot. President Trump's military and foreign policy advisers persuaded him that the value of the U.S.'s major air base in the Middle East, Al Udeid near Doha, Qatar, was too high to be jeopardized by this quarrel. Despite U.S. attempts to get the parties to settle, the dispute continued to be stalemated through the fall of 2018 and in all likelihood will not have an early solution. Most concerning, it has led to the virtual collapse of the Gulf Cooperation Council (GCC), made up of Kuwait, Saudi Arabia, Bahrain, Qatar, the UAE and Oman), supposedly a shield against external threats and a model for regional cooperation.

Iran at a Crossroads

In Iran, the withdrawal of the U.S. from the nuclear accord and re-imposition of sanctions has led to consternation, a feeling of betrayal and serious economic consequences. The Iranian currency rapidly plunged in value, from 43,000 rials per dollar at the start of 2018 to 190,000 per dollar in early October. European companies that had rushed to invest, such as Daimler, Siemens and Peugeot, were forced to pull

Iranians stage a protest against Trump's decision to withdraw from the Iran nuclear deal after Friday Prayer at Tehran University's campus in Tehran, Iran on May 11, 2018. (FATEMEH BAHRAMI/ANADOLU AGENCY/GETTY IMAGES)

out or face secondary sanctions. The French company Total, which planned to develop natural gas in the Persian Gulf, cancelled and the concession was awarded to the Chinese.

Iranian oil exports, which amounted to 2.5 million barrels per day (bpd) in April 2018, have fallen steeply and by October only came to 1.1 million bpd. With fluctuating exchange rates, rampant corruption and lack of protection under the law, many foreign companies were not about to enter or re-enter Iran whether it was under sanctions or not. Iranian banks are cut off from the world financial system and suffer from mismanagement, capital shortfall and a lack of transparency. Although the government blames its economic woes on U.S. actions, the lack of reform has turned away potential investors despite the large consumer market.

The multiplying internal problems have led, since January 2018, to widespread protests. So far they have attracted a different demographic than the Green Movement of 2009, which appealed to the middle and upper classes and was focused on Tehran. At that time initial protests about a fraudulent presidential vote count morphed into demands for a complete overhaul of the political system, with an emphasis on the republican rather than the Islamic part. Today, poorer Iranians who have been the worst hit by government blunders have risen up spontaneously all over the country and condemned clerical leaders for a gamut of woes, ranging from high prices and shortages of water and electricity to ruining the environment and imposing strict Islamic rules. So far there is no clear leadership or agenda and these protests are not a serious threat. However, they amount to a vote of no confidence and demonstrate that, as in other parts of the Middle East, people have lost fear of their government.

Hardliners have increased pressure on President Hassan Rouhani, a relative moderate, who was chastised by supreme leader Ayatollah Khamenei for selling out to the Americans. The Revolutionary Guard has widened its role in foreign policy at the expense of the Foreign Ministry and has been in the forefront of exerting Iran's influence abroad. Iran has created and worked closely with Shi'i militias to implement its goals of being the power behind the scenes in Iraq and keeping President Bashar al-Assad in office in Syria. Because Iran lacks the funds to modernize its army (in 2017 it spent $16 billion on defense while Saudi Arabia spent $76.7 billion), it has specialized in asymmetric warfare, exemplified by small speedboats harassing American warships. According to Nasr, "if Iran's behavior appears more threating today than it once did, that is not because Iran is more intent on confronting its rivals and sowing disorder than before but because of the drastic changes the Middle East has experienced over the last decade and a half."

In light of the anti-Iranian rhetoric emanating from Washington, Riyadh, Abu Dhabi and Tel Aviv, Iran feels vulnerable. The Saudi crown prince ominously warned in May 2017 that any future battle would be fought inside Iran, not the Gulf states, hinting

Iranian Supreme Leader Ali Khamenei (L) presents his official approval to Hassan Rouhani, who was re-elected in presidential elections in May 2017, during a ceremony at Khamenei's office in Tehran, Iran on August 3, 2017. (IRANIAN LEADER'S PRESS OFFICE/ANADOLU AGENCY/GETTY IMAGES)

at Saudi support for Iranian minorities such as the Arabs, Kurds and Baluch. Iranians were shocked by an attack on Revolutionary Guard forces during a parade in Ahwaz (in southwest Iran) last September 22, claimed by a local Arab liberation group. (The Islamic State dubiously also claimed credit, while Iran blamed the U.S. and Saudi for being behind the attackers.)

Ayatollah Khamenei, the Supreme Leader since the death of Ayatollah Khomeini in 1989, is 79 and ailing and at his death all issues will be on the table. The original "reign of the ayatollahs" has now morphed into rule by the security services, above all the Revolutionary Guard, who are expected to fight hard to preserve their power and exclude reformists and moderates. In a recent exchange of vitriol with President Trump, Qasem Soleimani, the head of the Quds Force, the section of the guard that operates abroad, said the U.S. should deal with him, not Rouhani, indicating where the real power lies. Over the years Khamenei has built up a "deep state" of loyalists among security, intelligence and economic elements, according to analysts Sanam Vakil and Hossein Rassam. The Guard seeks to preserve Iran's revolutionary legacy and has strong economic interests in a state that has rewarded them well. They will make it very difficult to select a moderate successor, however much the majority of Iranians may wish it.

Brief takes

Iraq and Syria

U.S. forces occupied Iraq from the 2003 invasion down to their exit in 2011, when the Iraq War ended. Many returned in 2014 to battle ISIS, and about 9,000 remained in the fall of 2018. A major U.S. concern is that pro-Iranian militias do not gain the upper hand and the Baghdad government remains friendly. The largest winner in parliamentary elections of May 2018 was a party led by the anti-American cleric Moktada al-Sadr. In October a new government was formed under prime minister Adel Abdul Mahdi and a new president, Barham Salih, who is Kurdish. They are regarded as capable technocrats who are non-sectarian, have good relations with both Tehran and Washington and are expected to maintain continuity. The future role of Iran in Iraq is problematic, as Iraqi nationalism is rising and many Iraqis resist their influence.

Syria has been tearing itself apart since a major anti-government insurgency broke out seven years ago. There are actually two conflicts taking place, a civil war centered in the west, and the fight against Islamic State in the east. Thanks to major assistance from Iran and Russia, the Bashar al-Assad government is on the brink of regaining control. The U.S. has few troops on the ground (currently about 2,000 to fight the Islamic State). President Trump, like Obama, does not want to commit U.S. troops. In response to use of chemical weapons by the Assad government, Washington mounted airstrikes in 2017 and 2018. The Gulf Arab states, mainly Saudi and the UAE, have funded some of the insurgents, and Turkey, burdened with 3.5 million Syrian refugees, has also sent troops, making it a dangerous and volatile arena. In a "shadow war," Israel has launched airstrikes against military assets of Iran in Syria. The Islamic State is much weaker now than a year ago, and an open question is whether U.S. troops may clash with Iranian troops or pro-Iranian militias there in the future.

Israel and the Palestinians

As soon as he assumed office Trump, noted for his "bromance" with Prime Minister Netanyahu, announced he would focus on the peace process between Israel and the Palestinians. Progress, however, has stalled. Designating Jerusalem the capital of Israel, cutting aid to the United Nations Relief and Works Agency (UNRWA), which provides support to Palestinians in the West Bank and Gaza, and shutting the Palestine Liberation Organization office in Washington reinforced a perceived tilt toward Israel that had been avoided by previous administrations. By late 2018 the peace plan being developed by Jared Kushner, the president's son-in-law, still had not been announced and it was evident that the U.S. has lost all credibility as an interlocutor. Robert Malley, president of the International Crisis Group, observed "by punishing the Palestinians, the administration unwittingly is liberating them from former restraints under which they had operated since [the] Oslo [Accords of 1993] in order to placate the U.S. and

People walk past signs in Jerusalem on May 13, 2018, that show support for U.S. President Donald Trump's decision to move the country's Embassy to the city.(KYODO NEWS/GETTY IMAGES)

Yemeni soldiers loyal to the Shi'ite Houthi rebels march in the capital Sana'a on October 16, 2018, to protest against the Saudi-led intervention in the country. (MOHAMMED HUWAIS/ AFP/GETTY IMAGES)

Israel. What gradually removing those shackles from Palestinians will mean in terms of the future is unclear."

Stalemate in Yemen

Perhaps the greatest tragedy in the region is unfolding in Yemen. The war there started in 2014, when the Houthis, a rebel group loosely aligned with Iran but following a different form of Shi'ism, took control of the northwest, including the capital, Sana'a. A military coalition led by Saudi Arabia began bombing Yemen in March 2015 to oust the Houthis and restore the government to power. However, so far this has not been successful and according to the UN, more than 16,700 civilians have been killed or injured. The Saudis regard the Yemen conflict as a war of necessity against a failed state on their border that is a haven for terrorists and nonstate actors that are proxies for Iran. A UN report issued in August 2018 accused the coalition of actions that may amount to war crimes, including air strikes on civilians, torture and rape of detainees. The Houthis, also, came in for criticism and may also have committed war crimes. The coalition has imposed major restrictions on shipping and air travel, preventing the delivery of food and medical supplies and leading to widespread starvation. Water and sewage systems have been disabled and a major cholera epidemic broke out in 2016 which was ongoing in the fall of 2018.

Terrorism

Fighting terrorism was part of the rationale for the wars in Afghanistan and Iraq. However, an assessment released by the White House last October concluded that 17 years of counter-terrorism strategy by the U.S. had only been a "mixed success." Although the Islamic State only controls 1% of the territory it formerly held in Iraq and Syria, it remains a global threat and still attracts recruits. It has recently mounted operations in Afghanistan, Iraq, the Sinai peninsula in Egypt, Libya, and Yemen. Al Qaeda likewise retains a global network of jihadists. Countering terrorism remains a primary mission of the U.S. military and a reason for the U.S. presence in the Middle East.

U.S. policy in the age of Trump

The current disorder in the Middle East poses a formidable challenge to the U.S. This is a reflection of the regional confusion about what to do: all governments feel vulnerable and at the mercy of transnational forces they cannot control. The advent of the Trump administration has made things worse since many states do not know what U.S. policies are and how long they will be in place. *The New York Times* editorialized, "articulations of foreign policy by President Trump may not always be what they seem.... Mr. Trump has a well-established record of undermining [his officials'] pronouncements, and even his own, with a tweet." The result is that, in the opinion of Robert Hunter, "U.S. policy goals in the region, defined primarily in terms of American interests, are still opaque, and may not have been formulated at all, and certainly not in any comprehensive way."

Reversing Obama's legacy

President Trump has been severely criticized for rolling back policies that were supported by a consensus of foreign policy experts, such as the Iran nuclear accord and not moving the embassy in Israel. His overall goal of reversing any policy put in place by President Barack H. Obama (2009–17) is wreaking havoc in the region. "The Trump administration's decision to double down on support for autocratic regimes while ignoring the profound structural changes that stand in the way of restoring the old order will neither produce stability nor advance U.S. interests," according to Marc Lynch. The administration's lack of interest in promoting democratization and human rights has been a stepdown from the Obama and Bush II eras and is out of synch with the wishes of the youthful population that makes up a majority of local societies.

Calibrating the U.S. response to the events of the Arab Spring was one of the greatest foreign policy challenges faced by the Obama administration, and it was not met effectively. Repeatedly, the US was forced to take sides between a popular uprising demanding democracy, and the autocratic rulers it had long worked with who ensured security and "stability." In the case of Tunisia, few U.S. interests were at stake and it was not difficult to cut ties to the leader. Egypt, however, was a different story. President Mubarak had been a close U.S. ally for 30 years and had kept the peace with Israel. After equivocating at first, eventually the US voiced support for the demonstrators and accepted that Mubarak had to go.

However, events in the Gulf were a different matter. When confronted with the uprising in Bahrain the US held back on criticism of the ruling Al Khalifa due to the island's strategic importance. The US urged them to find a peaceful solution, but this advice was disregarded. In the case of Saudi Arabia, where there were some demonstrations, the US was notably silent and supportive of the ruling family. The Al Saud were greatly angered at the forced departure of Mubarak, and feared that the U.S. would abandon them next. Israel also was distressed at the loss of their longtime partner for peace.

When Syria crossed Obama's redline by using chemical weapons in 2013 and the US did not respond, the Saudis questioned US credibility. Worst of all, it seemed to them that the US preferred Iran to the Sunni Gulf monarchies which historically were the closest US allies in the region. When Obama was asked if he regarded the Saudis as friends, he replied, "it's complicated." Obama pressed the Saudi king to be willing to "share" the neighborhood with Iran—an appeal he did not appreciate. He criticized the kingdom's harsh human rights record, and expressed dissatisfaction with the war in Yemen. Obama also believed that Saudi Arabia and the GCC states in the future needed to rely less on the U.S. for their security.

The U.S. participated in the seven-month long NATO intervention in Libya's civil war in 2011, helping to enforce a no-fly zone. This was an example of the "right to protect" civilians as endorsed by the UN in 2005 and was done without congressional backing. The Libya intervention was remembered in the US for the attack on American diplomats in Benghazi on September 11, 2012 by a militant Islamic group resulting in the death of US Ambassador to Libya J. Christopher Stevens. Libya has been divided into competing political and military factions based in Tripoli and the east since 2014 and remains in a state of civil conflict.

In Obama's second term his administration, led by Secretary of State John Kerry, focused on Iran and achieved their signal foreign policy victory. With its partners, the U.S. negotiated a comprehensive agreement that achieved the paramount goal of preventing Iran from acquiring a nuclear weapon, in return for an easing of sanctions and normalization of relations. The agreement was widely praised but also had vocal critics, while as a presidential candidate Trump disparaged it as "the worst deal ever." By the time Trump took office, disillusionment with the U.S. stoked by the invasion of Iraq, U.S. equivocation during the Arab Spring, and the expansion of Iranian influence, was widespread in the Middle East.

Trump's policies

Donald Trump comes to foreign policy with a weak understanding of regional dynamics. "Where his predecessor hoped to win hearts and minds, Mr. Trump champions the axiom that brute force is the only response to extremism – whether in Iran, Syria, Yemen or the Palestinian territories," according to international correspondent David D. Kirkpatrick. "He has embraced the hawks of the region, in Israel and the Persian Gulf, as his chief guides and allies."

Like Obama, Trump would prefer to avoid being hopelessly bogged down in the Middle East. In August 2018 he approved a new defense budget that instead of fighting terrorism there prioritizes countering China and Russia. The U.S. military has reduced its presence in the Gulf, with no aircraft carrier there since March 2018 and the removal of Patriot missile-defense systems from Kuwait, Bahrain and Jordan. The problem with a U.S. drawdown is that there is no obvious alternative to maintain regional security. Looking East, where much of the oil now goes, neither India nor China (nor Russia) are willing to provide it.

The primary reason for U.S. involvement in the Middle East since World War II, security of its energy supply, is now less important as U.S. shale oil production has soared. Total U.S. oil production is expected to reach 11.5 million bpd in 2019, up from 9.4

White House Adviser Jared Kushner watches alongside a member of the Saudi delegation during a meeting between President Donald Trump and Crown Prince Mohammed bin Salman of the Kingdom of Saudi Arabia in the Oval Office at the White House on March 20, 2018. (KEVIN DIETSCH/POOL/GETTY IMAGES)

million bpd in 2017, according to U.S. Energy Information Administration forecasts. Imports from the Gulf (which in 2017 amounted to 17.3% of the total) are declining. The price of West Texas Intermediate crude, the North American benchmark, was trading in the $56 range in mid-November. Saudi supplies less than 5% of U.S. imports, but it could opt to cut exports which would lead to rise in prices. The basis of the longstanding understanding in which Saudi provides oil in return for security provided by the U.S. has been increasingly called into question.

Personal diplomacy is a hallmark of Trump's foreign policy, which has been carried out to a large degree on a personal basis between MbS and Jared Kushner, with many U.S. experts on the region sidelined. This likely contributed to the Khashoggi fiasco of last October, as the crown prince probably counted on Trump to look the other way. Senior U.S. experts Aaron David Miller and Richard Sokolsky wrote in an op-ed in *Politico* last August that "the most successful Saudi foreign policy initiative in recent memory is the successful capturing and bamboozling of Donald Trump."

By late 2018, it seemed clear that the expectations of the U.S. on the one hand and the Gulf Arabs on the other were exaggerated and unrealistic. The priorities of the Gulf states lie in preserving regime security at any cost and in persuading the U.S. to take the lead in opposing Iran, plus providing funding if not forces for proxy wars. Trump's comments on banning Muslims from entering the U.S. and use of the term "radical Islamic terrorism" has not helped. He has also said (like Obama) that the Gulf monarchies were "free riders" that were dependent upon the U.S. for their security and have to "pay their way" in return for the U.S. defending them.

The president rejects multilateralism and has always emphasized that his priority is "America First." His personal view runs against military intervention, and instead of sending forces to Syria to counter Russian and Iranian influence he is trying to pressure his Gulf allies to step up their involvement. He is also relying on them to keep oil prices low, confront Iran and persuade the Palestinians to make peace with Israel. The Gulf states complain about American fidelity, but as Lynch points out, "no amount of reassurance from the U.S. can ever be enough."

The Trump administration shares a belief with some of the Gulf monarchs and Israel that Iran is the source of most problems in the Middle East because of its nuclear program, ballistic missiles, and military interventions in Iraq, Syria and Yemen, in addition to its support for Hezbollah and Hamas. Although the national security adviser, John R. Bolton, has denied it, many analysts conclude that the U.S. aim in Iran is regime change. By withdrawing from the nuclear deal in May 2018, reimposing punishing sanctions in August (targeting currency, gold, automobiles and commercial airplane parts and services) and November (targeting banks, petroleum and shipping) and possibly aiding internal opposition groups among Iranian ethnic minorities, the administration appears to believe that it can stoke internal opposition that leads to the fall of the government. Most outside analysts think this is fanciful and will only contribute to regional chaos. U.S. relations with its European allies, who still remain in the deal, have come under unprecedented strain. As former ambassador and leading Iran expert John Limbert has pointed out, "[the U.S.] does not know what it wants beyond the end of the Islamic Republic."

There are a number of key issues over which U.S. policy is being contested, including:

THE IRAN NUCLEAR DEAL

Iran and the other signatories, except the U.S., maintain that they are adhering to the deal, although Iran has not received the economic benefits it expected.

Without U.S. participation, Iran will not be able to normalize its relations with the rest of the world and will be tempted to resume its nuclear program. Trump has repeatedly announced that he is willing to initiate negotiations with Iran for a "better deal." But his advisers have issued preconditions that make this a non-starter. A future president might seek to return to the deal, a prospect Iran may be waiting for. Better relations with Iran should not wait, though, as the U.S. needs Iran's help with many regional issues from narcotics and smuggling to keeping the peace in Iraq and Syria. Iran played a key role in defeating ISIS in Iraq. Wendy R. Sherman, who led the team of American negotiators, observed that "Trump has turned Iran into a nearly impossible problem for future administrations. His behavior has given U.S. allies less reason to trust Washington on future deals or to take U.S. interests into account. He has thrown away a hard-nosed nuclear deal that set a new standard for verification, and he punched a hole in a highly effective web of sanctions and international consensus that made the Iran deal—and future deals like it—possible."

RELATIONS WITH SAUDI ARABIA

Although the president has restored strong ties to Saudi Arabia, the Khashoggi affair has led to a crisis in relations. Many urged Trump to step back from tribal politics he does not understand, reduce blanket support for the new Saudi rulers, and push harder for a settlement of the war in Yemen and the quarrel with Qatar. The U.S., in short, should not let the Gulf Arabs dictate the regional agenda. The U.S. could cut back on massive arms sales to Saudi as a sign of displeasure – something Congress may mandate. Although Saudi does cooperate with the U.S. on antiterrorism measures, the Financial Action Task Force, an international watchdog, issued a report last September criticizing it for weak measures against money laundering and financing terrorism. As remarked by F. Gregory Gause III of Texas A & M University, "The U.S. needs a stable Saudi Arabia, as well as a Saudi Arabia that isn't destabilizing the Middle East."

RESET RELATIONS WITH THE PALESTINIANS

The U.S. is no longer seen as a credible interlocutor between Israelis and Palestinians, and as the possibility of a long-envisioned two-state solution recedes relations between the two can only worsen. Questionable acts such as moving the U.S. embassy to Jerusalem, cutting aid to the Palestinians and closing their office in Washington have led to despair and regular outbreaks of violence in Gaza and the West Bank. If the U.S. has a new peace plan, it should not delay further in unveiling it, and must take actions to rebuild trust with the Palestinians.

■ CONTRIBUTE TO A SOLUTION IN SYRIA

As we reach the endgame in Syria, it seems likely that President Bashar Assad will prevail over his opposition. Although the U.S. wants to help shape a solution, one may be imposed instead by an evolving axis of Russia, Iran, and Turkey. U.S. troops in eastern Syria are tasked with defeating the Islamic State. Since this has largely been achieved, when will they come home?

■ ENDING THE WARS IN YEMEN AND LIBYA

Many note that U.S. complicity in arming and advising the Saudis goes against U.S. interests and perhaps U.S. laws. Its role now should be to pressure its allies, Saudi Arabia and the UAE, to find a face-saving way out. The U.S. has acknowledged providing midair refueling (which it recently announced will end), intelligence support and other advice to the Saudis, but maintains it does not approve target selection. There has been rising concern in military and congressional circles in Washington, however, that the U.S. was getting bogged down in a hopeless conflict. There has been widespread international condemnation of the U.S. role in the war; for example, the charity Oxfam, which provides assistance to civilians in Yemen, declared, "The State Department demonstrated that it is blindly supporting military operations in Yemen without any allegiance to facts, moral code or humanitarian law. This administration is doubling down on its failed policy of literally fueling the world's largest humanitarian crisis."

A child walks among graves of people who were killed in the ongoing war including children killed by airstrikes, at a cemetery on October 12, 2018 in Sana'a, Yemen. A United Nations body has requested Saudi Arabia to halt its deadly air raids against civilians in war-torn Yemen immediately and to prosecute officials responsible for child casualties. (MOHAMMED HAMOUD/GETTY IMAGES)

■ HUMAN RIGHTS

The state of human rights throughout the Middle East is currently dismal, especially in major states such as Egypt, Iran, Turkey and Saudi Arabia. Although traditionally a concern for U.S. foreign policy, Trump has indicated this is not an issue he is interested in, but a successor might feel differently.

★ ★ ★

The current situation in the Middle East is troubling and confusing, and regional leaders are not fulfilling their duty to govern effectively. Instead of working with their neighbors and compromising to get things done and make things better, they engage in blame games and rely on outside powers to provide solutions. States and societies will grow further apart if governments continue to refuse to provide needed reforms, and the possibility of further upheaval is very real.

While solving longstanding internal problems in the region is beyond the ability of the U.S., American policies that are contributing to regional instability can change due to public pressure. Already Congress is forcing the Trump administration to reduce support for the Yemen war, and some have suggested that Saudi Arabia, not Iran, is the most destabilizing force in the region. Many U.S. policies are out of synch with regional realities, and the insistence on "America First" is not practical in today's globalized and transnational world where the state is only one of many actors.

Trump's inclination not to send troops to the Middle East and to reduce U.S. involvement there will find widespread support at home from a public weary of decades of involvement, expense and casualties. However, with a reduced footprint on the ground, the U.S. needs to find a way to work with regional states as well as Europe, Russia and China, plus international organizations such as the United Nations, to achieve the policy results it wants. It seems clear that congressional hearings on U.S. policy and a thorough rethinking of policy by the State Department are in order.

Many believe that the Middle East is at a tipping point, in which all stakeholders must step up and contribute to solutions. While outsiders cannot impose a regional order to their liking, they can provide incentives for all interested parties to come to the table, defuse tensions, and arrive at agreements for the good of all.

discussion questions

1. Is Iran a greater cause of problems in the Middle East than Saudi Arabia? Which country could make a better ally in the future?

2. So far, the U.S. has usually backed autocrats in the Middle East, as long as both had good security relations. Should the U.S. accord higher priority to democracy and human rights, goals that usually get sidelined?

3. Many experts believe that canceling the Iran nuclear deal and reimposition of sanctions was a bad idea. What do you think?

4. Do you agree that the U.S. should increasingly extricate itself from the Middle East and "pivot to Asia" instead?

5. Why are there so many failed states in the Middle East? Is this region an exception?

6. How do non-state actors now challenge the state for influence in the Middle East?

7. Do you expect the state system, and its current borders, to survive in the Middle East, or do you think other arrangements are possible?

suggested readings

Al-Rasheed, Madawi, ed.. **Salman's Legacy: The Dilemmas of a New Era in Saudi Arabia**. 320 pp. Oxford: Oxford University Press, 2018. Leading experts explain the transition Saudi Arabia is experiencing under King Salman and his son.

Cook, Steven A. **False Dawn: Protest, Democracy, and Violence in the New Middle East**. 313 pp. Oxford: Oxford University Press, 2017. Surveys the Arab Spring revolts and explains why they did not succeed, while considering the role of the U.S. in the region.

Hanna, Michael Wahid. "Explaining Absence: The Failure of Egypt's Liberals." 24 pp. New York: **The Century Foundation, Report,** March 21, 2017. Explains the lack of liberalism in Egypt and Arab world and its replacement by authoritarianism and Islamist militancy. https://tcf.org/content/report/explaining-absence/

Hiltermann, Joost, lead contributor. **Tackling the MENA Region's Intersecting Conflicts**. 47 pp. Brussels, Belgium: International Crisis Group, December 22, 2017. A major study of the clusters of conflict in the Middle East and policies to tackle them.

Kamrava, Mehran. **Troubled Waters: Insecurity in the Persian Gulf**. Ithaca, NY: Cornell University Press, 2018. New study by leading scholar examines the security dilemmas of regional states and why they have led to continuing tensions.

Khouri, Rami G. "The Citizen and the State: The Decline of Sovereignty in the Arab World." **World Policy Journal**, vol. 33 no. 3 (Fall 2016): 114-21. An insightful article by leading Lebanese journalist that distills the true problems of the region, which result from a failure to transition to pluralistic democracies.

Lynch, Marc. "The New Arab Order: Power and Violence in Today's Middle East." **Foreign Affairs**, September/October 2018, pp. 116-26. The disorder in the Arab world created by the failure of the Arab Spring and the Trump administration's mistake in supporting autocratic regimes

Sherman, Wendy R. "How We Got the Iran Deal and Why We'll Miss It." **Foreign Affairs**, September/October 2018, pp. 186-97. The lead negotiator of the deal explains why it was a mistake to cancel it.

Don't forget: Ballots start on page 103!

To access web links to these readings, as well as links to additional, shorter readings and suggested web sites,

GO TO www.greatdecisions.org

and click on the topic under Resources, on the right-hand side of the page.

Nuclear negotiations: back to the future?

by Ronald J. Bee

This August 29, 2017, photo distributed by the North Korean government shows what was said to be the test launch of a Hwasong-12 intermediate range missile in Pyongyang, North Korea. (KOREAN CENTRAL NEWS AGENCY/KOREA NEWS SERVICE/AP PHOTO)

In 1986, over 70,000 nuclear warheads had amassed in world arsenals, according to the Federation of American Scientists (FAS). In January 2018, the FAS Nuclear Notebook estimated the total number of nuclear weapons worldwide at 14,485. At first glance, today's numbers seem like a measurable improvement. The end of the Cold War (1947–91) led to 85% reductions in U.S. and Russian arsenals, and the two powers agreed to the Strategic Offensive Reductions Treaty (SORT, 2003) and the New Strategic Arms Reduction Treaty (New START, 2010). The latter, which is set to expire in 2021, reduced the number of strategic missile launchers by 50%, and limited each country to 1,550 strategic nuclear warheads on bombers, submarines and missiles. Even with this treaty in place, the U.S. and Russia still control 93% of all nuclear weapons internationally.

New tensions and conflicts in world politics today threaten to renew strategic nuclear competition between the major powers. A nuclear war ignited by using a small fraction of 9,300 warheads could mean the end of civilization as we know it—a situation that Daniel Ellsberg (famous for leaking the Pentagon Papers report on the Vietnam War in 1971) calls "omnicide."

Since the U.S. bombed the Japanese cities of Hiroshima and Nagasaki on August 6 and 9, 1945, no state has used nuclear weapons in an attack. Why? For those who support the strategy of deterrence, the fact that no state

RONALD J. BEE *has served at the International Atomic Energy Agency, the Congressional Research Service, the Pentagon, the University of California Institute on Global Conflict and Cooperation, and as Director of the Charles Hostler Institute on World Affairs. He currently works as the Director of the Hansen Summer Institute on Leadership and International Cooperation at the University of San Diego, as an adjunct professor, as well as a lecturer at the Oxford Study Abroad Programme in international relations in the UK.*

Dr.Herbert F.York, the Defense Department's research chief, is shown at a press conference on October 5, 1959, where he said Americans must be prepared for the "acute embarrassment" of seeing Russia launch bigger space vehicles than the U.S. for several more years. The press conference was called in the wake of Russia's new moon-rocket success. (BETTMANN/GETTY IMAGES)

with nuclear weapons has attacked another state with nuclear weapons is an affirmative sign. The superpowers came close to mutual assured destruction in the Berlin and Cuban Missile Crises of 1961 and 1962, but when push came to shove, no politician, American or Soviet, was about to risk nuclear annihilation.

The yin and yang junction of disarmament and deterrence has existed in the nuclear weapons discourse since at least World War II (WWII). In his memoir, *Making Weapons, Talking Peace: A Physicist's Odyssey from Hiroshima to Geneva*, Herbert F. York reveals his ambivalence along these lines by noting the need to build nuclear weapons while simultaneously using them as leverage to negotiate for peace. York, a Manhattan Project scientist, advised six presidents. He became a staunch advocate for dialogue and nuclear arms control. He fully recognized the need to protect the U.S., yet felt anxious about any international breakdown in deterrence that might lead to the destruction of his country and others.

! Before you read, download the companion **Glossary** that includes definitions, a guide to acronyms and abbreviations used in the article, and other material. Go to **www.greatdecisions.org** and select a topic in the Resources section on the right-hand side of the page.

"Peace through strength," a phrase coined by the Roman Emperor Hadrian in the first century AD, would become a motto of U.S. President Ronald Reagan (1981–89) some 19 centuries later. While "Peace through strength" has consistently appeared in Republican Party platforms in the years since Reagan left office (including in 2016), Democratic Presidents Bill Clinton (1993–2001) and Barack Obama (2009–17) favored another approach: Their "lead but hedge" strategy sought to take the lead on arms reductions and nuclear nonproliferation while maintaining a viable nuclear arsenal to hedge against unforeseen geopolitical developments.

The possibility of "unforeseen developments" lies at the heart of states' rationales for keeping nuclear weapons. Such weapons provide some guarantee of survival in an unpredictable and confrontational world. Every leader of a nuclear-weapons state, no matter their preferred political or economic system, has thus far coveted this hedge. No state, whether democratic or totalitarian, has thus far risked self-destruction by attacking another nuclear-weapons state. Yet as regions become more crowded and less stable, as in the Middle East, it is only prudent to interrogate the status quo.

York, who served as the U.S. ambassador and chief negotiator for the Comprehensive Test Ban Treaty (CTBT) talks, published the second edition of his book in 1989, one month before the Berlin Wall fell and two years before the Soviet Union dissolved. York concluded that "Two great realities dominate the world scene. One is that the strategy of maintaining peace through the threat of mutual annihilation cannot work forever, no matter how stable it may currently be. The other is that finding an effective, moral, and permanent replacement for the current strategy will take serious effort, and a long time, generations at least."

While the U.S. and Russia have reduced their nuclear arsenals, they have not eliminated them. Furthermore, the other three nuclear-weapons states recognized by the Treaty on the Non-Proliferation of Nuclear Weapons (NPT, 1968), the UK, France and China, also maintain their arsenals, and four other countries outside the NPT now possess nuclear arsenals (Israel, India, Pakistan and North Korea).

As the U.S. and Russia ponder renewing the New START Treaty to 2026, competing interests on the world stage threaten to jump-start new nuclear arms races. In February 2018, the U.S. Department of Defense (DoD) released its Nuclear Posture Review (NPR), which determines the role of nuclear weapons in U.S. security strategy. Citing an "uncertain international security environment," the NPR notes that "While the U.S. has continued to reduce the number and salience of nuclear weapons, others, including Russia and China, have moved in the opposite direction...North Korea continues its illicit pursuit of nuclear weapons...[and] Iran retains the technological capacity and much of the capacity necessary to develop a nuclear weapon within one year of a decision to do so." The review warns that "nuclear non-proliferation today faces acute challenges" in North Korea and Iran, and concludes with the statement that "The U.S. remains willing to engage in a prudent arms control agenda."

That prudence looks much like York's "making weapons, talking peace." The U.S. will modernize its nuclear triad, and new tit-for-tat rhetoric between U.S. President Donald Trump (2017–present) and his Russian counterpart Vladimir Putin (2000–08, 2012–present) in 2018 indicates that both of their countries have begun development of hypersonic cruise missiles that could carry nuclear warheads and circumvent ballistic missile defenses. China has also invested in developing this technology.

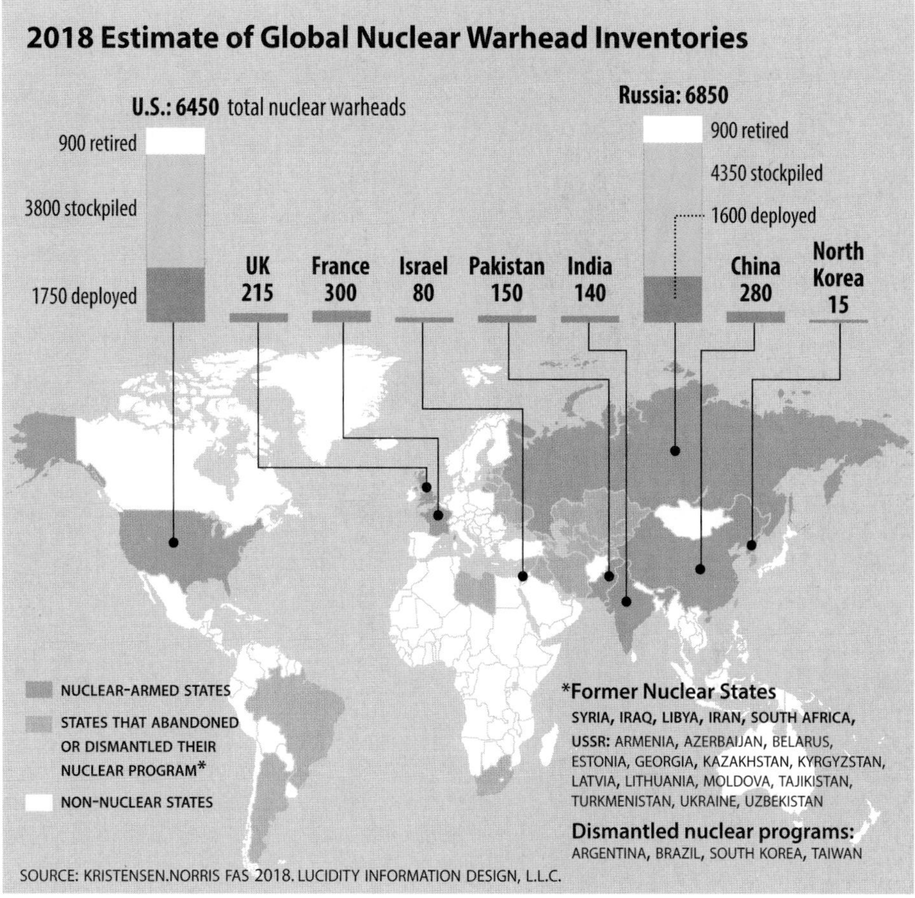

The Permanent Five (P5) of the United Nations Security Council (UNSC)—the U.S., the UK, France, Russia and China—all retain nuclear arsenals, despite the best intentions of the NPT, which calls upon those states to eventually destroy their weapons. Hoping for general and complete disarmament as promised in that treaty, however, has become the nuclear equivalent of waiting for Godot. Any nuclear aspirant can readily see by the structure of the United Nations (UN), and the veto power of the P5, that having a nuclear arsenal promises power, prestige and protection.

In June 2018 President Trump announced the establishment of a U.S. Space Force to, among other goals, counter anti-satellite weapons developed by Russia and China. A space race could very well risk the placement of nuclear weapons in space and the deployment of advanced ballistic missile defense systems. Such actions would violate the New START Treaty and the Outer Space Treaty (1967), whose provisions compel the parties "not to place in orbit around the earth, install on the moon, or any celestial body, or otherwise station in outer space, nuclear or any other weapons of mass destruction."

The Intermediate-Range Nuclear Forces Treaty (INF, 1987) has also come into question, with Russia appearing to have abrogated that accord. The U.S. claims that President Putin has plans to build a land-based nuclear missile system that could attack Europe on short notice. Such a system would violate the INF Treaty. On October 2, 2018, the U.S. permanent representative to the North Atlantic Treaty Organization (NATO), Kay Bailey Hutchison, put Russia "on notice," announcing that if Moscow continued to develop the missile system, "countermeasures [by the U.S.] would be to take out the missiles that are in development by Russia in violation of the treaty." On October 20, President Trump announced his decision to terminate the INF Treaty because Russia has built a prohibited missile designated as the 9M729 that could threaten European NATO, and China, not a party to INF, has built intermediate-range missiles that could threaten U.S. and allied interests in Asia. This withdrawal implies that any future talks on intermediate range nuclear missiles should include China.

Secretary of State Hillary Clinton presents Russian Foreign Minister Sergey Lavrov with a device with a red button symbolizing the intention to "reset" U.S.-Russian relations during their meeting in Geneva,Switzerland, on March 6, 2009. (AP PHOTO)

Before and after his election, Trump severely criticized the "reset" policy with Russia that had been spearheaded by his predecessor President Obama and Obama's Secretary of State Hillary Clinton (2009–13). Trump claimed that the policy led directly to the Russian annexation of Crimea, a civil war in Eastern Ukraine and the insertion of Russian troops into Syria to support the Syrian dictator Bashar al-Assad. Trump also criticized the Obama-Clinton approach of "strategic patience" with North Korea, taunted North Korean leader Kim Jong Un (2011–present) by calling him "a maniac" and "little rocket man," and suggested that Japan (steadfastly

anti-nuclear since the events of WWII) might need to develop nuclear weapons to deter Kim. In his first speech to the UN, President Trump warned that if the U.S. "is forced to defend itself or its allies, we will have no choice but to totally destroy North Korea." Mr. Trump also railed against President Obama's nuclear agreement with Iran as "the stupidest deal of all time." The president has since withdrawn the U.S. from that agreement.

President Trump must now deal with Russia, China, North Korea and Iran on the nuclear front, and has juxtaposed fiery public rhetoric with cordial face-to-face dialogue. He has personally met with President Putin, Kim Jong Un and Chinese President Xi Jinping (2013–present), and has said he would be willing to meet with Iranian President Hassan Rouhani (2013–present) with "no preconditions." At the same time, Trump has imposed economic sanctions on Russia for its invasion of Ukraine, on China for unfair trade practices, on North Korea for missile and nuclear tests, and on Iran for supporting terrorism throughout the Middle East.

President Trump's gambits carry high stakes for a variety of constituencies: for U.S. citizens; for the U.S. government as the leader of the free world; for U.S. allies in Europe, Northeast Asia and the Middle East; and for rivals in the not-so-free world that perceive nuclear weapons as an ultimate hedge for political survival. Can a businessman-turned-president apply "the art of the deal" to the age-old dilemma of "making weapons, talking peace," and if so, what can we expect from pending nuclear negotiations, and for the future of arms control talks in general? What options does the president have, and what lessons should he consider in navigating today's nuclear waters?

The economics of nuclear weapons

Since the beginning of the nuclear age, much debate has unfolded over the question "how much is enough?" How many nuclear weapons do we need to deter our enemies, and how much money should we invest in that arsenal to protect the peace? Tracking the actual money expended by the U.S. for nuclear weapons over time should provide salient insight into how the country has answered these questions.

In a 1998 Brookings Institution book, *Atomic Audit: The Costs and Consequences of U.S. Nuclear Weapons Since 1940*, the authors calculated that the U.S. spent $5.5 trillion on nuclear weapons and weapons-related programs through 1996—some 29% of all military spending during that period. In 2014, the James Martin Center for Nonproliferation Studies released a report estimating that the U.S. would spend a trillion dollars over the next 30 years to modernize or replace the full triad of air-, land- and sea-based nuclear weapons. The DoD, in a 2018 fact sheet, "U.S. Nuclear Modernization," had a more moderate estimate: "Recapitalization, including plans for sustainment and modernization, will cost approximately 6.4% of the DoD base budget ($230–290 billion in 2018 dollars) spread from 2018 to 2040."

As the percentage of the military budget devoted to nuclear weapons has gone down, the budget for post-9/11 conventional operations has drastically gone up. The total U.S. defense budget enacted for fiscal year 2018 equals $700 billion, and fiscal year 2019 will amount to $716 billion. After WWII, in fact, the U.S. turned to nuclear weapons as a *cost-saving measure*. In 1953, President Dwight Eisenhower (1953–61) announced his New Look strategy, which reduced costs by bringing U.S. troops home to contribute to the postwar economy; the U.S. would now rely on deploying nuclear weapons in Europe to deter Communist aggression. At the time of this decision, President Eisenhower had just witnessed a bloody Korean War (1950–53) that ended in stalemate, and a Soviet buildup of huge conventional forces in Eastern Europe that required a counterbalance in Western Europe—both hugely expensive endeavors.

Non-nuclear conflicts since 9/11 have certainly borne out Eisenhower's warnings about the long-term costs of conventional conflicts. In a May 2018 report from the Stimson Center, a nonpartisan study group concluded that the total spending on counterterrorism since 9/11 amounted to $2.8 trillion from fiscal year 2002 to 2017. These expenditures included "governmentwide homeland security efforts, international programs, and the wars in Afghanistan, Iraq, and Syria."

Some ask why we should continue to expend so much money, labor and opportunity costs on weapons that prove useful only if they are never used. Indeed, *Atomic Audit* concludes that "The time has come to consider carefully the costs of and consequences to the U.S., and the world, of producing tens of thousands of nuclear weapons and basing national security on the threat of nuclear annihilation." The contrasting school of thought argues that nuclear weapons have proven their worth every day by deterring attack from our adversaries. This view holds that nuclear weapons kept the peace during the Cold War, until the Soviet Union unraveled from within, and that they continue to keep the peace with Russia today.

In reviewing the U.S.-Soviet nuclear contest, James Schlesinger, former secretary of defense and director of central intelligence, argued that nuclear weapons "shaped the outcome." He added, "It is far, far harder to argue that the West generally, and Western Europe in particular, would have been better off without nuclear weapons. Without the nuclear deterrent, the kind of semi-darkness that held the nations of Eastern Europe in its grip for more than four decades might also have afflicted much of Western Europe. Despite the worries of the past and the prospect of concern about nuclear weapons in the future, in this century their benefits have exceeded their costs."

These words continue to ring true to a national security community faced with new risks from troubled state and non-state actors. Secretary Schlesinger and political scientist Kenneth Waltz subscribed to a "nuclear peace theory" of international relations, which maintains that under some circumstances nuclear weapons induce stability and reduce the chances of escalation. Waltz's famous *Adelphi Paper #171*, "The Spread of Nuclear Weapons: More May Be Better," argues in favor of this perspective. The counterargument, made by Scott Sagan at Stanford University, asserts that "more will be worse" due to lack of civilian control over nuclear policy, and the potential for accidental use with catastrophic consequences.

Since the Berlin Wall fell on November 9, 1989, nuclear weapons have done nothing to deter ethnic conflicts in the former Yugoslavia and sub-Saharan Africa (Somalia, Sudan and Rwanda), a war in Afghanistan (Operation Enduring Freedom, 2001) two wars in Iraq (Operation Desert Storm, 1991, and Operation Iraqi Freedom, 2003), terrorist attacks in the U.S. and Europe, civil wars in the wake of the 2011 Arab Spring (Egypt, Syria, Libya and Yemen), and the invasion of Ukraine (2014).

Only in Syria have nuclear states—the U.S. and Russia—backed different factions with troop deployments. In this particular case, both parties coordinate their air force movements via a "deconfliction line" to reduce the likelihood of a collision between aircraft. This provides a modern-day conventional weapons equivalent of the 1963 hotline agreement, which built a direct communications link between the U.S. and the Soviet Union in order to prevent an accidental nuclear war. Since 1963, additional hotlines have been established, including between the U.S. and Russia, the U.S. and China, France and Russia, the UK and Russia, and between India and Pakistan.

States with smaller arsenals have also calculated the costs and benefits of developing nuclear deterrents. The usual conclusion is that minimal nuclear deterrence with smaller arsenals will prevent attack from potential adversaries. The UK, France, China, Israel, India, Pakistan and North Korea have all made those calculations to protect their respective national interests. In the case of North Korea and now Iran, authoritarian regimes have embraced what we might call "making weapons, talking survival" as part of a long-term gambit to protect their power.

Both the UK and France have recently re-invested in nuclear deterrence. In 2016, UK Parliament voted to renew its arsenal with a commitment to a new fleet of Trident submarines, which will come into service in the 2030s. In February 2018, on the heels of the U.S NPR, France announced that it would invest 37 billion euros in upgrading its nuclear deterrent.

Nuclear weapons, whether we like it or not, continue to serve a political purpose. For liberal republics, they hedge against illiberal regimes. For authoritarian and totalitarian regimes, they deter regime change from abroad and instill fear in their citizens at home. Tolerating costs to budget and population, nine states have chosen to build and keep nuclear weapons.

Indian military forces display an Agni II missile during the Republic Day Parade on January 26, 2002. The Agni II is the most powerful missile capable of carrying nuclear warheads in the Indian arsenal. Earlier that week, India had tested a shorter range nuclear-capable ballistic missile, heightening tensions with Pakistan. (AMI VITALE/PANOS PICTURES/REDUX)

Nuclear weapons cooperation agreements: maintaining deterrence

The U.S. has nuclear weapons cooperation agreements with its two nuclear allies in NATO, the UK and France. The UK and the U.S. have, since WWII, worked together on nuclear weapons development. In 1958, they signed a mutual defense pact to improve each party's "atomic weapon design, development and fabrication capability." In 2014, President Obama announced an update to that agreement that will last until 2024: The UK "intends to continue to maintain viable nuclear forces into the foreseeable future," he explained, adding that it remained in the U.S. interest to help the UK retain "a credible nuclear deterrent."

U.S. nuclear cooperation with France began during the administration of President Richard Nixon (1969–74), when both countries quietly cooperated on ballistic missile design, and, later, safety and security of nuclear weapons. On June 19, 1974, the U.S. signed the NATO Ottawa Declaration, which recognizes the role of British and French nuclear forces in NATO. In 1996, according to the *Washington Post*, the Clinton administration entered into an agreement with France to share nuclear weapons data from simulated explosions, and to increase cooperation between nuclear scientists.

While the French sharply disagreed with the 2003 U.S. invasion of Iraq and with President Trump's decision to withdraw from the 2015 nuclear deal with Iran, the two countries remain on the same page regarding Syria and the value of nuclear deterrence for collective security.

Since November 2, 2010, via the Lancaster House Treaties, the British and French also cooperate on nuclear stockpile stewardship, including working together at a joint facility in Valduc, France, to "model performance of nuclear warheads and materials to ensure long-term viability, security and safety."

Atoms for Peace?: nuclear energy cooperation agreements

The U.S. also enters into nuclear cooperation agreements with non-weapons states. These are designed to promote peaceful nuclear energy while thwarting the proliferation of nuclear weapons. Known as 123 Agreements, after Section 123 of the 1954 Atomic Energy Act (AEA), Congress formally calls them U.S. Bilateral Agreements for Peaceful Nuclear Cooperation.

The 123 Agreements have their origin in the Atoms for Peace program, part of President Eisenhower's Operation Candor—an effort to create an informed and cautious U.S. public in the nuclear age, and to project to the world that the U.S. had more interest in peace than in war. Atoms for Peace grew out of a December 1953 address by President Eisenhower to the UN General Assembly. The speech came in the wake of fears generated by the destruction of Hiroshima and Nagasaki, as well as by the 42 U.S. nuclear tests conducted since the end of WWII, among them the detonation in 1952 of a thermonuclear device with a blast effect over 60 times larger than that of the Hiroshima bomb.

The Atoms for Peace program has a mixed legacy of success. It supplied nuclear materials and know-how to India, Pakistan, Iran and Israel. In these cases, honorable intentions led to the diversion of technology for military purposes. Leonard Weiss, an expert on nonproliferation, has noted, "[I]t is legitimate to ask whether Atoms for Peace accelerated proliferation by helping some nations achieve more advanced arsenals than would have otherwise been the case. The jury has been in for some time on this question, and the answer is yes."

(Original Caption) Washington, D.C.: Postmaster General Arthur E. Summerfield announced that a special 3-cent stamp to commemorate "Atoms for Peace" will be first placed on sale at Washington, D.C. on July 28, 1955. The stamp will be blue in color and the central design is composed of two spheres showing each side of the atlas encircled with the orbital emblem which has become symbolic of atomic energy.(Bettmann/Getty Images)

Eisenhower's initiative also called for the establishment of the International Atomic Energy Agency (IAEA), which eventually occurred on July 29, 1957. The IAEA serves as an independent wing of the UN and promotes peaceful and safe uses of atomic energy, while acting as a nuclear watchdog agency. It has become an essential component of the NPT, which is itself the cornerstone of international efforts to stop the spread of nuclear weapons. The NPT calls for a grand bargain wherein nuclear-weapons states promise to negotiate the reduction of their arsenals (Article VI) and refrain from helping non-nuclear states to acquire nuclear weapons (Article I). In exchange, non-nuclear states agree not to build nuclear weapons (Article II), and place all of their nuclear facilities under international safeguards (Article III). Those safeguards require IAEA inspectors to verify compliance by visiting nuclear facilities of member states to ensure that nuclear materials, equipment and know-how do not get diverted for military purposes. Inspectors report any non-compliance to the UNSC. Most of the nuclear weapons controversies in North Korea, Iraq and Iran began when those countries denied access to IAEA inspectors.

Since Atoms for Peace, the U.S. has entered into 123 Agreements by selling nuclear reactors, critical parts of reactors and reactor fuel. The U.S. requires 123 Agreements for companies that wish to sell materials overseas that can be used to construct energy-producing nuclear reactors. The U.S.

has 123 agreements with 48 countries, the IAEA and Taiwan. In 2015, the U.S. negotiated new agreements with China and South Korea, and in 2018, renewed its agreement with Japan. Saudi Arabia and Mexico are currently seeking agreements. The UK plans to exit the European Union (EU) in 2019, and will then require a new 123 Agreement with the U.S., as the current accord exists under the rubric of the European Atomic Energy Community.

In testimony to the House Foreign Affairs Subcommittee on the Middle East and North Africa in 2018, Henry Sokolski, executive director of the Nonproliferation Policy Education Center, warned that the Middle East was at risk of becoming a "nuclear Wild, Wild West." In particular, he criticized the Trump administration proposal for a 123 Agreement with Saudi Arabia that would not require the kingdom to stop enriching or reprocessing nuclear fuel (the processes used to make a nuclear weapon). This oversight, Sokolski argued, "risks pouring kerosene on the embers of nuclear proliferation already present in the Middle East."

Some of those embers can be found in Iran, a regional rival of Saudi Arabia. Saudi Arabia is already fighting alongside other Arab states against Iranian-backed Houthi rebels in Yemen. Saudi Crown Prince Mohammed bin Salman (2017–present) has threatened to withdraw from the NPT, and he claimed in a March 15, 2018, CBS *60 Minutes* interview that "If Iran developed a nuclear bomb, we will follow suit as soon as possible." Israeli Prime Minister Benjamin Netanyahu (1996–99, 2009–present), in a meeting with the U.S. Senate Foreign Relations Committee, advised Washington not to cut a nuclear deal with Saudi Arabia unless the deal prohibits enrichment and reprocessing.

The Saudi 123 Agreement points to the U.S.' paradoxical interest in creating nuclear business while preventing proliferation. If the U.S. requires a "gold standard" that outlaws enrichment and reprocessing, U.S. companies are likely to lose business to other states like Russia and China with fewer nuclear scruples. Sokolski believes the U.S. must coordinate between all key nuclear reactor suppliers (France, Russia and China) and uranium fuel suppliers (France, a British-Dutch-German consortium and Russia) to stop proliferation. Moreover, we should consider placing an international moratorium on sales of nuclear reactors to the Middle East.

Henry D. Sokolski, executive director of the Nonproliferation Policy Education Center, in the Capitol Visitor Center on October 20, 2017. (TOM WILLIAMS/CQ ROLL CALL/GETTY IMAGES)

Sokolski further warns that the Trump administration "may also renew, revise, or cut additional nuclear cooperation agreements with Jordan, Egypt, Turkey, Morocco, and the [United Arab Emirates]. As a practical matter, there will be tremendous pressure to have these understandings take whatever we allow the Saudis," thus creating conditions for a nuclear arms race in the Middle East. Sokolski believes that Congress should revise and update the AEA to require the gold standard for all nuclear cooperation agreements

Setting this standard would also send a signal to other regions and countries. South Korea, for instance, has expressed a wish to build its own nuclear submarines, which would require enriched uranium fuel. South Korea's current nuclear cooperation agreement with the U.S. compels Seoul to acquire permission to enrich uranium. If the Trump administration acquiesced, this would certainly complicate denuclearization talks underway with North Korea.

How we got here: five nuclear races

We can conceptualize nuclear weapons issues and their related negotiations in terms of five chronological and overlapping races:

1. The ***original*** race against the Nazis during WWII to build the first atomic bomb.

2. A ***vertical*** race between the U.S. and the Soviet Union during the Cold War, which may be reemerging between the modern-day U.S. and Russia.

3. A ***horizontal*** race after the Cuban Missile Crisis to quell state-based proliferation, which endures today in Northeast Asia (North Korea) and the Middle East (Iran).

4. A race of ***denial*** to prevent non-state actors from acquiring nuclear weapons after 9/11, which continues unabated.

5. A nascent ***space race***, in which new cyber, artificial intelligence and space-based technologies may affect the future stability of nuclear deterrence.

The first two nuclear races involved competitions to acquire nuclear weapons; the third and fourth races became imperatives to stop the spread of nuclear weapons to state and non-state actors; and the fifth race, a competition in outer space, now looms as our next nuclear challenge.

The original race: against the Nazis

The first nuclear race began in 1938, when German scientists Otto Hahn and Fritz Strassmann discovered nuclear fission in Berlin. The Nazi government quickly formed a German atom bomb project—the Uranium Club—in April 1939. A group of prominent German and Hungarian Jewish refugee physicists, including Albert Einstein, warned U.S. President Franklin Roosevelt (1933–45) about the German project. Roosevelt formed his own Uranium Committee to hedge against the possibility that the Germans might wish to attack the U.S. This committee remained highly secret because the U.S. formally remained neutral until attacked by the Japanese at Pearl Harbor on December 7, 1941. Germany declared war on the U.S. four days later on December 11, which led to accelerated spending on the Manhattan Project, the U.S. secret effort to beat Hitler to the atomic bomb.

The U.S. project led to the first successful test of a nuclear weapon, in New Mexico, on July 16, 1945—over a month after Germany had surrendered in Europe. After the defeat of Germany, President Harry Truman (1945–53) pivoted toward Japan, warning the empire to surrender or face a "rain of ruin." The first nuclear race thus ended with the defeat of Nazi Germany and the use of nuclear weapons against Japan, the only use of such weapons in wartime to date.

While the devastation in Japan led to attempts to curtail nuclear weapons proliferation internationally—including via the U.S.-backed Baruch Plan, introduced at the UN in 1946—such proposals fell on deaf ears. The call for "international control of nuclear weapons" did not resonate in an era in which capitalism and Communism competed in a world destroyed by war. Soviet dictator Joseph Stalin (1924–53) fast-tracked his own nuclear weapons program, underway since 1942. The U.S. started testing nuclear weapons again in 1946, only reinforcing Soviet commitment to their own arsenal.

The vertical nuclear race: between the superpowers

The second nuclear race saw the U.S. and the Soviet Union competing to build and deploy a large array of nuclear weapons—short-, medium- and long-range—in an effort to prevent the opposing side from gaining an advantage. The vertical nuclear arms race also witnessed atomic standoffs in Berlin and Cuba, and proxy wars in Korea, Vietnam and Afghanistan. In 1963, after close shaves in Berlin and Cuba, leaders chose to establish the first hotline agreement, as well as the Limited Test Ban Treaty, which banned nuclear testing in the atmosphere, underwater and in outer space. They further committed to a nuclear nonproliferation regime, designed to stem the spread of nuclear weapons to other state actors. The NPT lies at the center of this regime.

With the emergence of a new Soviet leader, Mikhail Gorbachev (1985–91), President Reagan negotiated the Intermediate-Range Nuclear Forces Treaty (INF), which came into effect in 1988. With the end of Communism and the rise of Putinism, however, a new strategic competition has emerged between the U.S., Russia, and China and the INF as of October 2018 President Trump has scrapped the agreement. In February 2014, Russia invaded and annexed Crimea, and began support for Russian separatists in an ongoing civil war in Ukraine. The Obama administration and the EU imposed economic sanctions on Russia for its actions, and those remain in place today. NATO counterbalanced Russian actions by deploying more forces in the region, including ballistic missile defenses to its eastern flank. This move challenged the stability of the New START Treaty: For the Russians, New START hinges on the U.S. not developing its ballistic missile defenses.

In March 2018, Presidents Trump and Putin, in dueling State of the Union speeches, proposed modernization of their respective nuclear arsenals, including new weapons. Putin announced that Russia had developed a new array of "invincible" weapons, including a hypersonic nuclear-powered cruise missile with worldwide range that can evade ballistic missile defenses. The second nuclear race threatens to reemerge, if it has not already.

The horizontal race: preventing the spread of nuclear weapons to states

The third nuclear race, which began in 1962, refers to the ongoing global policy challenge of preventing proliferation of nuclear weapons by states. The NPT is the glue of the international nonproliferation regime, and can claim success for establishing a norm against proliferation.

Several states, like Argentina, Brazil and South Africa, have decided against developing nuclear weapons. After liberalizing their politics, these countries weighed the costs of owning atomic bombs and found that they paled in comparison to the benefits of remaining in the community of non-nuclear states. Others, including Taiwan, South Korea and Japan, have security guarantees provided to them by the U.S. that obviate the need to develop their own weapons. Still others—Israel, India, Pakistan and North Korea—have chosen a different course. For them, the benefits of building and maintaining nuclear weapons outweigh the economic and diplomatic costs. Israel neither confirms nor denies the existence of its ambiguous nuclear arsenal, yet everyone assumes it has one. India and Pakistan both exploded nuclear weapons in 1998, but the U.S. response to their nuclear programs has been complicated by strategic interests (interests in India, as a democratic country and marketplace of over 1 billion people; interests in Pakistan, which provides essential bases for U.S. operations in Afghanistan).

Rogue states: building weapons, negotiating concessions

The original grand bargain of the NPT holds out peaceful nuclear technology to non-nuclear states in exchange for their never building nuclear weapons. Nuclear safeguards, including inspections by the IAEA, provide oversight. But a number of NPT signatories, including Iraq, Libya, North Korea and Iran, have used the NPT to secretly develop their own nuclear weapons capabilities. In these cases, non-nuclear states abrogated their NPT obligations and built nuclear "sticks" so that they could leverage both political and economic "carrots." This "new nuclear bargain" has turned the NPT on its head.

The events of 9/11 changed the calculus for dealing with rogue regimes. The George W. Bush administration (2001–09) created the Department of Homeland Security to defend against terrorism domestically, and went after threats from abroad by invading Afghanistan (2001) and Iraq (2003), and conducting a global "war on terrorism." President Bush wanted to prevent a *nuclear* 9/11 and used "preemptive nonproliferation" to inhibit Iraq from aiding terrorists.

In 2003, Libyan dictator Muammar Gaddafi (1969–2011) watched the overthrow of Iraqi dictator Saddam Hussein (1979–2003) with trepidation. Gaddafi saw this as a wake-up call for his own regime, since Libya, too, had a not-so-secret weapons of mass destruction (WMD) program. Italy had seized a ship bound for Libya with parts for nuclear centrifuges. Gaddafi worried that the U.S. would invade Libya next, so he entered into secret talks with the U.S. and the UK: He would give away his nuclear program in exchange for regime survival and the end of economic sanctions. The U.S., UK and IAEA dismantled Libya's WMD program in 2004.

Then in February 2011, during the Arab Spring, Gaddafi's army brutally killed scores of peaceful protestors in the city of Benghazi. A civil war ensued, and the UN re-imposed sanctions on Libya for human rights abuses. The U.S., the UK, France and several other NATO members attacked Libya in support of the rebels (Operation Unified Protector). On October 20, 2011, rebel forces captured Gaddafi and killed him on the spot. While President Obama hailed this operation as an example of how collective security should work, nuclear proliferators like North Korea and Iran likely drew the conclusion that the U.S. could not be trusted to keep its nuclear deals.

U.S. President Donald Trump (R) gestures as he meets with North Korea's leader Kim Jong Un (L) at the start of their historic summit, at the Capella Hotel on Sentosa island in Singapore on June 12, 2018.(SAUL LOEB/AFP/GETTY IMAGES)

The "Libya model" for North Korean disarmament, proposed by John Bolton after he became President Trump's third national security adviser in April 2018, likely raised eyebrows in Pyongyang. Since the U.S. and North Korea negotiated an agreed nuclear framework in 1994, North Korea has always used its nuclear program as leverage for economic and political benefits in negotiations. (On the table then were two reactors for peaceful energy production and heavy oil transfers). Twelve years later, in 2006, North Korea detonated its first atomic weapon, and shortly thereafter left the NPT—the only country ever to have left the treaty.

Since 2011, Kim Jong Un's regime has also conducted scores of long-range missile tests, as well as five nuclear weapons tests, and made threats against Guam and the U.S. Kim has called President Trump a "mentally deranged U.S. dotard," and claimed "I have a nuclear button on the desk in my office. All of the mainland U.S. is within the range of our nuclear strike." Not one to back down from a war of words, Trump retaliated, calling Kim "little rocket man" and tweeting the message, "Will someone from his depleted and food-starved regime please inform him that I too have a Nuclear Button, but it is much bigger and more powerful than his, and my button works!" Amidst this schoolyard banter, three U.S. aircraft carriers were deployed around North Korea.

Under pressure from the U.S., the Chinese supported UN sanctions against North Korea, and warned that China would not come to Kim's defense if he launched missiles aimed at U.S. territory. Meanwhile, South Korean President Moon Jae-in (2017–present) has met twice with his North Korean counterpart, and has invited him to visit Seoul. Many South Koreans have relatives in the North, and President Moon has always supported peaceful unification of the Koreas.

On June 12, 2018, President Trump and Kim met in Singapore—the first summit meeting ever between a sitting

U.S. president and a North Korean leader. President Trump apparently conceded to stop U.S.-South Korean naval exercises, without first informing the U.S.'s South Korean allies. This led to "a joint statement committing to denuclearization of the Korean peninsula. Similar commitments have been made before, and now we await the devil in the details. The U.S. wants the North Koreans to denuclearize as a precondition for any concessions such as ending the Korean War, recognizing North Korea as a state or promising not to invade. North Korea, for its part, says that the U.S. needs to officially end the Korean War as a minimum prerequisite for denuclearization. Talks continue and a second summit may occur. In a positive development, North Korea has not conducted any nuclear or missile tests since the meeting.

Iran, for its part, used its nuclear program to negotiate an end to U.S. and EU economic sanctions through the Joint Comprehensive Plan of Action (JCPOA, 2015), signed by Iran, the P5 of the UN, and Germany. A signature achievement of the Obama administration, the deal has been intensely criticized by President Trump and by Prime Minister Netanyahu. In May 2018, President Trump announced that the U.S. would withdraw from the deal and re-impose sanctions on Iran.

The Iranian threat in Lebanon and Syria, and Tehran's abiding interest in atomic weapons, has increased the level of panic in Israel. It is possible that Israel could attack Iran should the kingdom decide to re-start its nuclear program. Israel has employed "preemptive nonproliferation" before: On June 7, 1981, it struck Iraq's Osirak reactor, and on September 6, 2007, it hit a Syrian nuclear compound. Moreover, Saudi Arabia, other Sunni states and Israel now have common cause against the growing Iranian threat.

The race of denial: denying non-state actors access to nuclear weapons

The fourth nuclear race emerged after 9/11. It aims to keep nuclear weapons out of the hands of terrorists. Indeed, the invasions of Afghanistan and Iraq were carried out on the pretext of protecting against a hypothetical nuclear terrorist attack. We now know that in fact, Saddam Hussein had bluffed about having WMDs in an effort to deter invasion and to intimidate his enemies at home. In September 2003, the U.S. and ten other countries established the Proliferation Security Initiative (PSI), with the mission of stopping WMD trafficking by state *and* non-state actors. This effort helped uncover the Libyan nuclear program, as well as the Abdul Qadeer (A.Q.) Khan proliferation network that supplied nuclear technology to Libya, North Korea and Iran from Pakistan. Today, 105 countries have committed to the PSI.

States still pose the biggest proliferation threat. The excessive costs of buying or building weapons prove prohibitive to terrorists; moreover, rogue nuclear states prefer to avoid the risk of having any weapons they might hand over to non-state actors traced back to them. Nonetheless, loose nuclear materials pose a threat as dirty-bombs—conventional explosives laced with radioactive materials. Keeping a lid on the spread of nuclear materials to terrorists remains a high priority.

Race five on the horizon: the new space race

In 1957, the Soviet Union launched the Sputnik satellite into space. The exorbitant financial costs of the ensuing "space race" between the U.S. and the Soviet Union eventually led to arms control efforts and the Anti-Ballistic Missile Treaty (ABM, 1972). The ABM Treaty came under fire during the Reagan administration, when the president began his Strategic Defense Initiative (SDI, 1983), also known as Stars Wars. This well-funded research and development program sought to produce viable ballistic missile defense systems. President Reagan marketed the idea as one that could render nuclear weapons obsolete. But the Soviets accurately saw it as the next expensive chapter in the arms race.

Reagan decided to rebuild the U.S. military to better compete with the Soviet Union. The Soviets had been under strain for years, with a collapsing economic system and military overspending. The Pentagon's Competitive Strategies plan involved leveraging U.S. economic strengths against Soviet weaknesses. Secretary of Defense Caspar Weinberger (1981–87) outlined the approach in his 1986 Foreign Affairs article "US Defense Strategy"; SDI became one of the fronts for that strategy. Speaking at Princeton University in February 1993, Mikhail Gorbachev admitted that SDI had helped end the Cold War, and that any attempt to compete with it would have come at unrecoverable cost to the Soviet economy.

On June 18, 2018, nearly 30 years after the collapse of the Soviet Union, President Trump signed a presidential directive to create a U.S. Space Force as a sixth branch of the Armed Forces. Congress initially raised the issue of a separate Space Force out of "concern over the slow pace with which the Department of Defense...and the Air Force have addressed the growing threat to U.S. national security in space from adversaries, particularly Russia and China, and to a lesser extent North Korea and Iran." Congress has passed, and the president has signed into law, the fiscal year 2019 National Defense Authorization Act (NDAA), which includes the creation of a subordinate Space Command under the auspices of U.S. Strategic Command.

Has President Trump taken a page out of the Reagan strategy? Are we going back to the future by strengthening the economy at home, rebuilding the military abroad, modernizing our nuclear forces and building a new space force to compete with Russia, and possibly China? The Russian economy has many structural problems, and the Chinese economy has sputtered since Trump levied sanctions for unfair trade practices. Russia, China, North Korea and Iran all currently have U.S. sanctions levied against them. Could this prove a set-up for second-term negotiations to reduce threats to the U.S. and its allies?

Options for alternative nuclear futures: between hope and fear

A number of options have emerged for how and when to proceed with nuclear weapons negotiations. They include moving toward a global ban—eliminating all nuclear weapons; moving toward a deterrence-only posture—fewer, and ultimately zero, nuclear weapons; and prioritizing the modernization of U.S. nuclear arsenals, followed by an assessment of the potential for negotiations.

Nuclear weapons ban: On July 7, 2017, the UN passed a Treaty on the Prohibition of Nuclear Weapons. It represents the first legally binding international agreement to prohibit nuclear weapons. The accord urges that nuclear-weapons states fulfill their obligations to general and complete disarmament. In addition, UN Secretary General António Guterres (2017–present) has proposed a five-point plan to achieve nuclear disarmament:

1. Urge nuclear-weapons states to work toward this goal, specifically at the Conference on Disarmament in Geneva, Switzerland;

2. Ask the UNSC to convene a summit on nuclear disarmament;

3. Resume talks on a CTBT and a Fissile Material Cut-off Treaty, and reaffirm nuclear-weapons-free zones;

4. Improve transparency on numbers of weapons, stocks of fissile material and disarmament efforts; and

5. Bolster efforts against WMD terrorism and put limits on conventional arms, with new bans on missile and space weapons.

Deterrence-only posture: Bruce G. Blair, a nuclear security expert currently at Princeton University, has written "The End of Nuclear Warfighting: Moving to a Deterrence-Only Posture," an alternative to the 2018 NPR. He suggests that we reduce U.S. and Russian arsenals while maintaining nuclear deterrence. This plan calls for eliminating all silo-based intercontinental ballistic missiles (ICBMs), reducing deployed nuclear weapons by two thirds to 650 warheads, and deploying those warheads on five nuclear submarines backed by a small reserve of 40 strategic bombers. A "deterrence only" posture, Blair argues, should have a no-first-use clause for nuclear weapons, no counterforce options against ICBMs, and a no-hair-trigger response to avoid accidental nuclear war. This plan would provide an interim step toward negotiating a nuclear-free world. The international non-governmental organization Global Zero endorses this approach, and believes it can help reach total world disarmament by 2030.

Modernize nuclear weapons, then negotiate: This option reflects the 2018 NPR's conclusion that the world remains a dangerous place, with the existence of potential adversaries—Russia, China, North Korea and Iran—necessitating the modernization of the U.S. triad. By modernizing existing ICBMs, submarines and bombers to maintain deterrence, the U.S. can negotiate from a position of strength in the future.

All three of these approaches see a role for nuclear negotiations, but at different times: one immediately, the second a little later and the third, once conditions prove correct. The U.S. should renew the New START treaty with Moscow, stay focused on reducing proliferation threats from North Korea and Iran, and insist that U.S. nuclear cooperation agreements—especially in the Middle East—uphold the gold standard of preventing uranium enrichment and reprocessing. The PSI must also remain focused on preventing the illicit sale and transfer of nuclear materials to state and non-state actors.

The Trump administration has a tall order of nuclear business ahead of it. It must negotiate between ideals of disarmament and fears of losing strategic advantages to potential enemies. In his 1987 book *The Art of the Deal*, Trump signaled that he likes to think big: "Most people think small, because most people are afraid of success, afraid of making decisions, afraid of winning." What will "winning big" mean in terms of the future of nuclear peace? As the president likes to say when planning his next move, "we'll see what happens."

Pictured in this screen grab is the Russian Navy Northern Fleet's Project 955 Borei nuclear missile cruiser submarine Yuri Dolgoruky as it launches Bulava missiles from the White Sea in north-west Russia at the Kura testing grounds on Kamchatka Peninsula on Russia's Pacific coast during a military drill in May 2018. (TASS/ GETTY IMAGES)

discussion questions

1. What are the political factors driving nuclear production and negotiations today? Why are nuclear weapons still produced if there are treaties and agreements in place not to utilize them?

2. How have nuclear agreements impacted negotiations in the past? How will President Trump's withdrawal from agreements such as JCPOA impact the United States and its allies?

3. North Korea is arguably the nation with the most unpredictable nuclear arsenal and capabilities. What role can the United States play in disarming this threat? How can past strategies of disarming be useful in this current situation?

4. Developed in the 1940s, nuclear weaponry is relatively recent issue in foreign policy. How has history influenced current nuclear negotiations? How have nuclear negotiations evolved since its emergence in the 20th century?

5. Last summer, Donald Trump announced and took steps towards creating a Space Force to protect American interests in outer space. How would the creation of this branch of military impact nuclear negotiations? Would it increase security against nuclear attacks? Why or why not?

6. Is a nuclear-free world possible? Why or why not? If so, what are the pathways to achieve this goal? What will nuclear negotiations look like in the future?

suggested readings

Ellsberg, Daniel. **The Doomsday Machine: Confessions of a Nuclear War Planner**. 432 pp. New York, NY: Bloomsbury Publishing, 2018. A memoir by the famous Pentagon Papers whistleblower of his time in the Pentagon as a nuclear war planner. He warns that the specter of nuclear war remains upon us and that we must disarm or face "Omnicide."

Feiveson, Harold et. al. **Unmaking the Bomb: A Fissile Material Approach to Nuclear Disarmament and Nonproliferation**. 296 pp. Cambridge, MA: MIT Press, 2016. The authors, based at Princeton University, believe that we can disarm as well as prevent nuclear proliferation and nuclear terrorism by focusing on the production, stockpiling, and disposal of highly enriched uranium and plutonium.

"From the Archive: Nuclear Weapons," **Foreign Affairs**, 1948–2005. Anthology of 12 articles from a leading journal on foreign policy with pieces written by government leaders and experts on the history of nuclear weapons and efforts to control them.

Roberts, Brad. **The Case for Nuclear Weapons in the 21st Century**. 352 pp. Stanford, CA: Stanford University Press, 2016. The Director of the Center for Global Security Research at Lawrence Livermore National Laboratory argues that other nuclear states are not prepared to join the U.S. in reductions and as a result, we must balance the reduction of future dangers with a nuclear strategy to deter potential enemies.

Sagan, Scott D. and Waltz, Kenneth N. **The Spread of Nuclear Weapons: An Enduring Debate (Third Edition)**. 288 pp. New York, NY: W.W. Norton & Company, 2012. Two prominent political scientists lay out the opposing arguments for whether the spread of nuclear weapons makes the world more or less peaceful.

Schultz, George P. and Goodby, James E. **The War That Must Never Be Fought: Dilemmas of Nuclear Deterrence**. 450 pp. Stanford, California: Hoover Institution Press, 2015. Secretary Schultz and Ambassador Goodby challenge the assumptions of classical deterrence theory, while reviewing problem regions in a series of articles that conclude that the global commons must build a new conceptual and institutional foundation for nuclear restraint.

Walt, Stephen M. "The World Does Not Need Any More Nuclear Strategies," **Foreign Policy**, February 6, 2018. The Harvard professor critiques the 2018 Nuclear Posture Review because it implies the Pentagon wants to create a new generation of smaller, usable nuclear weapons.

Don't forget: Ballots start on page 103!

To access web links to these readings, as well as links to additional, shorter readings and suggested web sites,

GO TO www.greatdecisions.org

and click on the topic under Resources, on the right-hand side of the page.

Discovery. Discussion. Decision.
GREAT DECISIONS
1918 • FOREIGN POLICY ASSOCIATION
2019 EDITION

4

European populism and immigration

by James Kirchick

...paign meeting of the party leader of the far-right Sweden Democrats, Jimmie Akesson, in Stockholm, Sweden, ...day before legislative elections. (JONATHAN NACKSTRAND/AFP/GETTY IMAGES)

Across the West, apprehensions over immigration and fraying national identity are boosting the electoral fortunes—and in some cases, bringing to power—political forces hostile to the liberal world order. In the U.S., President Donald Trump unexpectedly rode into office by promising to deport millions of illegal immigrants and to build a wall along the country's southern border. Trump's radical departure from traditional Republican Party foreign policy nostrums like support for free trade, international alliances like the North Atlantic Treaty Organization (NATO), the promotion of liberal values abroad and a tough posture toward Russia—in sum, his repudiation of key elements of the U.S.-led, post-1945 liberal world order—has done little to dent enthusiasm among his supporters, who are willing to overlook or endorse his policy heresies because of his restrictionist position on immigration.

This text is adapted from a report simultaneously published by the Brookings Institution.

Opposition to mass immigration has had similar electoral effect on the other side of the Atlantic. The rise of right-wing populism, at least in Europe, is mainly attributable to the migration crisis that began in 2015. Between 2015 and 2016, over 2 million asylum seekers and migrants arrived in Europe illegally, overwhelming the system in place to deal with them. The 2016 "Brexit" decision by the British people to leave the European Union (EU), the unprecedented share of the vote won by far-right nationalist candidate Marine Le Pen in the 2017 French presidential election, the entrance of the right-wing nationalist party Alternative für Deutschland into German parliament in 2017, and the formation of a populist coalition government in Italy between the far-right Northern

JAMES KIRCHICK *is a visiting fellow at the Center on the U.S. and Europe at the Brookings Institution and author of* The End of Europe: Dictators, Demagogues and the Coming Dark Age *(Yale University Press, 2017).*

Hungarian Prime Minister Viktor Orbán waves to the audience after delivering his address on the national holiday marking the 62nd anniversary of the outbreak of the Hungarian revolution and war of independence against communist rule and the Soviet Union in 1956, at the House of Terror in Budapest Hungary, October 23, 2018. (TAMAS KOVACS/MTI/AP PHOTO)

League and the leftist Five Star Movement are all political expressions of the increasingly popular belief that national borders have become too porous and that immigrants are not assimilating quickly and thoroughly enough into receiving societies. Meanwhile, Hungarian Prime Minister Viktor Orbán has earned an international profile far out of proportion to that which would usually be afforded the leader of a small, Central European country of just 10 million people. This is solely a result of his fierce and overtly xenophobic opposition to what he characterizes as the EU's elite, cross-partisan consensus in favor of mass immigration from Africa and the Middle East.

While the number of irregular migrants entering Europe has declined significantly over the past three years, the lingering after-effects of the deluge—namely, the sense that European governments had lost control over the situation, combined with a pessimistic view toward European societies' ability to integrate so many newcomers—have had a profound effect on the politics of the West. According to the Spring 2018 Eurobarometer poll, which measures public opinion across the EU, Europeans list immigration and terrorism as the two most important issues facing the EU—issues that have become increasingly intertwined in the minds of ordinary citizens as a result of their association with Islam. Across Europe, the failure to control external immigration and the inability to effectively integrate newcomers risk elevating into power parties that are not only nativist and (in some cases) outright racist, but which are also fundamentally opposed to the liberal world order constructed so painstakingly by the U.S. and its allies over the past 70 years.

Since the twin shocks of Brexit and Trump in 2016, the world has been inundated with a slew of books, think tank reports, films and media analyses on the subject of populism and the threat it poses to liberal democracy. To that extent that populism can be defined as a political tendency which demonizes any and all opposition to it as inherently illegitimate, it is indeed a menace to liberal democracy, a constitutive element of which is pluralism, or the belief that for a society to be decent it must make room for various perspectives and political formations.

But what if the phenomenon that is near-universally described as "populism" is not so much an expression of hostility to liberal democracy per se, but rather of frustration that liberal democracy has not been democratic enough? What if populism is being driven, mainly, by deep dissatisfaction with the Western political establishment for not heeding the popular will on an issue of major importance to voters, that is, mass immigration? The rise of populist politics in the West is often laid at the feet of the 2008 financial crisis. Indeed, a range of economic factors—from the growing gap between rich and poor to declining wage growth—have all played a part in fanning the flames of populism, on both the left and right. But in countries as diverse as Germany, Poland and Sweden, the rise of populist politics cannot be blamed on the usual suspect of poor economic performance, as all three countries have posted impressive growth and low unemployment since the 2008 crisis.

Our purpose here is not to weigh the morality of the liberal or restrictionist approaches to immigration. Immigration is ultimately a national competency, a realm best left to individual governments in consultation with their citizenries. While one can certainly oppose restrictive immigration policies on economic, humanitarian or even cultural bases, there is nothing inherently illiberal in reducing immigration levels, even reducing them drastically. The specific matter of asylum excepted, a liberal democracy does not have an obligation to open its doors to foreigners in the same way that it is obliged to protect the basic freedoms—of speech, of religious practice, etc.—of its own citizens.

What should concern all of us with a stake in upholding the liberal international order is how increasing popular opposition to mass immigration across the Western world is politically channeled. For what all of the aforementioned political leaders and movements share, in addition to their anti-immigration fervor, is skepticism if not outright opposition to that liberal order, as well as a positive disposition toward its chief external threat: the regime of Russian President Vladimir Putin. In Europe, it is becoming increasingly ap-

! Before you read, download the companion **Glossary** that includes definitions, a guide to acronyms and abbreviations used in the article, and other material. Go to **www.greatdecisions.org** and select a topic in the Resources section on the right-hand side of the page.

parent that mass immigration and the liberal order (and maybe even liberal democracy itself) are incompatible. So opposed to mass immigration are they, a large and growing number of citizens are voting for parties which, in addition to their anti-immigration stance, also threaten to dismantle democratic institutions and their nations' role in upholding the liberal democratic order.

When it comes to immigration, European policy, on both the national and supranational levels, has for years been engaged in a game of catch-up with public opinion. In no case has this refusal of the political class to meet the demands of the public had more momentous consequence than with Brexit. After the EU welcomed ten new member states from Central and Eastern Europe in 2004, the United Kingdom (UK) government of Tony Blair was one of only three EU governments which chose not to avail itself of temporary immigration controls applicable to citizens from those countries. Seven years later, an online survey by the UK polling organization YouGov would find that 67% of the British public believed that immigration over the previous decade had been "a bad thing for Britain." In the minds of a growing number of UK citizens, then, the EU had become associated with mass immigration, and the drastic step of leaving the bloc became the only means of bringing immigration numbers down to manageable levels. Cognizant of these worries, the Conservative-led coalition government of Prime Minister David Cameron promised to reduce immigration. But Cameron was either unwilling or unable to slow immigration, to the point where it actually increased to a high of 330,000 people annually in 2015. It was in this context of repeatedly thwarted expectations that the mantra of "take back control" found an audience, and citizens voted in favor of Brexit.

It is not just Britain where public and elite opinion on immigration have been dangerously out of sync. Divergence on immigration is noticeable across Europe, according to political scientists Markus Wagner and Thomas M. Meyer, as "voter positions are generally to the right of mainstream party consensus, so that shifts to the right on immigration and on law and order are in fact shifts towards the median voter." A 2017 Chatham House survey found that, in eight out of ten European countries, majorities oppose any further immigration from Muslim countries (corresponding with President Donald Trump's highly controversial calls for a ban on Muslim immigration in the U.S.). Some 53% of Germans, whose country made a highly visible humanitarian gesture during the 2015 migrant crisis, agree with the idea of a Muslim immigration ban. In no country did more than 32% disagree with a complete ban.

Such figures are no doubt dispiriting to those who believe in the inherent virtue and workability of multiculturalism. But if preservation of the liberal international order is the foremost concern of political leaders—and given the catastrophic potential consequences of a breakdown in that order—then more important than moral judgments on public attitudes regarding Muslim immigration is how political leaders handle those attitudes. Voters across Europe want and expect stricter immigration and assimilation policies. In an electoral democracy, they will eventually get those policies either from mainstream political leaders, who also support NATO, the EU, market economies and other elements of the liberal order, or from demagogues who support none of these things. "It would be a major political mistake if liberals simply ignore or ridicule these fears," writes political scientist Ivan Krastev of the anti-immigration feeling rising across the West. His is a sentiment echoed by European Council President Donald Tusk, whose native Poland is one of the European countries most hostile to immigration. Speaking of the EU's controversial efforts to partner with various African governments to limit external immigration into the bloc, Tusk put it bluntly: "If we don't agree on them then you will see some really tough proposals from some really tough guys."

To be sure, populist parties often exaggerate the downsides of immigration and scapegoat immigrants as terrorists and criminals. But to echo Krastev's warning, "In democratic politics, perceptions are the only reality that matters." If a perception exists among European voters that their governments are unable or unwilling to control immigration, and if this perception festers, then political forces that would upset Europe's postwar political, economic and security settlement will continue to gain strength.

Handling immigration

The first step in bridging the gap between elites and the public is acknowledging that opposition to mass immigration is not necessarily always the direct result of racism or xenophobia. It can be grounded in serious and well-founded concerns about crime, social cohesion and cultural adaptation. Sweden, which touts itself as a "humanitarian superpower," provides a compelling illustration of how not to handle the issue of immigration. In 2013 alone, Sweden accepted more than twice as many migrants per capita as any other country in the world. This intake reached its height during the 2015–16 crisis, when the country accepted over 160,000 people. Over the past five years, Sweden welcomed 600,000, an enormous number for a country of less than 10 million.

Unfortunately, migrants have disproportionately been involved in certain types of crime in Sweden; namely, sexual assault, gang violence, grenade attacks and car bombings. According to statistics compiled by Sweden's public broadcaster, 58% of men convicted of rape and attempted rape over the past five years were born abroad. "Scarcely a day has gone by in the past few years without a shooting, burned-out car, or even a grenade attack being reported in one of the cities," the *Financial Times* reported about migrant gangs last summer in the run-up to Sweden's parliamentary election.

With the unemployment rate among the foreign-born four times higher than the rate for native Swedes (and six times higher for non-Europeans), Sweden's unemployment gap is the second highest among members of the Organization for Economic Cooperation and Development (OECD). This disparity is due to the low educational achievement of most migrants and a lack of unskilled jobs in the highly advanced Swedish economy. "Sweden is statistically one of the worst countries at the integration of foreigners," Aje Carlbom, a professor in social anthropology at Malmö University tells the *Financial Times*. "Why? Mainly because this is a highly complex country where you can't get a job without education. Many of those who come are uneducated — that is the main problem."

Sweden's approach to immigration and assimilation has been the subject of frequent criticism among its neighbors. "I often use Sweden as a deterring example" of how not to deal with these issues, former Danish Prime Minister and NATO Secretary General Anders Fogh Rasmussen said in an interview on Swedish television. Many Swedes would agree. In 2014, a year before the migrant crisis, 44% of Swedes supported cuts in the country's generously high annual intake of immigrants. Three years later, after the government was forced to announce the deportation of 80,000 people (a full half of the number it had admitted during the brunt of the crisis), 48% of Swedes expressed agreement with the sentiment that "there are too many immigrants in our country" and 44% endorsed the statement that "immigration is causing my country to change in ways that I don't like." And while only 7% of Swedes said immigration and/or integration was one of the most important issues the country faced in 1987, that figure skyrocketed to 43% by 2017, making it the single most important issue for voters. That year, 53% of Swedes agreed with the sentiment that accepting fewer refugees was a "good proposal."

Yet despite the problems presented by mass immigration, and the large portion of the public opposed to it, no mainstream political party in Sweden would broach the subject. This unfortunately left a massive vacuum. When the Sweden Democrats party (SD) first entered parliament in 2010, it barely passed the electoral threshold with 5.7% of the vote. The SD has its origins in the neo-Nazi movement, and while it has certainly moderated its message and expelled some of its more visibly extremist members over the years, it nonetheless opposes Swedish membership in the EU and proposed membership in NATO, and seeks better relations with Russia. In the most recent election, the SD achieved nearly 18% of the vote, a rapid and lamentable rise that would likely never have occurred had Sweden's mainstream parties effectively represented the views of nearly half their population on immigration. Support for the SD and its anti-establishment message has coincided with the longest economic expansion in Sweden in four decades, an indication that issues related to national identity and immigration transcend the vicissitudes of economic boom and bust.

Belatedly, the Swedish center right is acknowledging its failure to represent voter concerns, and realizing that such condescension has only emboldened the far right. "When voters are discontent, don't blame them," the recently elected leader of the center-right Moderate Party, Ulf Kristersson, says. Over the past two decades, he adds, Swedish governments of both the right and left have pursued "very unsuccessful integration policies." The Moderates' 2018 election manifesto called for a "strict migration policy" that reduced the number of people granted asylum, "faster integration" with a greater emphasis placed on language acquisition, and welfare benefits contingent on employment.

Adopting tougher policies on immigration, to the point of actually inviting a far right party into government, is the strategy currently underway in Austria. There, the young Chancellor Sebastian Kurz of the Christian-democratic Austrian People's Party (ÖVP) has been governing since 2017 in coalition with the Freedom Party (FPÖ), which was founded by former SS officers and which motivated the EU to introduce sanctions when it last entered into a coalition government in the early 2000s. Many criticized Kurz for agreeing to work with the FPÖ rather than prolonging a coalition with the Social Democrats. Yet a poll taken before the 2017 parliamentary election found only 15% public support for continuation of such a "grand coalition" government. While establishing a cordon sanitaire around the far right might lend the appearance of constraining its influence, such maneuvering does not come cost-free. These frequent pacts between the country's two main political parties—which have been the norm in postwar Austria—are viewed by many citizens as a form of elite collusion, thus discrediting democracy and contributing to the rise of the far right as a protest force.

Though it's far too early to make any categorical conclusions, early signs indicate that what the Austrian journalist Franz-Stefan Gady calls "Kurz's populism lite" may be working. Addressing popular concerns about immigration and integration "not only helped him gain voters who previously cast their ballot for the FPÖ (168,000) as well as for two other far-right, populist parties (158,000), but also managed to attract 84,000 votes from former Green Party supporters, 60,000 votes from the New Austria and Liberal Forum (a liberal party), and 121,000 nonvoters, including first-time voters, from the previous election." Taking a harder line on these issues has not led Austria toward the "illiberal democracy" of its neighbor Hungary, nor has it encouraged Kurz to adopt the anti-pluralist rhetoric which is the hallmark of populists left and right. In fact, Kurz directed his members of the European Parliament (EP), the EU's directly elected legislative body, to vote to censure Prime Minister Orbán's government for its anti-democratic policies. The EP's move divided the transnational center-right European People's Party, of which both Kurz's ÖVP and Orbán's ruling Fidesz party are members. Kurz's decision was all the more significant given the warm personal ties Kurz has developed with his Hungarian counterpart.

The Austrian government's turn away from liberal immigration policies, its crackdown on Islamism and its emphasis on integration have inspired something close to hysteria in Germany, where liberal elites see signs of incipient fascism in any deviation from the Willkommenskultur ("welcome culture") toward migrants that Chancellor Angela Merkel expounded in 2015. "What we are talking about here is the question of whether Germany's neighbor is, bit by bit, bidding farewell to the democratic way of life," warned the German news magazine *Der Spiegel*. "Whether its society still wants pluralism and if it is capable of enduring the thousand varieties of multiculturalism and the processes of migration despite all the difficulties they present." But there is nothing in the writings of John Stuart Mill, John Locke, the documents of the American founding or any of the other foundational texts of Western liberalism mandating that a country "endure the thousand varieties of multiculturalism" in order to classify as a liberal democracy. Reducing non-EU immigration will not adversely affect the quality of European democracy (on the contrary, by reducing the number of immigrants from the non-democratic world to more manageable numbers, it might increase it). We may not be able to say the same thing should (more) populist parties come to power as a consequence of liberal governments ignoring public opinion on immigration.

Migration debate

In many European nations, large pluralities or even majorities believe that most immigrants coming to their country are not refugees or asylum seekers fleeing violence and persecution—as they are usually portrayed in the media, and in which case Europe has a legal duty to shelter them—but rather economic migrants. In light of the 2016 statement by EU Commission Vice President Frans Timmermans that around 60% of the people entering the bloc over that past year had been jobseekers, they are not wrong in this assumption. Political leaders must be more discriminate, therefore, in how they apply the terms "refugee" and "economic migrant," as a continued blurring of the clear, legal distinction between the two will only play into the hands of populists who would deny entrance to both.

The inability—real or perceived—of mainstream European political leaders and parties to stop illegal immigration and alleviate its negative consequences has simultaneously decreased popular backing for the European project and increased support for extremist parties. Neither of these developments is a good omen for the future health of the liberal world order, which depends upon a strong, coherent EU, governed by mainstream parties committed to the transatlantic alliance with the U.S. and a values-based foreign policy. Opposition to immigration correlates strongly with opposition to European integration, as membership in the EU has become increasingly perceived as entailing the opening up of a country's borders to migrants not just from within the bloc but from outside Europe as well. In turn, voters are increasingly willing to overlook the illiberal tendencies of anti-immigration parties, a dangerous development. For instance, the proportion of citizens who see Marine Le Pen's National Front party (now the National Rally party) as a threat to democracy has fallen over the past 15 years from 70% in 2002 to 58% last year as the issue of immigration has gained salience.

The vast majority of Europeans want drastic decreases in immigration. Eventually, they are going to get them. (Indeed, in the form of Brexit, the British people already have). The great question in European politics over the next decade is who will deliver this policy goal. To ensure that the answer is not the far right, the center right will need to find solutions that are both workable and humane. Supporting economic development in Africa, the Middle East and other regions of the world that are sending migrants toward Europe is one way to reduce migratory pressures over the long term. Pushing the asylum process outside the continent via the creation of "regional disembarkation platforms" where potential asylees will have their claims processed, a proposal the European Commission has endorsed, is also one that center-right parties should fully support. Funding for the EU's Border and Coast Guard Agency (Frontex) is a cause around which the vast majority of the European public can rally.

Voters intuitively (and correctly) realize that once a migrant makes their way into the EU, there is little chance of them being deported if their asylum claim fails. Extreme examples fuel the perception of bureaucratic and politi-

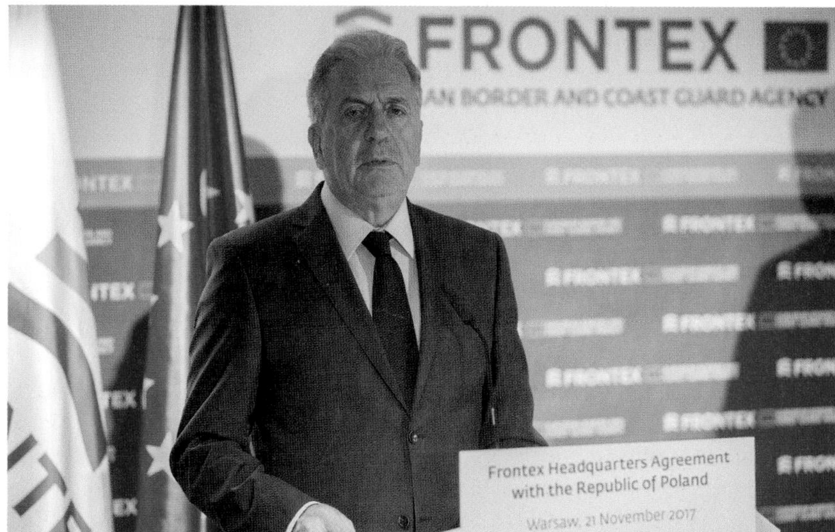

Dimitri Avramopoulus, EU Commissioner for Migration, Home Affairs and Citizenship, attends the press conference after the inauguration ceremony for the FRONTEX headquarters, in Warsaw, Poland, in November 2017. (JAN A. NICOLAS/PICTURE ALLIANCE/GETTY IMAGES)

cal incompetence on this issue. Take the case of the Swedish court that overturned a decision to deport a Palestinian refugee who had firebombed a synagogue on the basis that he would be under threat from the Israeli state were he to be sent back to Palestine. The decision sent different messages to different constituencies: For potential migrants to Sweden, it signaled that the bar for deportation was practically nonexistent; for Jewish Swedes, it implied that the well-being of an anti-Semitic criminal migrant was more important than their own safety and freedoms as citizens. According to European Commission data, just 36.6% of failed asylum claimants are sent back to their home countries. In Germany, some 233,000 rejected asylum seekers remain in the country, and in 2017, German authorities only carried out about 24,000 deportations. The low deportation rate isn't necessarily a result of political obstacles; rather, the cost of removing an unsuccessful asylum applicant can be prohibitively high.

In another symbolically resonant case, a failed asylum seeker from Tunisia killed 12 people in a December 2016 truck attack on a Berlin Christmas market. The attack demonstrates the most acute weaknesses and potential dangers of the current system, and why increasing numbers of European voters are falling into the arms of the far right. Denied an Italian residence permit in 2011, the perpetrator was then imprisoned after setting fire to a government shelter. Upon his release, he moved to Germany, where his applications for asylum (under several false identities) were rejected. Though he was subject to deportation, the German government lost track of his whereabouts; moreover, the Tunisian government refused to accept him back. It was in the midst of this bureaucratic confusion and incompetence that he was radicalized and carried out his deadly attack. Preventing such worst-case scenarios from occurring by making it harder to enter Europe illegally is a way to both protect against real threats from terrorism and to earn back the trust of European publics.

Unfortunately, many European elites and commentators are taking the opposite tack, establishing a totalizing, and false, dichotomy between proponents and opponents of liberal immigration policies, which correlates perfectly with a dichotomy between proponents and opponents of liberal democracy itself. According to Financial Times columnist Gideon Rachman, because "mass migration into Europe is unstoppable," there today exists a "battle between nativists and liberals" with the former waging an "all-out war on democracy and on migration"—as if a "war" on migration (by which Rachman presumably means reducing the numbers of immigrants) were equivalent to dismantling democracy. A Politico op-ed by Swedish Moderate Party Member of European Parliament (MEP) Anna Maria Corazza Bildt, calling upon the European People's Party to expel Viktor Orbán's Fidesz party, consisted almost entirely of complaints about his migration policies—policies which are democratically legitimate and popular with the vast majority of Europeans, never mind Hungarians.

Scenes of a devastation at the Breitscheidplatz Christmas market after a heavy goods vehicle ploughed into crowds of people during a terror attack in Berlin, Germany, December 20, 2016. (MICHAEL KAPPELER/DPA/NEWSCOM)

In no place is this conflation between the liberal world order and a liberal immigration regime more an article of bien-pensant faith than in Germany, often seen as symbol and center of the European experiment and even the liberal Western order. There, Chancellor Angela Merkel and those who share her views in the domestic and international media have framed the debate such that criticism of her position on immigration amounts to nothing less than an attack on liberal democracy itself. "This isn't a debate about the future of the chancellor, it's about the future of Europe," the editor of the business newspaper Handelsblatt warned after a dust-up over migration between Merkel and her more conservative allies in the Bavarian Christian Social Union.

But the conflation of an increasingly unpopular liberal immigration dogma with the liberal world order is becoming a disaster all around. One consequence of associating liberal immigration policies with both the liberal world order and its component parts (of which the EU is a major one) is that it risks tainting the latter in the minds of voters. It also plays right into the hands of proto-authoritarians like Orbán, who has instrumentalized widespread anti-migration sentiment into hostility against liberal democracy writ large. "Liberal democracy is pro-immigration, while Christian democracy is anti-immigration," he said in the summer of 2018, as the EU debated various migration policy proposals. Contra Orbán, liberal democracy is not inherently "pro-immigration." But given the rhetoric and behavior of many of its leading practitioners, it's not hard to see why many voters would fall for this simplistic rendering.

A political leader worth emulating on these questions is Donald Tusk, who, as a Pole and a committed European, can speak to the concerns of those made uneasy by mass immigration without resorting to crude nationalism and beggar-thy-neighbor policies. In a letter to the members of the European Council, Tusk made an unsubtle dig at the Hungarian prime minister and those like him:

> *There are voices in Europe and around the world claiming that our inefficiency in maintaining the external border is an inherent feature of the European Union, or—more broadly—of liberal democracy. We have seen the creation of new political movements, which offer simple answers to the most complicated questions. Simple, radical and attractive. The migration crisis provides them with a growing number of arguments. More and more people are starting to believe that only strong-handed authority, anti-European and anti-liberal in spirit, with a tendency towards overt authoritarianism, is capable of stopping the wave of illegal migration. If people believe them, that only they can offer an effective solution to the migration crisis, they will also believe anything else they say. The stakes are very high. And time is short.*

If the European debate over migration is framed as one between the Willkommenskultur of Angela Merkel and the harsher position adopted by Viktor Orbán and his ilk, then it is the latter, unfortunately, who will win. The optimal immigration policy—one that balances a commitment to humanitarian concerns with an alertness toward the negative consequences that high numbers of poorly educated migrants from vastly different societies can bring—lies somewhere in between. But for that policy to be achieved, the terms of the immigration debate have to change. Out of a desire not to aid the far right, many Germans choose to ignore issues like migrant criminality, and attack anyone who does

President of the European Council Donald Tusk speaks during a press conference after a European Council Meeting at the Council of the European Union on March 22, 2018, in Brussels, Belgium. (JACK TAYLOR/GETTY IMAGES)

draw attention to them as crypto-fascist.

The task for Europe's centrist parties on matters of national identity and immigration, then, is not a particularly difficult or novel one: Represent the views of your constituents. Adopting stricter immigration policies is not "co-opting" the far right or a betrayal of democracy, but may be the affirmation of it. "It's not that national populism reflects an abandonment of democracy," writes Matthew Goodwin, professor of politics at the University of Kent in England, on Twitter. On the contrary, it may indicate a yearning for more democracy, as "it reflects the fact that people want a different conception of democracy. One where 'the people' get 'more voice' while 'elites' get less."

This is a particular duty of center-right and Christian democratic parties, whose traditional role in postwar Europe has been the articulation of a healthy patriotism, and respect for authority and national traditions. It must have struck many German voters as bewildering that the issue which threatened to torpedo government coalition talks in early 2018 was not a bread-and-butter concern for German citizens, like pensions or the minimum wage, but family reunification for migrants. The discourse on migration, so heavily influenced by pro-migration non-governmental organizations and media voices, too often has the tenor of an elite preoccupation woefully out of touch with mainstream perceived and real concerns about crime, terrorism and social cohesion.

Despite the best intentions of its proponents, mass immigration is having a destabilizing effect on European democracy by abetting populist parties hostile to both liberal democracy and the liberal world order. As these parties exploit the gap between public opinion and public policy, the dilemma that Western political leaders, in Europe especially, have to confront is whether to sacrifice the stability of the liberal international order on the altar of a liberal immigration regime. To save liberal democracy from its illiberal antagonists, they will need to decouple the highly charged subject of immigration from the suite of metrics—respect for checks and balances, adherence to the rule of law, protection of minorities, pluralism, freedom of the press, support for democratic alliances, a values-based foreign policy—that truly determine whether a nation is a liberal democracy and plays a productive role in maintaining global peace and prosperity. If leaders who are genuinely committed to preserving that order ignore or dismiss popular opinion on immigration, they will lose ground to far-right movements committed to neither.

discussion questions

1. Populism is becoming increasingly common in Europe; is populism just a trend or a political movement here to stay?

2. Migrants, asylum-seekers, and refugees have contributed to the populist movement in Europe. Is it possible to have high volumes of migration without a political reaction? How can other regions prevent such backlash when faced with large-scale migration?

3. What role do trans-European organizations, such as the European Union, play to dissipate tensions brought on by populism?

4. What similarities and differences can you see between populist parties in different countries? For example, the National Rally party in France and the Sweden Democrats of Sweden, the Fidesz party of Hungary, etc.

5. How does the rise of populism in Europe affect the world? What are ways that Europe's populism will impact the world?

6. How can pro-immigration groups and anti-immigration groups find common ground in a period of high demand for migration to Europe?

suggested readings

Barker, Vanessa. **Nordic Nationalism and Penal Order: Walling the Welfare State**. 168 pp. New York, NY: Routledge, 2017. Swedish case study challenges several key paradigms for understanding penal order in the 21st century.

Büllesbach, Daphne. **Shifting Baselines of Europe: New Perspectives Beyond Neoliberalism and Nationalism (X-Tests on Culture and Society)**. 212 pp. Bielefeld, Germany: Transcript-Verlag, 2017. This book discusses the future of Europe and criticizes the false dichotomy between nationalism on the one hand and a neoliberal version of Europe on the other.

Müller, Jan-Werner. **What is Populism?** 136 pp. Philadelphia, PA: University of Pennsylvania Press, 2016. Brief book grounded in history that draws on examples from Latin America, Europe and the U.S. to define the characteristics of populism and the deeper causes of its current electoral successes.

Finchelstein, Federico. **From Fascism to Populism in History**. 352 pp. Berkeley, CA: University of California Press, 2017. A history of transnational fascism and postwar populist movements that informs ways to think about the state of democracy and political culture on a global scale.

Judis, John B. **The Populist Explosion: How the Great Recession Transformed American and European Politics**. 184 pp. New York, NY: Columbia Global Reports, 2016. Good background for anyone hoping to grasp a global political system that is just beginning what will be a long-running and highly consequential readjustment.

Rydgren, Jens. **The Oxford Handbook of the Radical Right (Oxford Handbooks)**. 760 pp. New York, NY: Oxford University Press, 2018. This provides an authoritative overview of the topic and will set the agenda for scholarship on the radical right for years to come.

Teitelbaum, Benjamin R. **Lions of the North: Sounds of the New Nordic Radical Nationalism**. 232 pp. New York, NY: Oxford University Press, 2017. Exposes the dynamic relationship between music and politics, but also the ways radical nationalism is adapting in some of the most liberal societies in the world.

Don't forget: Ballots start on page 103!

To access web links to these readings, as well as links to additional, shorter readings and suggested web sites,

GO TO www.greatdecisions.org

and click on the topic under Resources, on the right-hand side of the page.

Decoding U.S.-China trade

by Jeremy Haft

Containers sit stacked at the Yangshan Deep Water Port in Shanghai, China, on July 10, 2018. China told companies to boost imports of goods from soybeans to seafood and automobiles from countries other than the U.S. after trade tensions between the world's two biggest economies escalated into a tariff war.(QILAI SHEN/BLOOMBERG/GETTY IMAGES)

Anyone who wears eyeglasses knows how it feels when you need a stronger prescription. You're reading a book, doing a crossword, or peering at a road sign in the distance, and you suddenly realize your vision looks fuzzy. The longer you wait to calibrate the strength of your lenses, the fuzzier things get.

The same could be said about economic numbers. Like eyeglass lenses, they're designed to help see the world around us more clearly, but they need to be updated from time to time. The U.S.-China trade war illustrates why modern, accurate economic numbers are so important, and how damaging misleading, out-of-date numbers can be.

One participant in this trade war is a big, populous nation far away. In order to perceive it, we peer through two statistical lenses. With one eye, we look at China through the lens of trade balances: how much the U.S. sells China versus how much the U.S. buys from China. With the other eye, we see China through the lens of Gross Domestic Product (GDP): China's economic size versus the size of the U.S.

Peering through these lenses, China looks like Goliath and America more like David. On the trade side, China sold the U.S. about half a trillion dollars-worth of manufactured goods in 2017, while the U.S. sold China about $129 billion. That's a $375 billion trade deficit. And on the GDP side, it seems to be the end of the American century. The World Bank ranks China as the world's number one economy at about a $23 trillion GDP, with the U.S. in second place at a $19 trillion GDP. Waging a trade war in these economic eyeglasses, the U.S. is the underdog, fighting a superior antagonist.

But we're peering through economic lenses that are cen-

Entrepreneur, author and teacher, **JEREMY HAFT** *is a 20-year business veteran of the U.S.-China import-export sector, where he traded everything from auto parts to oil rigs, honey to pork sides. He is the writer of two popular books on China trade—*Unmade in China: The Hidden Truth About China's Economic Miracle *(Polity Books: 2015) and* All the Tea in China: How to Buy, Sell, and Make Money on the Mainland *(Penguin: 2007).*

turies old. They are statistical antiques, meant to measure a world before globalization. They present a version of economic reality so distorted that it's like looking through the wrong end of a telescope, shrinking the image of the U.S. to a fraction of its true size and power, while magnifying China's size beyond proportion.

First, let's consider the macro-economic lens, GDP. We've been hearing for over a decade that China is the world's second largest economy and catching up to the U.S. quickly. According to the World Bank, that happened. China overtook the U.S. to be the largest GDP in the world in 2015.

But what is GDP? This statistic has become synonymous with "the economy" at large. We use the two interchangeably. GDP is actually a very old number. It makes its first appearance in history in the 1600s, when an English landholder sought to tally up national accounts. (The most modern iteration was formulated in the 1930s in the Franklin D. Roosevelt administration to grapple with economic policy amid a major depression. The name, however, is misleading. The figure does not measure the total amount that a country produces, as "gross domestic product" might lead one to believe, further indicating that this number somehow encapsulates an entire economy. The most common formulation for GDP (used by the World Bank, the U.S. government, and mainstream economists) is to add up expenditures—that is, the combined spending of consumers, businesses and government—plus the value of exports (how much one country sells to other countries) minus the value of imports (what one country buys from other countries). GDP is a broad measure of the value of spending and trade as a snapshot of economic size.

In the 1930s, when the U.S. was in the depths of a depression and spurring consumer demand and spending was of paramount importance, gauging economic health through measuring expenditures in this way made sense. But nearly a century later, looking through this antique lens at the macroeconomy causes severe myopia. A tally of national expenditures tells very little about the size and vitality of a modern economy.

If you build a bridge, tear it down, build it again, tear it down, and build it again, you are adding to GDP but not adding to the value of your economy. This may sound like an academic example, but after the onset of the 2008 Great Recession, to keep its economy afloat, China's government began a series of mammoth stimulus programs, pumping billions of newly printed *renminbi* into its money supply. These funds flowed into the coffers of local governments, which spent them lavishly on infrastructure, much of which still sits idle, as empty ghost cities or bridges to nowhere. Sheer volume of spending tells nothing about the quality of economic growth.

In fact, in China's case, its GDP growth—its expenditures, driven by massive government investment spending—is causing severe economic problems. As China's central bank continues to print money, which it keeps pumping into the economy in a long, continued series of stimulus programs, its vast and expanding broad money supply is estimated to be 75% larger than that of the U.S. (but no one knows for sure). Since China's currency system is closed and not freely exchanged, and China artificially sets consumer prices, the money has nowhere to go but toward creating asset bubbles in real estate and manufacturing. While spending in the U.S. is primarily driven by consumers, in China, it remains driven by sustained, massive government investment. The more the government spends, the more overcapacity and overproduction increase, such as in the steel, aluminum, and cement industries. Hundreds of billions of stimulus dollars' worth of funds have been pumped into China's provinces and cities, which must keep balanced budgets, so the money has been squirreled into off-the-books entities to keep the debt off of municipal ledgers. In so doing, China's stated national debt of $25 trillion has ballooned to something much larger in the form of shadow debt.

In the case of China, GDP figures are especially misleading because they are famously fabricated. Li Keqiang, China's premier, once laughingly referred to China's economic numbers as "man-made" and "for reference only." In China, each province has its own economic statistical bureau tasked with measuring GDP, at the same time that the Chinese Communist Party puts paramount importance on GDP growth, promoting officials who preside over fast growth over those who don't.

That's one reason why, year after year, the total GDP of the provinces is larger than the GDP of the whole country, defying the law of math that the sum of the parts can't be more than the whole. It also explains China's torrid, though slowing, GDP growth rate. According to their official statistics, the rate of China's provinces is growing faster than the rate of the country as a whole. Again, a mathematical impossibility. The provinces famously cook their books and inflate their numbers. Chinese officials don't believe their own economic statistics, yet when making comparisons about economic size, the World Bank and U.S. government take Chinese GDP numbers at face value.

To make GDP even more specious, the World Bank tries to make up for the fact that a unit of currency spent in Beijing will buy a different amount than a unit of currency would buy in Manhattan by employing a statistic to adjust GDP called purchasing power parity (PPP). PPP seeks to make apples to apples comparisons between two economies' currencies but is highly imprecise. It fails to consider how prices change within a country's borders, as well as over time. And, when it comes to China, PPP fatally fails to accurately reflect a key driver of price, inflation. The inflation rate in China is a government secret, and World Bank economists must guess at China's number. Once a few years ago, in a

! Before you read, download the companion **Glossary** that includes definitions, a guide to acronyms and abbreviations used in the article, and other material. Go to **www.greatdecisions.org** and select a topic in the Resources section on the right-hand side of the page.

demonstration of the arbitrariness of its calculations, the World Bank upwardly revised its inflation estimates, and with the stroke of a key, cut China's GDP by about 40%. When China is called the world's number one economy, it is China's GDP which is being referred to, which is, statistically speaking, a fiction wrapped in a mirage.

Putting all of this aside, GDP is the wrong number to size an economy. Let's say you apply for a loan. Would the bank officer ask you how much you spent in the past year? Of course not. The bank would consider your spending in the broader context of your net worth, or what CFOs call the balance sheet. What are your assets and liabilities? How much do you own minus what you owe? This is a more accurate picture of financial health. Spending is just one aspect of it.

The same can be said for national economies. The combined assets and liabilities of households, businesses, and government tells a lot more about the size and vitality of an economy than spending can. First consider what's called net private wealth, a tally of the balance sheet value of all households in a country. The Federal Reserve and Credit Suisse in separate studies have concluded that American net private wealth was around \$93–96 trillion in 2017 compared to Chinese net private wealth of \$29 trillion. That's more than a \$60 *trillion* difference in America's favor.

Factoring in the assets and liabilities of businesses and government and then adding those to net private wealth, yields what economists call national wealth—the balance sheet of a nation at large. America's national wealth, the sum of private, corporate and government balance sheets, in 2017 was \$45 trillion greater than China's. And that gap is growing, not shrinking, as China's economy stagnates, while America's continues to grow.

Peering through the antique lens of GDP, we fail to see true economic wealth and size. Yet from the point of view of the balance sheet, what a nation owns minus what it owes, the U.S. is nowhere close to being number two. It is, far and away, still the wealthiest economy in the world. It can be debated whether that wealth is equitably distributed, but what cannot be debated is the fact that America's national wealth dwarfs that of its economic rival, China. The fear that China is about to plow over the U.S. in the global economy is mistaken. If anything, the U.S. is getting wealthier as a whole, while China slows and heads toward stagnation. The antique GDP lens distorts one's perspective, making China look bigger than it is, and the U.S. smaller than it is.

To truly get an understanding of the size of the U.S. economy compared with China's, though, requires looking beyond financial resources. In addition to financial resources, economies are also endowed with human and natural resources. Both are unfavorable for China and favorable for the U.S. In terms of demographics, China has become old before it has become rich. Decades of the One Child Policy have created more elderly than working age people, which will present a significant headwind to economic growth. Before Japan's lost decade, it grappled with similar demography. Since China's government owns and controls all the arms of its financial system, a full-scale economic collapse is unlikely, but demographics point to economic stagnation. The U.S., on the other hand, is a relatively younger nation with a history of immigration policies that favor dynamic economic growth. It remains to be seen what long-term impact on demographics and economic growth the current administration's new, more restrictive immigration policies will have.

In terms of natural resources, China has 20% of the world's population but just 8% of the world's arable land. Though China on the map seems like a vast country, you could fit China's arable land on the state of Texas. And that land is shrinking by about 1,900 square miles per year because of deforestation and desertification. Meanwhile, China faces a full-blown environmental crisis. China's air, land, and water are all under severe stress. Coal still provides 70% of China's energy needs, one chief reason why China is home to 16 of the world's 20 most polluted cities.

Tourists wear face masks due to severe air pollution in Beijing on November 14, 2018. (KYODO NEWS/GETTY IMAGES)

The very act of breathing for children in China's major cities is like smoking two packs of cigarettes a day. Cancer cities have sprung up all over China, as well, in which the population has an abnormally high degree of cancer sufferers, near industrial zones or downstream from them. Wanton dumping has contributed to a poisoning of the land with heavy metals, and as much as 10% or more of China's farmland has been officially reported to be too polluted to farm, but the real number is expected to be much higher. About 435 of China's 660 cities have less water than required; 100 Chinese cities are much worse off, already suffering severe water depletion. America's arable land and water, though disproportionately concentrated east of the Rockies, is sufficient to sustain its population; China's is not.

In all three measures of economic resources—financial, demographic and geographic—the U.S. enjoys significant advantages. The antique lens of GDP, which is used to size economies and which shows China as number one, needs its prescription updated. So does the second antique statistical lens used to perceive China: the balance of trade, which was designed with a worldview dating back to the 1600s. The balance of trade seeks to measure a country's imports and exports, what it buys from other countries versus what it sells to other countries. That may sound simple enough, yet today's economy is a globally interconnected, dynamic web, where many countries collaborate in the making of consumer products. Everyday goods like coffee, blood thinner, dog food and cell phones crisscross the world, logging thousands of transportation miles and multiple countries before arriving at your grocery store, pharmacy, big box retailer or doorstep.

Yet, balance of trade statistics do not account for trade flows that way. They attribute 100% of the value of an imported product to the last country that shipped it. It's as if we were still living in the 17th century. I sell you the wine I made in my cellar, you sell me the cloth you wove on your loom. Of course, most imported products are made by many countries, not one. To see them as being made entirely by the last country that shipped them severely distorts one's perspective of how global trade works—it magnifies the last country in the chain, while ignoring all the other countries that participated in the making of a product, including the U.S.

Since China typically occupies the last node of the global production platform—as a vast assembler for intermediate goods mostly made elsewhere—China appears much larger in trade stats than it actually is. Squinting through our pince-nez, China looks like a trading Goliath, America more like David. But the reality is closer to the opposite.

The curious case of the shrinking iPhone

Let's try an experiment. Let's swap out our Ben Franklin lenses for some modern Warby Parkers. Now let's direct our eyes at a smartphone. Suddenly, we're no longer looking at the surface of the object, attributing 100% of its value to China because that's the last country that shipped it. Now we can see all the components inside the phone, their value and what country made them.

Magically, China's share shrinks before our eyes—from 100% of the phone's value to around 3% to 6%. The cost of materials for an iPhone X is around $378 dollars. China contributes only $8 in value for the assembly of the phone and $6 for the battery pack for a combined value contribution of $14 or about 3% of the total cost of manufacturing. The rest of the parts are made by suppliers in the U.S., South Korea, Japan, Taiwan and the EU.

Men walk past an ad for the new Apple iPhone X on November 22, 2017, in London, UK. (RICHARD BAKER/IN PICTURES/GETTY IMAGES)

With the crisp new clarity of 21st century economic lenses, we can see China for what it really is. Not so much the legendary factory floor of the world, but the world's assembler—the last node on a long journey, in which raw materials are transformed into semi-finished goods by suppliers in many countries, to finally converge in China to be put together, packaged and exported. China looms so large in trade stats because they ignore all the value created by the other countries that preceded China in the chain.

The fact is that most of the major supply chains that run through China are owned by American or European firms, such as Apple, the world's first trillion-dollar company. Computer electronics may be the top Chinese product export to America, clocking in at $167 billion in 2017, but Apple and its U.S. suppliers and distributors are the overwhelming economic winners with regard to these imports, not China. China's value participation per phone is about 3% to 6%, most of which goes to a Taiwanese-owned company, Foxconn, for assembly. American suppliers provide about a third to a half of the value of materials for an iPhone X. Plus, Apple commands around a 60% profit margin, which supports American jobs, research and development, and distributions to shareholders. The antique trade lens shows China flooding the U.S. with $167 billion-worth of electronics, but with new lenses, we can see how little actual value participation China commands in the finished product of these electronics. Though China may be the last country that shipped the finished goods, American firms like Apple sit atop the global supply chain and receive the lion's share of its riches.

Step back from smartphone imports and use 21st-century trade lenses to examine China's trade deficit with the U.S., a *casus belli* for the trade war. In 2017, the U.S. imported about $505 billion worth of manufactured goods from China and exported around $129 billion to China. The trade deficit with China—the difference between the values of imports and exports—was $375 billion. That is to say, the *gross* trade deficit. Economists call these numbers "gross trade balances" because the numbers do not discern where the value came from; they ascribe 100% of value to the last country that shipped the goods. When you hear the term "gross trade balances," think antique 17th century lenses.

The U.S.'s "value-added trade deficit," which measures how much China *actually* contributes in value to the products the U.S. imports from there, is something quite different. A comprehensive analysis of America's value-added trade balance with China has not yet been conducted. Japan and the World Trade Organization have begun to shift their trade accounting to a value-added system, but the U.S. has not, insisting on looking at trade through a 17th-century economic paradigm, which makes the

U.S. appear tiny and China gigantic. If the U.S. were to consider its trade deficit in manufactured goods with China in value-added terms, it is estimated by mainstream economists and trade experts that the deficit would be cut by about one third to over one half. And that does not consider trade in agriculture and services, where the U.S. was running big surpluses with China before the trade war.

Wearing our modern lenses that allow us to see value-added instead of gross trade, China does not loom so large anymore. Suddenly, we also can see the U.S.' vital participation in the global manufacturing platform. Because hidden inside of many of the products the U.S. imports are American-made raw materials or parts. Even relatively basic products that China sells, like clothes, toys and hardware, often contain hidden U.S. content. America is a major grower and exporter of cotton, China a major importer. So that t-shirt that says Made in China will often contain American cotton. The more of these t-shirts the U.S. imports, the more cotton the U.S. exports. The U.S. is a major supplier of recycled metals; China, which lacks a robust recycling capability, is a major importer. So that imported Chinese faucet will often contain U.S. recycled steel. The more faucets the U.S. imports, the more scrap it exports. The U.S. is a major supplier of chemical resins, like plastic; China is a major importer. The more auto parts the U.S. imports, the more plastics it exports. And so on.

If it sounds symbiotic, it usually is. When it comes to production, the U.S. and China are typically arrayed in the form of a smile curve. America participates at the beginning of the product cycle—with design, engineering, raw materials and semi-finished goods—and at the end—with transportation, warehousing, retailing and servicing. China usually performs the middle functions—parts fabrication and assembly.

A dollar spent on Chinese imports, therefore, does not *all* go into Chinese coffers. The U.S. Federal Reserve estimates that about 55 cents of every dollar spent on Chinese imports goes to U.S. firms. That 55 cents pays for all the services associated with bringing a product to market. But it does not include any U.S.-made content that also may be hiding in the imported products, which trade numbers obscure. In the case of an iPhone or a fish stick, for example, both are imported from China, but both contain a high degree of U.S. content. Meaning that one dollar spent on an iPhone or a fish stick is closer to 60 or 75 cents going to U.S. firms.

The assertion that China's imports kill U.S. jobs is premised on the economic assumption that a dollar spent on Chinese goods is not a dollar spent on American goods. Less money spent in an economy means fewer jobs. Yet this is a 17th century view of trade which does not discern the value contributed by the U.S. in an interconnected globalized economy. In fact, one dollar spent on Chinese imports is around 55 to 75 cents spent in the U.S. economy. That income supports millions of jobs across America.

If Chinese imports kill American jobs, the employment data would show that as U.S. imports from China rise, employment would fall. Yet, looking at imports from China over the past 30 years and compare that to U.S. employment, reveals zero correlation. U.S. imports from China keep rising and rising, yet American employment levels also generally continue to rise, with the exception of recessions that hit every decade or so, when net job creation falls.

U.S. employment levels rise and fall based on the cycles of the U.S. economy—or when Wall Street runs amok, as in 2008—not in response to import levels from China. Otherwise, rising Chinese imports would trigger net job losses. Actually, imports *support* millions of jobs in America. All of those products need to be stevedored off the ships, loaded onto trains, transported to warehouses, wholesaled, retailed and serviced. And when those imported products contain American-made inputs, that supports domestics jobs, too. As imports rise, employment rises.

America, we should remember, is a big, dynamic economy, where 4–6 million jobs are churned through each month. The employment numbers that are announced by the Commerce Department are the net jobs created or lost *on top of the churn*. No doubt, as America began to array its supply chains across the globe in the 1990s and 2000s, many domestic jobs were lost as functions in the middle of the manufacturing smile curve—such as, primary fabrication and assembly—were outsourced overseas; and imports from China put American companies out of business, such as in the furniture and clothing industries. But any jobs lost to Chinese outsourcing or imports are statistically subsumed in that 4–6 million per month job churn; because the graph of the past 30 years of employment in America shows steady net job creation with the exception of recessions, irrespective of rising Chinese import levels.

This is not to minimize the dislocation that exposure to Chinese trade has caused communities across America. But a testament to the dynamism of the U.S. is that for every example of American carnage, there are five more of American renaissance. Across the very same Rust Belt that witnessed the closure of steel and saw mills, arising in their place have come advanced manufacturers of auto and aerospace parts, chemicals and pharmaceuticals. These companies are mostly comprised of small to midsized firms and employ hundreds of thousands of skilled workers across the Rust Belt.

The cruelty of the capitalist system is that while these jobs may look fungible on paper, they're not in real life; and many of the higher paying advanced manufacturing jobs that have come to the Rust Belt are not occupied by those who were doing the lower value jobs before. So, while it is a testament to U.S. economic resilience that advanced manufacturers have taken the place of relatively lower-value companies shuttered by Chinese competition, it is also a testament to the failure of the U.S. government and politicians of succeeding administrations to substantively help those put out of work by trade. It is politically more expedient to blame the Chinese for problems the U.S.' own policies have created.

The scythe of tariffs

We can perhaps forgive Americans, then, for feeling that hitting back with tariffs at least is doing *something* to protect American workers, after hearing for 30 years that China has been stealing U.S. jobs and intellectual property. A broad swath of voters across party lines feel that tariffs are justified in combatting China's trade abuses. They think that, with tariffs, if imported Chinese products are a bit more expensive, as long as they're protecting American workers and helping the country, so be it.

The problem, however, is that the opposite is happening. Tariffs are not protecting American workers, they are killing many more jobs than they're saving. One stark, recent example of the impact of a 17th century trade remedy on a 21st century supply chain can be seen in the Obama administration's 2010 tariffs on imported Chinese solar panels. The policy was meant to protect workers in the solar industry, but what happened was the opposite. It not only triggered a net loss of solar jobs, it decimated an entire domestic upstream industry and ceded significant market share to China.

The news kept reporting that China was flooding U.S. markets with cheap solar panels. Raising tariffs against this onslaught seemed like the right thing to do. But the policy backfired. You wouldn't know it from the trade numbers, but hidden inside imported Chinese solar panels was a lot of American-made content. A key raw material in making solar panels is photovoltaic (PV) polysilicon, the ingredient that converts light into energy. Before the 2010 tariffs, if you looked across the span of the solar supply chain—not just the single node of panel production—the U.S. was a net exporter to China. The U.S. sold China $247 million more in value than it bought in 2010. This is what's known as a "trade surplus." The value of exports exceeded the value of imports. Most of this value was attributed to PV polysilicon, and some of it, to capital equipment—the machines used to make the panels. So, the more panels the U.S. imported from China, the more PV polysilicon and capital equipment it exported to China to make the panels.

Then tariffs were levied on the imported panels. China retaliated by raising tariffs on U.S.-made PV polysilicon. A vicious cycle began. Demand slackened for imported panels, driving down demand for the U.S.-made inputs. Many U.S. firms in the PV polysilicon industry went out of business, and there were significant job losses. REC Silicon cut half its workforce. Hemlock Semiconductor shuttered a $1.2 billion factory project in Tennessee. Today, there are only three U.S. PV polysilicon firms standing. From 2010–17, the U.S. share of global PV polysilicon production fell from 29% to 11%. In 2010, China barely produced any PV polysilicon at all. Today, China produces 70% of the world's supply. Given that PV polysilicon is a key ingredient in semiconductors, an industry where the U.S. still has a significant technological lead over China, a credible case could be made that this self-inflicted wound constituted a national security threat.

Solar panels are not an outlier. Time and time again, the modern history of tariffs is that of killing more jobs than saving. And the job-killing effects of the U.S.-China trade war are already apparent. Economists at universities, think tanks and trade groups are providing estimates that generally comport with what has been true in the past. For every job saved or created through tariffs, many more jobs are eliminated. The administration announced on May 31, 2018, a 25% tariff on imported steel and a 10% tariff on imported aluminum. Economists estimate that about 27,000 jobs would be created in the steel and aluminum industry from the tariffs in the next one to three years, yet about 430,000 jobs would be eliminated in the aggregate. Every job created in the metals industry through tariffs would kill 16 jobs in other industries, mostly ones that consume steel and aluminum.

A lot of these jobs will be eliminated in the Rust Belt. An example: Mid-Continent Nail of Missouri, which is losing money because the tariffs have destroyed its profit margins. The company laid off 60 workers in June 2018, announced an additional 200 job cuts in July, and may go out of business entirely, putting its 500 employees out of work. Another example is Ford Motor Company, which states that its comeback has been stymied by the tariffs. Hamstrung between the metal tariffs on one side and China's retaliatory tariffs on the other, the company recently declared a $1 billion loss in profits due to the trade war. Companies large and small across America are being hurt.

And the tariffs extend well beyond metals, as China has retaliated with tariffs on a broad basket of U.S. exports, including many in the agricultural sector, where it is estimated that 67,000 U.S. jobs will be lost, according to research done by trade groups National Retail Federation and the Consumer Technology Association. Since one out of every four rows of soybeans grown in Iowa had traditionally been exported to China, soybeans were one of the first products China targeted with its counter-tariffs. China is, also, America's second largest pork market after Mexico. In addition to soybeans, China targeted U.S. pork exports with two rounds of tariffs. There was an existing tariff already in place of 11%, plus the two rounds of retaliatory tariffs China applied, plus a value-added tax already in place, which brought the effective tariff rate of U.S. pork exported to China to around 67%. That essentially has priced America out of the market. Unfortunately for U.S. ranchers and farmers, once Chinese importers turn to other market sources, it is expensive and time consuming to try to win them back. So the administration's announced $12 billion aid package to farmers is not only a drop in the bucket of profits that will be lost in a single year by an entire sector of the economy; but once these Chinese export markets are lost, they're often lost forever; winning them back is not a certitude.

But tariffs are politically popular

with at least some of the electorate, and this administration is determined to pursue tariffs as a remedy to China's economic abuses, despite mounting evidence of widespread domestic job losses and forfeited market share. Indeed, another round of tariffs on solar panels is being pursued by this administration, despite its catastrophic impact the last time. The problem with the antique blunderbuss of tariffs is that its scattershot range inevitably kills jobs in a rain of friendly fire. But the benighted trade numbers obscure the fact that this is happening.

What's to be done?

In the case of China, pursuing a trade war with tariffs is tantamount to economic suicide. China will merely turn to other countries as sources for the goods they require, boxing the U.S. out of future opportunities, while they keep carrying on acting in what they see as their own economic best interests. All the while, the tariffs will kill hundreds of thousands of U.S. jobs.

There are other tools available that don't backfire and decimate U.S. industries, tools that "fix" trade and deal directly with China's negative impact on the U.S. economy. Here are three:

First, bolster safety protocols. The danger posed by China does not come from the trade imbalance; it comes from Chinese food and drugs and other products the U.S. imports. China has been rocked by literally thousands, probably tens of thousands, of safety breaches in the past decade alone, spanning every aspect of China's manufacturing—from food and drugs to high-speed rail and shipbuilding to aerospace and consumer electronics. No one knows the exact number, as in most cases, China's local and national authorities try to cover up these incidents.

Most of these safety breaches have gone unnoticed by Americans, except for the really big ones. Like when baby formula tainted with the industrial chemical melamine poisoned over 300,000 infants. Or when Dora the Explorer toys were coated in lead paint. Or when the accelerator pedals of Aston Martins were too brittle, triggering a massive, multi-year recall. Or when the dry wall in FEMA-supplied homes after Hurricane Katrina began outgassing poison. Or when the flooring from Lumber Liquidators was found to be toxic. Or when there was a chemical explosion at a Chinese warehouse in the port of Tianjin so large, a 20-story high fireball could be seen from space. Or when school athletic fields were found to be toxic. Or most recently, when yet another scandal of widespread distribution of tainted vaccines to children was reported.

As grisly as these are, if you lived in China, you'd see another new, horrible safety breach nearly every day. From glow in the dark pork, to gutter oil being used in cooking, to chicken a decade past its sell-by date, to vegetables and fruit drenched in poisonous pesticides, fungicides and herbicides, day in, day out, in the cities or in the country, safety scandals happen with nearly numbing regularity. A CCTV news anchor, Qui Qiming, after the high-speed rail crash of Wenzhou in 2011, put it best, when he (bravely) went off script on national television and asked, "Can we drink a glass of safe milk? Can we live in apartments that do not fall down? Can the roads we drive on in our cities not collapse? Can we afford the people a basic sense of security? China, please slow down. If you keep going so fast, you may leave the souls of your people behind."

Each time another major safety breach occurs that affects American consumers, the reporting tends to single out individual malefactors. For the Dora lead paint, it was the owner of the factory tasked with painting the products. For the accelerator pedals, it was the tiny injection molder in the Chinese hinterland that was the culprit. China's authorities would tend to agree. In the past, they have characterized China's safety breaches as "a few bad apples."

But this misses the point. The sheer volume of the safety breaches—which continue unabated, and, if anything, are getting more lethal—suggests something deeper is going on here. It's more than a few bad apples. China's manufacturing platform is systemically risky. Modern manufacturing has evolved to the point where science is used to try to mitigate risk. As raw materials are transformed into finished goods, each node of the process is designed to minimize mistakes. The International Standards Organization awards its ISO certifications based, in part, on a factory's systems and effectiveness in scientifically measuring and mitigating risk.

Fire workers carry a body out of the blasts site on August 25, 2015, in Tianjin, China. A series of massive explosions in a chemical factory was one of China's worst industrial disasters in years with a death toll of 173. (VISUAL CHINA GROUP/GETTY IMAGES)

Yet, in China, each node of the manufacturing chain *adds* risk that the outputs will be unsafe. As raw materials wend their way through the supply chain, the safety risk increases. From unsafe raw material inputs, like poisonous baby formula or tainted active pharmaceutical ingredients, products move through a supply chain that is severely fragmented—what takes 3 to 5 firms in the U.S. to make a product still takes China from 15 to 20. Each of these firms adds risk, cost and time to the manufacturing process. In addition to this severe fragmentation, making quality control across a long opaque chain of firms difficult to impossible, primitive corporate governance, weak rule of law, and endemic corruption all contribute to a systemically risky production platform, to which Americans are increasingly exposed.

This is a terrifying proposition, when considering how much food and drugs the U.S. imports from China, often without a country-of-origin label. Eighty percent of the active pharmaceutical ingredients in drugs imported by the U.S. come from Chinese and Indian suppliers, and India imports its raw materials from China. Most kids would be surprised to learn that the apples in their morning apple juice come from China. Their parents would be disturbed to learn that China is rocked by persistent scandals of arsenic being discovered on Chinese-grown apples. The vitamin C in a Flintstone's Multivitamin was likely made in China, which makes most of the world's supply; so too, blood thinner and insulin. And, the same goes for many foods, like tilapia; 90% of tilapia consumed in the U.S. comes from China. One quarter of the garlic. One third of the processed mushrooms. China has one of the worst safety records in the world when it comes to food, drugs and consumer goods, yet it increasingly dominates the supply of critical products consumed every day in the U.S.

Japan, which has been importing food and drugs from China for a lot longer than the U.S., provides a good model to emulate. Japan has very stringent standards that Chinese suppliers must abide by before they can export into Japan. The U.S. doesn't. Essentially, the U.S. takes suppliers at their word that they comply with U.S. standards. The bad batches of raw heparin that went into the blood thinner that killed over 100 patients in American hospitals came from a Chinese supplier that drug wholesaler Baxter never inspected; they took the word of an inspection report done by another firm, years earlier.

That protocol must change. Chinese suppliers should have to comply with yearly audits of their physical plant and equipment, as well as their processes, organizational structure, accountability and corporate history. An audit of upstream supply should also be required. Yes, this would make products coming from China more expensive, but this price increase would be across the board; it would not discriminate one industry over another.

Japan also deploys giant quality-control clearinghouses in several of its ports, where large volumes of imported products pass through and are inspected. It is estimated that Japan inspects about 10% of its China imports this way; the current system in the U.S. inspects about 2%. That puts Americans at risk.

As part of a comprehensive safety upgrade, the U.S. would need to strengthen the mandate and resources of the FDA and USDA in China, as well. Right now, there are about 17 FDA inspectors in the field meant to inspect and police thousands of suppliers, exporting millions of pounds of food and drugs to the U.S. That's a big leap from the handful of inspectors in the field when the blood thinner scandal happened, but it's still a fraction of what's required to insure safety.

Also, regulations need to be tightened governing what the U.S. imports. Chinese processed chicken was recently determined to be "equivalent" to U.S. quality standards by the USDA. This determination was a long-time request of China's at the trade bargaining table. If the U.S. opened its market for Chinese processed chicken (think: the chicken in a McNugget or can of soup), China would open its market again to U.S. beef. There is nothing equivalent about China's chicken processing industry, however. A sneak peek inside a Chinese chicken processor would look like a scene out of *The Jungle* by Upton Sinclair. At U.S. chicken processors, USDA inspectors must be on site at all times. In China, terrifyingly, not so. In fact, inspectors must warn suppliers before they inspect. A big part of this problem—exposing the U.S. population to unsafe food and drugs—is the fault of the U.S. The FDA and USDA wear two hats; first, to protect consumers, but also, to advocate for American industry. You can't do both effectively and separately. You can't have the USDA pushing hard to open the Chinese market for beef, while at the same time, seriously pursuing its mission to keep consumers safe, because in order to open beef, they have to sell out safety on chicken. The mission of these agencies must be reformed. Let the U.S. Trade Representative or the Commerce Department advocate for U.S. industry. Governmental agencies like the USDA and FDA must focus strictly on the increasingly complex and challenging mission of protecting public health without conflict of interest.

Second, start pricing negative externalities into tradable goods. Though tariffs are the wrong way to fix trade, that doesn't mean "free trade," with no holds barred, is the right approach either. The global production platform inflicts harm on the environment and human populations. The average American uses more than double the CO2 emissions than counterparts in Germany or Japan, according to the UN. But these numbers do not include the CO2 emitted to make and transport the goods consumed in the U.S., which experts estimate more than *doubles* the country's individual carbon footprint.

The humble fish stick illustrates how. Over 80% of U.S. seafood is imported, not because there aren't abundant fish supplies on U.S. coasts, but because it is cheaper to ship fish thousands of miles away to be deboned, filleted, breaded, polybagged, boxed and then re-shipped thousands of miles back—burning bunker fuel, the dirtiest of fossil fuels, all the way. A single fish stick logs thousands of very dirty carbon miles. While CO2 emissions inflict a measurable economic cost to the planet and public health, they are not "priced in" to actual costs paid for a particular imported good. U.S. policies give businesses and consumers a pass on carbon emissions, effectively subsidizing the burning of fossil fuels to power the global supply chain.

Pricing in the cost of carbon in tradable goods would make imports more expensive across the board, but the prices would be more in line with the true costs of these goods. Companies and consumers would factor these extra costs into making purchase decisions. For many products, making them closer to home will simply make more economic sense. Trade would be rebalanced without arbitrarily picking politically connected winners (steel) over losers (PV polysilicon). The George W. Bush administration and its Republican Congress put forward a cap-and-trade system that would be a good place to start. A more precise system would involve tracking carbon emissions in each phase of the global supply chain and logging that data in an RFID chip that traveled with each product, then pricing these carbon miles accordingly. Given advances in blockchain technology, used, for example, by Walmart to track the pork supply chain in China, we may see an evolution to this product-specific carbon tracking sometime in the future.

Finally, economic number need to be updated. The fact that the U.S. still measures trade as if individuals were swapping wine for cloth keeps causing major economic policy misfires. The U.S. turns to tariffs again and again, when again and again, they kill more American jobs than they save, often ceding large swaths of markets to competitors in the bargain. Japan and the World Trade Organization are moving toward a value-added trading system. The U.S. should encourage its trading partners of Mexico, Canada, South Korea and the EU to do the same, and should follow suit. With a more granular understanding of where value is being created in the global supply chain, policymakers and economists could better understand where jobs are being supported in the economy—and where they are being destroyed. For the jobs being lost, politicians can work to create targeted policies that support those Americans in retraining, extended health care coverage, home mortgage leniency, and other support programs. Economic numbers, as accurate lenses on macroeconomics and trade, can become powerful tools to create more effective policies.

People pose for photos in front of a statue of a dog, with a resemblance to U.S. President Donald Trump, outside a shopping mall in Taiyuan, in China's northern Shanxi province on December 29, 2017. The statue is celebrating the year of the dog. (AFP/GETTY IMAGES)

Bolstering safety, pricing in negative externalities and updating economic numbers, however, are best done in the context of multilateral trade agreements. There is little sense, for example, in putting a tax on the carbon footprint of tradable goods as a country by yourself. You need many partners to go along with you. The Trans-Pacific Partnership, which includes NAFTA members Canada and Mexico, uniting together in a set of cap-and-trade protocols would have been a workable platform. Restricting yourself to bilateral trade deals impinges your ability to achieve scale. To impact China's economic behavior, or trade on a global level, it's more powerful to act in a big group of many strong economic allies rather than acting alone. The TPP was meant to be such an economic alliance. Imagine if the original TPP partners not only agreed to price carbon into trade, but also agreed to abide by common safety protocols that would raise the prices across the board on Chinese-made products by making quality controls much stricter, as Japan has done. That would make the world safer, while also helping to rebalance trade in an economically fairer way that does not advantage politically connected industries at the expense of others.

Without modernizing economic numbers across the board, however, we will continue to see the world myopically. Yes, there is an imbalance between the economies of China and the U.S., but financially, demographically and geographically, it is highly in the favor of the U.S. The trade imbalance, construed through 17th-century trade numbers, is a mirage. Looking at China's true value participation in the global supply chain, China shrinks before our very eyes. U.S. policymakers need to see this. Because the U.S.-China trade war, waged through tariffs to eliminate this illusory trade imbalance, will do nothing to deter China from following what it deems in its own best interests, but instead will kill jobs across America and cede large swaths of market share to U.S. competitors. The question is whether this time, after decades of the self-inflicted wounds caused by tariffs, America will wake up to the economic folly of these policies and, finally, lay its old eyeglasses aside.

discussion questions

1. Why do you think the U.S. uses outdated methods to measure trade and economic size? How can a new, more accurate system be developed? What benefits are there to keep using the current system of measurement?

2. The author points out misconceptions in China's contribution in the manufacturing of imports such as the iPhone and solar panels. Would awareness of these misconceptions affect trade policy ergarding China? Why or why not?

3. Do you agree that there is a trade war developing between the U.S. and China? How will this affect the U.S.'s relations with other trade partners, and the world economy?

4. How do environmental issues affect the U.S.-China trade relationship? Is it possible to create a system of trade that benefits both countries, as well as the environment? What would that look like?

5. The U.S. and China have a symbiotic relationship with trade. How should the U.S. respond to safety breaches in China? Does the U.S. have the right to intervene in unsafe manufacturing situations? If so, when? If not, why not?

6. How will recent tariffs between the U.S. and China affect the future of the U.S.-China economic relationship? Is it too late for policy changes to affect the relationship?

suggested readings

Allison, Graham. **Destined for War: Can America and China Escape Thucydides's Trap?** 389 pp. Boston, MA: Houghton Mifflin Harcourt, 2017. Harvard scholar Graham Allison blends history and current events to explain the timeless machinery of Thucydides's Trap—and to explore the painful steps that might prevent disaster today.

Bergsten, C. Fred and Gagnon, Joseph E. **Currency Conflict and Trade Policy: A New Strategy for the United States**. 230 pp. Washington, D.C.: Peterson Institute for International Economics, 2017. This book by two leading experts on trade, investment and the effects of currency manipulation traces the history, causes and effects of currency manipulation and analyzes a range of policy responses that the U.S. could adopt.

Blinder, Alan S. **Advice and Dissent: Why America Suffers When Economics and Politics Collide**. 351 pp. New York, NY: Basic Books, 2018. Blinder shows how both sides can shrink the gap between good politics and good economics.

McGregor, Richard. **Asia's Reckoning: China, Japan, and the Fate of U.S. Power in the Pacific Century**. 416 pp. New York, NY: Viking Press, 2018. The former bureau chief of the *Financial Times's* Beijing and Washington bureau chief shows how U.S power will stand or fall on its ability to hold its ground in Asia.

Nephew, Richard. **The Art of Sanctions: A View from the Field**. 232 pp. New York, NY: Columbia University Press, 2017. A framework for planning and applying sanctions that focuses not just on the initial strategy but also, crucially, on how to calibrate along the way and how to decide when sanctions have achieved maximum effectiveness.

Rachman, Gideon. **Easternization: Asia's Rise and America's Decline from Obama to Trump and Beyond**. 336 pp. New York, NY: Other Press, 2018. Rachman offers a road map to the turbulent process that will define the international politics of the 21st century.

Walt, Stephen M. **The Hell of Good Intentions: America's Foreign Policy Elite and the Decline of U.S. Primacy**. 400 pp. New York, NY: Farrar, Straus and Giroux, 2018. A look at the faults and foibles of recent American foreign policy—including why it has been plagued by disasters like the "forever wars" in Iraq and Afghanistan and outlining what can be done to fix it.

Don't forget: Ballots start on page 103!

To access web links to these readings, as well as links to additional, shorter readings and suggested web sites,

GO TO www.greatdecisions.org

and click on the topic under Resources, on the right-hand side of the page.

6

Cyber conflict and geopolitics

by Richard B. Andres

A picture taken on October 17, 2016, shows an employee walking behind a glass wall with machine coding symbols at the headquarters of Internet security giant Kaspersky in Moscow. (KIRILL KUDRYAVTSEV/AFP/GETTY IMAGES)

Across history, the geopolitical fortunes of great powers have often been closely connected with the rise of radical new technologies. In the current era, one of the most significant and controversial questions facing the U.S. is whether new cyber technology is facilitating the rise of Russia and China; more particularly, whether the growing competition in cyberspace is causing a geopolitical pivot that will eventually allow Moscow and Beijing to replace the U.S.-led liberal international order with one more conducive to their autocratic proclivities.

The idea that the U.S.' opponents are acting aggressively in cyberspace is not new. U.S. presidents have regularly pushed back against China's digital predations since at least 2009. Since 2017, the U.S. has significantly upped the ante, condemning Russian and Chinese actions, and using a variety of diplomatic demarches, tariffs and sanctions to back its demands.

Yet there is still a great deal of uncertainty about how serious Russian and Chinese actions are, and about what their behavior portends for future balances of international power. While U.S. security experts generally intuit that *something* important is happening, there is little consensus about what exactly that is or how significant it is compared to the many other threats currently faced by the U.S. and other democra-

The views expressed in this chapter are those of the author and do not reflect official positions of the National Defense University, the Department of Defense or any other U.S. government organization.

RICHARD B. ANDRES *is Professor of National Security Strategy at the U.S. National War College where his work focuses on developing national cyber security strategy. Across his career he has served as an adviser on strategy to the Bush and Obama National Security Councils and other senior leaders and institutions in and out of government. Dr. Andres holds faculty or board positions at the Johns Hopkins School of Advanced International Studies, the Georgetown University Security Studies Program, the American Enterprise Institute, and Pacific Northwest National Labs.*

cies. Officials are aware that Russia is using social media, doxing and various other methods to conduct what they call cyber psychological operations to increase political fear uncertainty and doubt across Europe and the U.S.; and they know that China is carrying out economic espionage and a variety of information operations. But they are unsure about how likely these actions are to undermine the post-World War II (WWII) international order, or if they will facilitate the rise of a new regional or global system in which Russia and China have significantly more say over the course of events.

Connected to this uncertainty is the question of whether the U.S. is a net winner or a net loser as a result of the struggle in cyberspace. The current generation of leaders responsible for formulating U.S. security policy came of age at a time when the U.S. lead in cyberspace was considered incontestable. For many, the idea that opponents might be gaining more than the U.S. from cyber competition is difficult to accept at either an intellectual or emotional level.

Among politically active groups in the U.S., and particularly among business leaders, the problem is equally tricky. In the private sector, there are often powerful incentives to maintain the status quo. The idea that, over a period of years or decades, foreign cyber psychological operations might undermine democracy, or that state-directed, cyber-enabled economic espionage could provide an opponent with an unassailable economic lead, can seem relatively abstract. On the other hand, economic sanctions threatened or enacted by the U.S. against Russia and China to curb specific bad behavior have immediate and tangible effects. On occasion, this dynamic has led Wall Street to oppose government actions that political and security professionals saw as necessary to constrain bad cyber behavior by Russia and China. For instance, in September of 2018, while conceding that the U.S. needs to confront China, Tom Donohue, President of the U.S. Chamber of Commerce argued in an interview with the *Christian Science Monitor* that "The single biggest threat facing the economy right now is the potential for a real trade war."

A serious theoretical problem underlies the lack of consensus on the geopolitical impact of the cyber struggle. Americans today often find it difficult to conceive of a world in which they face serious competition from other major powers. Americans have largely come to view the current world order as permanent, based on the national instruments of power that brought the U.S. to the fore during the Cold War (1947–91) and held it there after that competition ended. Thus, it is probably fair to say that most Americans (who think about this issue at all) tend to believe that so long as the U.S. maintains the world's most powerful military and does what it has always done economically, its ideals will dominate the international system. In fact, this assumption of permanent preeminence has become so strongly ingrained in U.S. thinking that the idea of great power competition and geopolitics has generally fallen out of most U.S. university curriculums. The overall result is that the current generation of leaders is ill-equipped to assess how Russian and Chinese innovations in cyberspace might undermine and eventually usurp the current system.

This lack of imagination is problematic not least because it is not shared by Russian and Chinese thinkers. Strategists in both of those states have regularly and publicly described the ways in which their countries are harnessing cyber technology to overcome the U.S. lead in more traditional instruments of national power. Moreover, Moscow and Beijing have been clear that they do not agree with important aspects of the current U.S.-led system. Should their plans prove successful, it is likely they will alter these systems in ways inimical to U.S. values and interests. Thus, the first step toward assessing how the competition in cyberspace is likely to affect geopolitics is to begin to expand the way Americans think beyond comfortable post-Cold War paradigms. American experts should reflect more generally on the historical connection between radical new technology and geopolitical pivots, and they should take a leaf out of Russia and China's book and apply some imagination to the issues at hand.

Understanding technology-based geopolitical pivots

The idea that new technology can alter geopolitical balances of power has long dominated the thinking of both historians and major power strategists. Writing in the fifth century BC, the Greek historian Herodotus described how Egypt was able to take advantage of new irrigation technology to expand its economic and military might, eventually becoming the most powerful state in the ancient world. Writing more than 2,000 years later, the American naval theorist Alfred Mahan described the role played by maritime technology in the rise of the states on Europe's Atlantic seaboard during the age of sail. A few years later, in a work that foreshadowed World War I (WWI) and WWII, British geographer Halford Mackinder predicted how new railroad technology would facilitate the rise of Europe's land powers at the expense of maritime nations like Britain.

While it is difficult to predict how any new technology might shift international balances of power, both Mackinder's and Mahan's theories provide some clues about what to look for. Mackinder first came to fame in 1904, when he published a paper in *The Geographical Journal* arguing that an emerging technology originally invented and championed by Britain would soon be used by its adversaries to upend its centuries-long position of primacy in world politics. In simplest form, Mackinder's argument was that the economic, military and political primacy of Britain depended on maritime technology. Railroad technology had largely originated there, and Britain appeared to maintain an unassailable technological lead. Yet, Mackinder contended, as continental powers like Germany and Russia developed new railroad networks to gain access to their hitherto inaccessible internal resources, their economies would come to eclipse Britain's. More than this, Mackinder believed that the incentive structure for violence that accompanied rail and continental expansion would alter the way states vied for power. All of this would lead to an international system in which Britain would be poorly equipped to compete. Mackinder's predictions proved accurate. Within a decade, Germany and Russia were battling for supremacy on the continent, and by mid-century, as the Soviet Union completed its rail networks and annexed Central Europe, a single victorious continental power emerged to eclipse Britain.

Russian army engineers seen here laying a track bed for a narrow gauge railway during the Russian campaign of March 1916 during World War I. (DAILY MIRROR ARCHIVE/MIRRORPIX/GETTY IMAGES)

Mackinder's and Mahan's work provide two general arguments about what is necessary for a new technology to change the geopolitical status quo. The first is that the new technology must be able to significantly change the way geography affects nations' ability to generate wealth and military power. As Mahan described it, in the five centuries preceding the advent of railroads, the diffusion of maritime technology radically improved the ability of states on Europe's Atlantic seaboard to create wealth. During this period, for instance, a sailing ship might circumnavigate the globe in the time it took a laden wagon or army to move a few hundred miles over land. Based on geographical variables such as access to ports and the presence of a population skilled in maritime commerce, states that were able to take advantage of this dynamic had the potential to build their economic and military influence much faster than states that did not. However, as Mackinder noted, when rail technology diffused across Europe, the new technology ended the upper hand enjoyed by maritime powers and provided an unassailable advantage for the economies of large continental powers.

Mahan and Mackinder's arguments further imply that a new technology can interact with geography to change the way that nations compete for security. According to Mahan, maritime technology created a set of incentives that had to be followed for a sea power to achieve primacy. Beyond working to benefit from maritime trade, a global power needed to control that trade by dominating the seas militarily. To control the seas, the state needed to be willing to fund a powerful navy, gain access to global basing and control the world's key maritime chokepoints. While Mahan's notion of control of the sea was assertive, it was not domineering, as maritime mastery depended on free trade and consortiums rather than on the conquest and domination of other states. Thus, the path that maritime technology provided to world power often incentivized nations to compete for military control of the sea, but not necessarily of the territory of other states.

Describing the diffusion of rail technology and the rise of continental power, Mackinder envisioned a significantly different set of incentives. He believed that the route to power lay in controlling the resources of Central and Eastern Europe recently opened up by rail. This territory not only offered access to the bulk of the world's industrial capacity, it also provided a secure base that was militarily inaccessible to peripheral powers. He argued that this created a nearly insurmountable security dilemma for the continental powers. Whichever was the first to conquer Central and Eastern Europe would become the master of Eurasia and thus the world. This type of incentive structure would lead inevitably to aggressive competition for control of territory.

Beyond these two characteristics, both Mahan's and Mackinder's work on geopolitics hint at a common irony. In the geopolitical pivot each author describes, the power that did the most to develop the relevant technology—the Hapsburg Empire in the case of maritime technology and the British Empire in the case of rail—eventually lost its primacy when adversaries adopted and adapted the technology for their own purposes. In the current era, the diffusion of cyber technology appears to be following a course with similarities to these geopolitical pivots.

A cyber geopolitical pivot

Like 15th century maritime technology or 19th century rail technology, cyber technology was originally championed by the world's leading state and, over a period of decades, eventually diffused around the globe. Maritime technology accelerated the economic growth of the Atlantic states and rail aided Europe's land powers; the effects of cyber technology are not as straightforward.

In the first place, the term cyber technology is not well defined. In general, it refers to computers and computer networks. This includes telephones, telecommunications networks, and data both in motion and at rest. In and of itself, this infrastructure is important. However, from the perspective of geopolitical power such a definition is incomplete. To truly understand why cyberspace is geopolitically relevant, it is necessary to understand that, over the last three decades, nations have connected virtually everything associated with their economies and national security to computer networks. Thus, the definition needs to expand to include much more than computers and data per se.

In terms of economics, the way wealth is generated and stored has changed in fundamental ways since the beginning of the cyber age. Leading up to the 1980s, around 80% of most U.S. companies' wealth was stored in tangible assets. From a security perspective, this meant that the key to national wealth was control of hard assets like land, natural resources and factories. In the worlds with which Mahan and Mackinder were dealing, the key to maintaining national power was maintaining control of economically productive territory and populations, as well as economic lanes of communication like land and maritime chokepoints. This is no longer true in the cyber age. Today, around 80% of most U.S. companies' wealth is stored in intangible goods, mainly trade secrets and intellectual property. These types of goods are not particularly vulnerable to territorial conquest or conventional seizure of land or maritime lanes of communication. They are, however, extremely vulnerable to certain types of cyber piracy, and their security depends on which actors control the cyber networks on which they are stored and across which they flow. In this sense, cyber technology has probably changed the way that wealth is generated, stored and transported at least as much as maritime and rail technologies did in previous centuries.

Cyber technology has also altered the character of military power. Before the cyber age, military power was generally measured in terms of the number of troops and weapons a nation could maintain. Today, as nations have computerized and networked their weapons, mere numbers have become increasingly irrelevant as indictors of military power. It has not been uncommon in recent wars for computerized and networked militaries, utilizing advanced sensors, communications and precision munitions, to inflict hundreds or even thousands of casualties for every one inflicted when fighting non-networked forces. Yet to achieve these results, modern forces have had to connect their systems to hardware and software that is often vulnerable to cyberattacks.

In an earlier age, the domestic critical infrastructure of strong advanced economies like the U.S. was often made all but invulnerable to attacks by foreign conventional militaries. Today, with most domestic infrastructure connected to computer networks, conventional defenses no longer offer much direct protection; any state with strong offensive cyber capabilities has the potential to do immense damage to a major power's critical infrastructure. Maritime and rail technologies once altered the fundamental requirements of military security for many states. Today, the security once derived from conventional military and geographical advantages is undermined by vulnerabilities inherent in networked domestic infrastructure.

Cyber technology is also altering geopolitical balances of power in more insidious ways. These have less in common with the maritime and rail models described above. In the pre-cyber era, nations generally had a good deal of control over the information their citizens received. In autocratic states, this control generally resided in the government; in democracies, it was located in civic institutions. While nations regularly conducted information operations against their opponents' citizens, these actions were relatively expensive and difficult. In the cyber age, information easily traverses national borders. This makes information operations far easier and cheaper to conduct, and it incentivizes states to attempt to influence the beliefs and behavior of foreign populations.

Yet understanding how states *might* use cyber technology is quite different from knowing how they are actually using it. The following section describes how the U.S., Russia and China have attempted to profit geopolitically from cyber technology over the last three decades, and how the competition in cyberspace has evolved to the benefit and detriment of each power over time.

The United States

The first power to take advantage of cyberspace for geopolitical gain was the U.S. As the originator of the technology, it had substantial first-mover advantage. As networking morphed from a small Department of Defense-centered project into the global Internet in the 1990s, U.S. intelligence agencies began to use cyberspace for espionage. One of the key lessons learned during this period was that, dollar for dollar, cyber espionage is hundreds-of-thousands or even millions of times more efficient at bulk data collection than traditional forms of spying. By the middle of the 2000s, U.S. intelligence had garnered a reputation in some parts of the world for supernatural clairvoyance.

In 2010, the role of cyber power in international politics changed radically in two ways. The first involved the Stuxnet "worm"—a piece of malware, or malicious software, that multiplied itself and spread between computers, in this case infesting critical infrastructure around the world. The cybersecurity and anti-virus provider Kaspersky Lab attributed Stuxnet to the U.S. government. Until this point, it had been widely assumed that states used malware exclusively for gathering information or, at worst, to sabotage adversaries' computers. Stuxnet turned this assumption on its head: It was designed to destroy hardware attached to a computer network. Specifically, it was designed to spread globally until it eventually infected an air-gapped (completely isolated from external networks) computer network at Iran's nuclear facility at Natanz. At that point, it slowly and stealthily destroyed the centrifuges connected to the network. While Washington did not take credit for the worm, it is widely believed that the U.S. and Israel designed the software with the goal of damaging Iran's nuclear weapons program without crossing a line that could lead to war.

In the same year that Stuxnet became public, the U.S. declared that it was engaged in a global effort to use its cyber capabilities against its autocratic adversaries. In January, on the heels of an announcement by Google that Chinese intelligence had hacked into its computers in order to track down dissidents, Secretary of State Hillary Clinton (2009–13) publicly rebuked Beijing, and delivered a speech on Internet freedom in which she stated that:

"[The U.S. is] also supporting the development of new tools that enable citizens to exercise their rights of free expression by circumventing politically motivated censorship. We are providing funds to groups around the world to make sure that those tools get to the people who need them in local languages, and with the training they need to access the Internet safely. The U.S. has been assisting in these efforts for some time, with a focus on implementing these programs as efficiently and effectively as possible. Both the American people and nations that censor the Internet should understand that our government is committed to helping promote Internet freedom."

Clinton's speech, which was representative of the Obama administration's larger goal of spreading democracy, provided the world's autocracies with indisputable evidence that the U.S. was attempting to undermine their systems of government. Not surprisingly, in the wake of the speech, China's Communist Party immediately began to complain of interference in its domestic affairs and greatly increased its spending on cyber based internet policing. (A year later Russian President Vladimir Putin [2000–08, 2012–present] accused Clinton of inciting unrest during the 2011 Russian elections.) When the social media fueled revolutions of Arab Spring began to spread across Northern Africa a few months after Clinton's speech, many observers in both democratic and autocratic nations took it as a sign that the programs Clinton had described were working. While scholars will long debate the actual impact of the U.S. freedom of information operations on the Arab Spring, what is clear is that the speech and the programs it described provided a wakeup call to China and Russia and were instrumental in how Russia chose to adopt and adapt cyber technology over the next few years.

Screen grab of the logo of the U.S. Cyber Command.(ALEX MILANTRACY/ZUMA PRESS/NEWSCOM)

Taken as a whole, the various uses to which the U.S. put its cyber capabilities were not revolutionary. While they extended and broadened Washington's role as *primus inter pares* in international politics, the U.S.' economic and military strength would almost certainly have accomplished something similar even in the absence of cyber tools. What they did do very well, however, was to provide a new means for countries to connect with each other and demonstrate to Russia and China that cyberspace could be used for geopolitical purposes. Both countries quickly followed the U.S. example but in innovative and revolutionary ways the U.S. had not anticipated.

Russia

Russia began the cyber age at a significant disadvantage. In the wake of the Cold War, Russia had a gross national product that was about the size of the U.S. defense budget. To make up for its lack of resources, in the late 1990s Moscow began to experiment with new ways to use cyberspace. Its first major adaptation was to develop a global network of criminal connections that it could use for economic purposes and as a tool of espionage. These irregular forces both improved Russia's economy, on the margins, and extended the reach of its intelligence agencies. Moscow's second adaptation involved uses of cyber technology against small local rivals: first to paralyze Estonian critical infrastructure during a diplomatic clash in 2007, and later to assist in the invasion of Georgia in 2008. Neither of these innovative uses of cyber technology appears to have done much to change Russia's influence among major powers.

In 2011, however, following Clinton's Internet freedom speech, the Arab Spring and Putin's accusations of U.S. meddling in its election, Russian cyber policy underwent a major change. Before the election, Russian leaders do not appear to have taken cyber information operations very seriously either at home or abroad. During the 2011 election, for instance, Putin appears to have relied chiefly on civilian supporters and criminal groups to disrupt attempts by protesters to organize. After the election, however, Russia's thinking about information underwent sweeping changes, as Putin became convinced that the U.S. had mobilized cyber technology to back protesters. In 2014, Russia's military doctrine was rewritten to include sections addressing information warfare that were absent

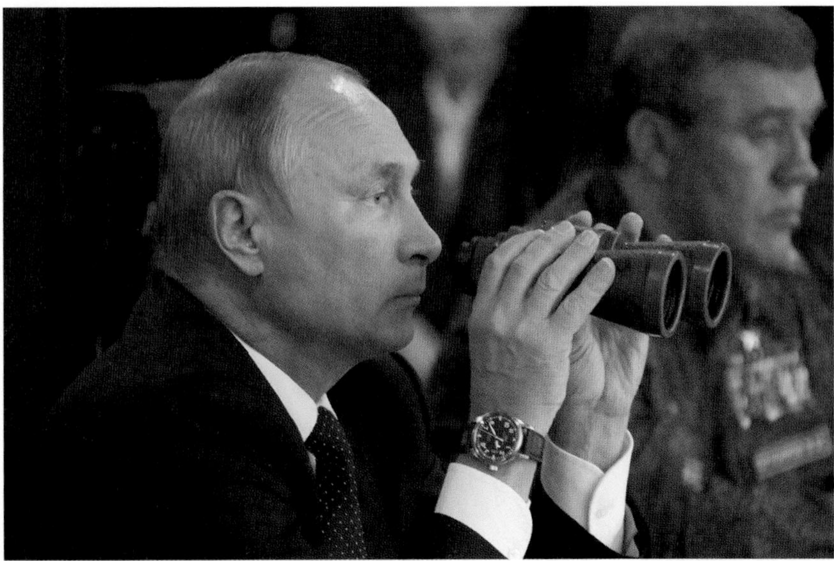

Russia's President Vladimir Putin (L) and Russia's First Deputy Defense Minister, Chief of the General Staff of the Russian Armed Forces Valery Gerasimov, attend the main stage of joint Russian and Belarusian military exercises, near Leningrad, September 18, 2017. (MIKHAIL METZEL/TASS/GETTY IMAGES)

from its 2010 military doctrine. While the 2010 doctrine discusses protecting information channels from hacking, the 2014 doctrine describes ways to use information to weaken states by exploiting popular protests and decreasing civilian patriotism and support for the state. Much of the thinking behind this change was expounded in a 2013 article written by Chief of the General Staff of the Russian Armed Forces Valery Gerasimov. In what came to be known as the "Gerasimov Doctrine," the article argues, among other points, that Moscow should adopt and adapt U.S. cyber methods to Russian purposes.

Between 2011 and 2018, Russia experimented with, and ultimately perfected the use of, cyber information operations to influence pro-Western nations. The program began in 2013 with a project led by Kremlin aide Vyacheslav Volodin aimed at the "systematic manipulation of public opinion through social media." Volodin established the Internet Research Agency (IRA), an organization tasked with spreading pro-Kremlin posts on social media and news sites in Russia and abroad. The IRA utilized a number of methods, but the main one involved employing individuals to write and repost stories to social media with the goal of fomenting dissention and undermining the legitimacy of established political institutions. The posters, often referred to as trolls, experimented with a wide variety of methods to achieve their goals.

In 2014, the IRA had some 250 employees. Although the organization's origins are shadowy, its first main foreign target appears to have been the Ukraine and its goal to increase turmoil during Russian operations there. Over time they expanded their operations to Europe and North America. In 2016, U.S. special counsel Robert S. Mueller indicted a group of Russians for interfering in that year's presidential election. The indictment accused the Russians of creating fake Facebook accounts with the goal of manipulating the election. Perhaps most interesting, it accused them of planning and promoting political rallies for Presidential candidates Donald Trump and Hillary Clinton.

Russia's cyber experiments have become increasingly bold and effective. In Europe, Russian operations seem to have played a significant role in increasing anti-U.S., anti-EU and anti-NATO sentiment, as well as support for nationalist movements including: the Basque Nationalist party in northern Spain, the Five Star Movement in Italy, the Vote Leave campaign in the UK, the National Front party in France and the Alternative for Germany party.

Beyond social-psychological manipulation, Russia also uses its cyber capabilities against physical infrastructure. In March 2018, as part of a package of sanctions against Russia, the Department of Homeland Security (DHS) issued an alert warning that Russia was placing malware on U.S. critical infrastructure. The alert shed light on November 2014 testimony by Admiral Michael Rogers, then the commander of U.S. Cyber Command (2014–18), before the House Intelligence Committee: Admiral Rogers stated that China and "probably one or two others" had the ability to flip the switch on the U.S. power grid and other critical infrastructure. The DHS alert also clarified reports from private industry going back to 2012 that implied that most electrical infrastructure around the world was infested with malware, much of it originating in Russia.

The problem of critical infrastructure attack is not well understood by the general public but is taken extremely seriously by the U.S. Department of Defense. Based on their assessment of the severity of the threat, the U.S. Defense Science Board proposed that the U.S. should consider nuclear retaliation as a possible instrument of recourse against this type of cyberattack.

Placing malware on its adversaries' critical infrastructure has the potential to significantly increase Russia's power projection capability and to provide it with diplomatic bargaining capital. Inasmuch as such attacks could be calibrated to affect different levels of damage, they are an inexpensive substitute for long-range conventional arms like aircraft carriers and bombers, which only the U.S. can currently deploy in large numbers. The threat of a Russian cyberattack undermines U.S. deterrence, particularly U.S. extended deterrence commitments to allies. In 2017 testimony to the Senate, former Director of National Intelligence James Clapper (2010–17) explained why the administration of President Barack Obama (2009–17) did not retaliate against Russian cyberattacks in 2016:

"...[W]e'll never be in a position to launch a counter attack...and we're always going to doubt our ability to withstand counter retaliation."

Where Russia appears to have successfully adopted methods to protect itself against cyberattacks, the West has proved highly vulnerable: It has fallen victim to Russian cyber psychological operations, and James Clapper's testimony suggests that it is at risk of critical infrastructure penetration. By adapting and adopting U.S. cyber methods, Russia has done disproportionate political damage. Nonetheless, with a gross domestic product (GDP) one fifteenth the size of the U.S.', it is unlikely that there is anything Russia could do to fundamentally improve its geopolitical fortunes or to catapult it to regional hegemonic status in Europe. While it could be argued that Russia is gaining proportionately from its strategic use of cyberspace, there is little chance that it will be able to use its cyber capability to achieve anything remotely resembling the geopolitical pivots described by Mahan and Mackinder.

China

China appears to have realized the importance of cyberspace in geopolitics as early as 2004. If General Gerasimov is the face of the Russian information doctrine, Major General Li Bingyan is a sort of standard-bearer for China. Writing in 2004, in the context of clear U.S. hostility to the autocratic excesses of China's Communist Party (CCP), rapid U.S. economic expansion, and a string of U.S. military successes in Central Asia and the Middle East, Li argued that China must use information and cyber capabilities to push back against U.S. primacy.

Applying a parable attributed to Chinese leader Mao Zedong (1949–76) about the best way to get a cat to eat a hot pepper, Li argued that China needed to adopt a cyber policy based on deception and reflexive control. As the parable tells it, the best way to get the cat to eat the pepper is not through violent force; rather, one should grind the pepper into powder and place it on the cat's fur. Since a cat cannot help but lick its fur, its instincts will lead it to consume the pepper of its own accord. As it applies to cyber conflict, the notion is that China cannot overcome U.S. technology directly, but can come to dominate the information arena by taking advantage of U.S. laws, instincts and customs, particularly the commitment to freedom of information.

To implement this approach, China began by adopting the cyber espionage tools pioneered by the U.S. and adapting them to its own needs and capabilities. Since the mid-1990s, the U.S. had gained a reputation for using the Internet to bypass geographical boundaries and take information from its adversaries' most protected institutions. In the mid-2000s, China began to replicate these methods. What it lacked in technical know-how, it attempted to make up for in sheer mass and audacity. In 2013, the U.S.-based telecom company Verizon reported that 96% of all state-affiliated cyber espionage attempts against intellectual property (IP) originated in China. In 2014, Federal Bureau of Investigation Director James Comey noted that "There are two kinds of big companies in the U.S. There are those who've been hacked by the Chinese and those who don't know they've been hacked by the Chinese." As Admiral Rogers' earlier quote suggests, China also appears to have used the access it developed to infiltrate its adversaries' critical infrastructure.

China adopted the tools of cyber espionage pioneered by the U.S., but it adapted them in one radical way: Where the U.S. had used cyber tools mainly for traditional state-centered espionage, China aimed mainly at commercial targets. Before 2004, China's economic growth had come to depend heavily on commercial espionage and IP theft. By taking advantage of cyber efficiencies, China was able to download millions of times more data than it had previously transmitted via paper and microfilm. In fact, in the mid-2000s, the intake became too much for China's existing espionage institutions to digest. To solve this problem, the CCP developed a series of national plans to manage the influx of digital IP and get it to commercial firms that

A wanted poster for five Chinese hackers charged with economic espionage and trade secret theft, released by the Justice Department in Washington, DC, May 19, 2014. The men are accused of being part of a Chinese military unit that has hacked the computers of prominent American companies to steal commercial secrets. (JUSTICE DEPARTMENT/THE NEW YORK TIMES/ REDUX PICTURES)

could convert it to market shares. This involved changing laws, developing bureaucracies and otherwise redesigning parts of China's commercial and civil society.

According to the methods laid out by General Li, however, the focus on commercial IP was only part of the new logic of cyber conflict. Cyber methods depended on a cooperative victim. If IP developing companies fought back, they could severely reduce China's access to their institutions. To reduce the chances of this occurring Li suggested that China should employ "thought control." In practical terms, this means using a combination of modern public relations techniques married with more traditional methods of infiltrating potentially hostile organizations and using economic and sometimes physical intimidation against potentially hostile individuals or organizations. Together, these information steering methods are often referred to both in China and abroad as "Magic Weapons." *The Economist* and *New York Times* have regularly written about these methods, generally with little result. China spends billions on these sorts of information operations every year. More worrying, though, are the more insidious forms of political-psychological operations it conducts abroad.

One of the cleverest methods China employs along these lines involves Hollywood. In the 1990s, political scientists argued that U.S. films were one of the strongest methods of broadcasting U.S. values abroad. Ironically, in the current era, it has become a truism in Hollywood that U.S. films and TV shows cannot make a profit unless they are shown in China. Because CCP censors screen Western media, in effect the CCP has the final say about content involving China in most movies and TV shows that come out of Hollywood. This does not only effect Chinese audiences. Because it is usually prohibitively expensive to film two versions of movies and televisions shows, scripts that are likely to be censored by the CCP are simply rejected. Moreover, because China has cultivated a reputation for doing business with trusted studios, companies often shy away from producing films even for non-Chinese audiences that might hurt their relationship with Chinese censors. The overall effect is that much of what U.S. studios produce is designed to "direct though" in the ways that further China's geopolitical goals.

China's Hollywood connection is only one of many ways the CCP works to reduce Western anxiety about China's policies. Recent studies have shown sophisticated programs to influence Western academia, business and politics. These methods involve holding out promises and threats that demonstrate little tolerance for Western academics or businesses that deviate from the CCP agenda. One particular anecdote is illustrative: Thwarting Chinese cyber espionage became a central goal of the Obama administration beginning in 2009. In 2015, after years of fruitless diplomatic efforts, President Obama invited Chinese President Xi Jinping (2013–present) to a summit in Washington, DC, to discuss Chinese cyber industrial espionage. In the run-up to the meeting, U.S. technology leaders (who had recently snubbed invitations to meet personally with Obama) accepted a public invitation to meet with President Xi. This unequivocal show of support for the Chinese leader undermined President Obama's bargaining leverage. The summit ended in little more than a symbolic promise by Xi to stop cyber commercial espionage. U.S. business leaders, fearful of losing profits in the short term, had enabled Xi's massive commercial espionage program to continue.

Xi Jinping, China's president (L) shakes hands with U.S. President Barack Obama as they depart following a joint news conference in the Rose Garden at the White House in Washington, DC, on September 25, 2015. The U.S. and China announced agreement on broad anti-hacking principles aimed at stopping the theft of corporate trade secrets though Obama pointedly said he has not ruled out invoking sanctions for violators. (PETE MAROVICH/ BLOOMBERG/GETTY IMAGES)

Three years after the Obama-Xi summit, the U.S. tried another tactic to reduce Chinese commercial espionage. In 2017, President Donald Trump's administration (2017–present) began to publicly describe the ways that China was using its cyber capabilities as part of a multipronged effort to improve its economy through commercial espionage. In June 2018, the White House Office of Trade and Manufacturing Policy laid out the administration's perspective in a report entitled *How China's Economic Aggression Threatens the Technologies and Intellectual Property of the U.S. and the World*. The report described an aggressive Chinese campaign with the potential to significantly damage the U.S. economy. Where previous diplomatic disputes with China had often been handled with distinct subtlety, the June report left no doubt as to the high geopolitical stakes involved.

In July 2017, citing unfair trade practices and emphasizing IP theft and illegal technology transfers, the U.S. imposed 25% tariffs on $34 billion-worth of Chinese imports, setting off a tit-for-tat escalation that eventually resulted in what could be described, in absolute terms at least, as the largest trade war in history between the two countries.

As the situation exists today, it is unlikely that U.S. actions will force China to halt its cyber espionage program. The problem is that the CCP is not likely to back down unless the total cost of U.S. tariffs is both economically and politically greater than the sizeable benefits it receives from its cyber espionage program: To a large extent, the CCP's domestic legitimacy is dependent on its record of economic growth; it believes that a sharp decline in this area would be a recipe for civil unrest. Concurrently, the U.S. economy would be likely to take a significant hit if it were to increase tariffs and sanctions to the level required to force Chinese cyber retreat. It is not clear that the American people would be willing to accept such a blow in pursuit of the relatively abstract goal of preventing a geopolitical pivot. Thus, there is a good chance that China will continue to pursue its current course.

With this in mind, it remains difficult to predict whether China's cyber economic espionage campaign will result in a geopolitical pivot. Calculating precisely how much China's economy gains from hacking commercial IP would be no easier than computing how much 18th century Britain's economy gained from its naval dominance, or 20th century Russia and later the Soviet Union gained from railroad technology. Official estimates do, however, provide some clues. In 2015, the Office of the Director of National Intelligence concluded that economic espionage by hacking cost the U.S. economy $400 billion per year. In 2017, the U.S. IP Commission calculated that the "annual cost to the U.S. economy continues to exceed $225 billion in counterfeit goods, pirated software, and theft of trade secrets and could be as high as $600 billion." In 2012, Director of the National Security Agency General Keith Alexander (2005–14) termed cyber commercial espionage "the largest transfer of wealth in history." These figures fail to consider IP taken from non-U.S. sources, which would increase these numbers considerably. In conjunction with China's astonishingly high and sustained economic growth, it is probably safe to assume that cyber commercial espionage has done as much to change the balance of wealth between major powers as did the advent of maritime or rail technology in earlier eras. It is probably also safe to assume that unless the West finds a way to curtail this use of cyber technology, China's economy will continue to grow faster than the economies it is exploiting.

Unlike Russia, China has a GDP comparable to that of the U.S. Given current trends, China's economic power will become much larger than that of the U.S. in coming decades. Accompanied by its domestic political shift toward autocracy and its increasingly assertive military posture, it is probable that China's economic growth foreshadows a geopolitical pivot. To the extent that this growth depends on cyber commercial espionage, it constitutes a cyber geopolitical pivot. Ironically, the cyber infrastructure and methods that paved the way for this shift were developed by the U.S. in the 1990s, and they continue today due to a perverse incentive structure that induces academia, business and politics to reflexively defend a system that is likely to alter the world system in ways these actors will ultimately regret.

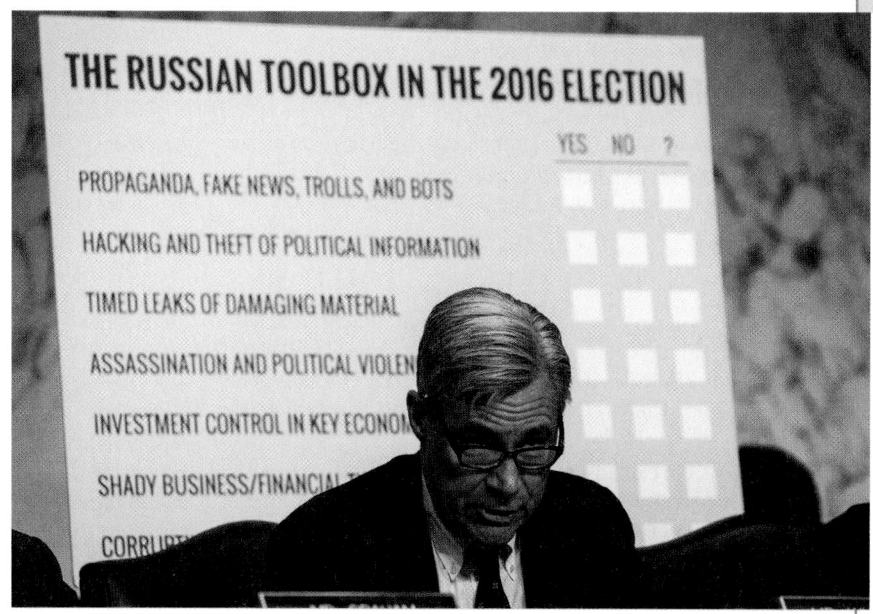

Senator Sheldon Whitehouse questions former Director of National Intelligence James Clapper and former Acting Attorney General Sally Yates during a Senate Judiciary Committee hearing on Russian Interference in the 2016 presidential elections in Washington, DC, on May 8, 2017. (SAMUEL CORUM/ANADOLU AGENCY/GETTY IMAGES)

Conclusions

Yet this version of a geopolitical pivot, based on China's information operations against the West, does not take into account the entire story. China's assertive use of cyberspace is based on a broad set of incentives that rewards states for covertly attacking each other via global computer networks. It originally encouraged the U.S. to spy on its adversaries and eventually to attempt to alter their governments through Internet freedom programs. Currently, it incentivizes Russia to foster nationalism, foment chaos in the West and infiltrate Western critical infrastructure in ways serious enough for U.S. defense leaders to draw parallels with nuclear war. It similarly encourages Chinese programs to embed malware in critical infrastructure and to loot Western companies for their IP.

The first two rounds of the international contest for cyber dominance have already unfolded: In round one, the U.S. government developed the cyber methods that Russia and China went on to adopt and adapt in round two. The game is unlikely to end here. Persistent access to adversaries' networks offers attackers the potential to affect virtually anything attached to a computer. Russia appears to have resolved its vulnerability to cyber psychological penetration, but has built an economic system susceptible to attacks on the computers that control its finances. Currently, China is increasingly using computers to assist in its attempts to control its population. Such a state may be easy pickings for hackers. Despite such potential weaknesses, autocratic states that do not traditionally value freedom of information appear to have an advantage in cyberspace.

It is no more inevitable that cyber technology will lead to a geopolitical pivot on Russian and Chinese terms than that the maritime and rail technologies of past centuries automatically resulted in the world systems described by Mahan and Mackinder. Prophecy is a fraught art. Yet the last two decades suggest that the incentives for low-intensity cyber conflict do exist, and, so far, the guardians of Pax Americana appear to be ceding ground.

discussion questions

1. President Donald Trump announced in 2018 the intent to create a Space Force to protect American interests in space. How will the creation of this military branch affect the U.S. in relation to cyber conflicts? Will it help protect American cybersecurity? Why or why not?

2. In 2011, Russian president Vladimir Putin accused then-Secretary of State Hillary Clinton of sparking conflict during Russian elections that year. How does this relate to the 2016 U.S. presidential election? In what ways has cyber conflict affected elections?

3. How does China and the U.S.'s economic ties affect their relationship with cyber politics? Can the U.S. afford to stop Chinese cyber espionage and face economic consequences?

4. Cyber space is not a tangible object. What are the ways in which geography affects cyber security and conflicts? How are geopolitics and cyber conflict related?

5. Cyber conflict is arguably the newest form of military and global conflict. How do you think the advancement of technology will affect global conflicts?

6. Cyber hacking has implicated both national and civilian security, with both government organizations and companies like Google reporting having been hacked. How will the potentially personal nature of cyber espionage affect individuals? How do individuals and/or companies fit into global cyber conflicts?

suggested readings

Buchanan, Ben. **The Cybersecurity Dilemma: Hacking, Trust and Fear Between Nations**. 282 pp. Oxford, UK: Oxford University Press, 2017. This book shows not only that the security dilemma applies to cyber operations, but also that the particular characteristics of the digital domain mean that the effects are deeply pronounced.

Chertoff, Michael. **Exploding Data: Reclaiming Our Cyber Security in the Digital Age**. 288 pp. New York, NY: Atlantic Monthly Press, 2018. Chertoff explains the complex legalities surrounding issues of data collection and dissemination today, and charts a path that balances the needs of government, business and individuals alike.

Futter, Andrew. **Hacking the Bomb: Cyber Threats and Nuclear Weapons**. 212 pp. Washington. DC: Georgetown University Press, 2018. A comprehensive assessment of this little-understood strategic development, this book explains how myriad new cyber challenges will affect the way that the world thinks about and manages the ultimate weapon.

Kaplan, Fred. **Dark Territory: The Secret History of Cyber War**. 352 pp. New York, NY: Simon & Schuster, 2017. The story of computer scientists and the NSA, Pentagon, and White House policymakers who invent and employ cyber wars—where every country can be a major power player and every hacker a mass destroyer.

Scharre, Paul. **Army of None: Autonomous Weapons and the Future of War**. 448 pp. New York, NY: W.W. Norton & Company, 2018. The author uses military history, global policy and cutting-edge science to argue that we must embrace technology where it can make war more precise and humane, but without surrendering human judgment.

Segal, Adam. **The Hacked World Order: How Nations Fight, Trade, Maneuver, and Manipulate in the Digital Age**. 320 pp. New York, NY: PublicAffairs Publishing, 2015. A description of how the internet has ushered in a new era of geopolitical maneuvering that also reveals the terrifying implications for our economic livelihood, security and personal identity.

Singer. P.W and Brooking, Emerson T. **LikeWar: The Weaponization of Social Media**. 416 pp. Boston, MA: Eamon Dolan/ Houghton Mifflin Harcourt, 2018. Two defense experts explore the collision of war, politics and social media, where the most important battles are now only a click away.

Don't forget: Ballots start on page 103!

To access web links to these readings, as well as links to additional, shorter readings and suggested web sites,

GO TO www.greatdecisions.org

and click on the topic under Resources, on the right-hand side of the page.

The United States and Mexico: partnership tested

by Michael Shifter and Bruno Binetti

A border fence maintained by the Homeland Security department, on private property in Douglas, Ariz., June 9, 2016. For all intents and purposes, the wall Donald Trump proposes is already there. (TODD HEISLER/THE NEW YORK TIMES/REDUX)

Few neighbors have such deep and wide-ranging ties as the United States and Mexico. Both countries are bound not only by geography, but also through economic, security and social connections. They share an almost 2,000-mile-long border, extending from the Gulf of Mexico to the Pacific Ocean, which was forged through conflict and war. More than 1 million people and $1.4 billion in trade cross the binational border every day. About 200,000 people have been killed in Mexico since 2006, when the country declared a "war on drugs," a conflict in which security forces are supported by the U.S. government, while drug cartels grow strong by selling to U.S. consumers and purchasing U.S. weapons. And 36 million people of Mexican origin live in the U.S.: Over 25% of them are American citizens.

Despite these strong connections—or perhaps because of them—the bilateral relationship is subject to strong pressures coming from domestic politics in both countries. Ever since he announced his candidacy for the U.S. presidency in 2015, Donald Trump has used Mexico as a proxy for two of his most central issues: He takes a protectionist stance on trade and a nativist and restrictive position on immigra-

MICHAEL SHIFTER *is president of the Inter-American Dialogue and an adjunct professor of Latin American Studies at Georgetown University. He speaks and writes widely on U.S.-Latin American relations and hemispheric affairs. Shifter is a member of the Council on Foreign Relations and a contributing editor of* Current History.

BRUNO BINETTI *is a non-resident fellow at the Inter-American Dialogue. He is a visiting professor at Torcuato Di Tella University in Buenos Aires, where he teaches U.S. Foreign Policy. He holds an MA from the Elliott School of International Affairs at George Washington University.*

tion—and accuses Mexico of being the problem in both areas. In doing so, Trump feeds negative prejudices and misconceptions regarding Mexico that were already present in parts of American society, and most of which have little basis in reality.

For example, Mr. Trump has pledged to "build a wall" (which he says would be paid for by Mexico) to stop the flow of migrants coming through the southern border. Yet since 2009 net immigration from Mexico has actually been negative, as more Mexicans have left than entered the U.S. Similarly, Trump blames the North American Free Trade Agreement (NAFTA) between Mexico, the U.S. and Canada for job losses and deindustrialization in the U.S. that are better explained by technological changes and the impact of China's growing manufacturing power.

Meanwhile, in July 2018 Mexico held a historic presidential election won by Andrés Manuel López Obrador, the country's first leftist president in generations. López Obrador secured a decisive victory against traditional parties by promising to transform the country and put an end to Mexico's pervasive poverty and inequality, widespread corruption, and rampant, drug-related violence. López Obrador will take office on December 1 and still hasn't met Trump, but they have held friendly phone conversations and have a good initial rapport. Further, after tumultuous and tense negotiations, in October 2018 the outgoing Mexican government reached an agreement to replace NAFTA with a new trade deal called "United States, Mexico, Canada Agreement" (USMCA), which addresses some of Trump's grievances.

At the same time, social and economic connections between the U.S. and Mexico thrive beneath political tensions and changes in diplomatic relations. Hundreds of students living in Mexico cross the border every day to attend U.S. schools. Passengers can check in at San Diego airport in Southern California and cross a binational bridge to board their flights at Tijuana airport, just across the border in Mexico. And because of NAFTA, U.S. and Mexican companies have integrated their production systems by building binational value chains, in which components of industrial goods are made in both countries.

In addition, since the 1990s the levels of cooperation between both governments in matters of trade, anti-drug efforts and even immigration have reached unprecedented levels. Economic interdependency, information-sharing to combat criminal networks, and a common effort to stem immigration from Central America have continued even under President Trump. Despite recent tensions, on fundamental levels the U.S. and Mexico are interrelated like never before.

Newly elected Mexican President Andres Manuel Lopez Obrador, running for "Juntos haremos historia" party, cheers his supporters at the Zocalo Square after winning general elections, in Mexico City, on July 1, 2018. (PEDRO PARDO/AFP/GETTY IMAGES)

Braceros and maquiladoras

Until recent decades, mutual distrust between Mexico and the U.S. hindered cooperation on the critical issues in the bilateral agenda, including immigration. A long history of U.S. disregard for Mexican sovereignty still affects the way Mexicans see their northern neighbor. In 1848, for instance, the U.S. annexed nearly half of what was then Mexico's territory—the current states of California, Nevada, Utah, New Mexico, Arizona, Texas and parts of Colorado—after a quick military victory. Further, the U.S. occupied the port of Veracruz in 1914 during the Mexican Revolution and sent troops into Mexican territory to hunt down revolutionary leader Pancho Villa, who had raided U.S. border towns. In the 1930s Mexico entered the long rule of the Institutional Revolutionary Party (or PRI), which would govern for seven decades with a combination of nationalism and restrictions on political freedoms. Under the PRI, Mexican-U.S. relations became more stable, allowing both nations to hold discussions on immigration, which was already the key issue on the bilateral agenda.

One of earliest and most successful results of bilateral cooperation on immigration was the Bracero Program, which regulated the entry of temporary laborers from Mexico to work on U.S. farms. The program was created during World War II, as the agricultural sector in the U.S. experienced an acute labor shortage. The U.S. government wanted to attract Mexican seasonal workers, but was wary of them staying permanently. Further, anticipating current discourse regarding immigration, U.S. labor unions criticized the allegedly unfair competition arising from Mexican immigrants, who accepted less pay than their American counterparts. The issue was also complex for Mexico. On the one hand, emigration helped to defuse social tensions in the impoverished north and provided valuable remittances for the families of those workers. But on the other, excessive flows to the U.S. might deprive the Mexican economy of the workers it needed to promote agricultural and industrial development.

Trying to come up with a mutually beneficial solution, in 1942 Mexico and the U.S. launched the first version of the Bracero Program. The program granted time-limited permits for Mexican guest workers, including a minimum wage and decent work conditions. Nearly 4.6 million contracts were signed until the program ended in 1964. Despite its relative success, this plan did not stop undocumented immigration of Mexican workers to the U.S., a phenomenon which was fueled by interests in both countries. Mexican workers kept entering the U.S. illegally in order to avoid the bureaucratic delays, eligibility criteria and time restrictions of the Bracero Program, and American farmers preferred paying workers less than what the program demanded. By the 1950s, the growing number of undocumented immigrants from Mexico had become a salient political issue in the U.S. that combined economic interests, rule of law concerns and racial stereotypes.

In the summer of 1954, the Dwight D. Eisenhower administration (1953–61) launched Operation Wetback, a massive immigration enforcement program that in a matter of weeks found, arrested and deported hundreds of thousands of undocumented immigrants of Mexican origin, while even more returned voluntarily, out of fear. This deportation plan was marred by xenophobia and abuses, including police brutality and the expulsion of U.S. citizens. Under an agreement with the Mexican government, those expelled from the U.S. were forcefully sent far from the border, to southern and central Mexico, to prevent them from returning. Many found themselves jobless and did not have the money to return to their families. Despite these many shortcomings, during the 2016 presidential campaign Donald Trump lauded Operation Wetback and promised to use it as a model for his own immigration policies.

Mexican migrant workers, employed under the Bracero Program to harvest crops on Californian farms, are shown picking chili peppers in this 1964 photograph. Bracero stems from the Spanish word for arm, "brazo," and refers to the hard manual labor. (AP PHOTO)

After a government crackdown on illegal immigration, legal immigration under the Bracero Program boomed in the 1950s, reaching its peak in 1956, when 445,000 Mexican workers entered the U.S. to work temporarily. Shortly thereafter, however, anti-immigrant sentiment became even stronger, leading to the end of the Bracero Program in 1964 when Congress refused to extend it. From that moment on, the U.S. has lacked a large and streamlined legal pathway for Mexican temporary workers. Since the U.S. economy still demanded relatively unskilled workers from Mexico, the end of the Bracero Program effectively promoted illegal immigration.

Paradoxically, the interruption of U.S.-Mexico cooperation on immigration opened the way for a deepening of economic interdependence between both countries. To tackle a massive rise in unemployment in the country's north after the Bracero Program came to an end, Mexico launched an industrialization plan for its border areas. Most of the new industries (known as *maquiladoras*) were established with U.S. capital: They imported U.S. components tax-free, assembled the final goods, taking advantage of Mexico's cheaper labor and devalued currency, and then re-exported them back to the U.S. By the 1980s, the maquiladora*s* were the most dynamic sector in the Mexican economy, representing nearly half of the country's exports and its largest source of foreign currency after oil exports. The rapid growth of these industries, however, did not trickle down to the rest of Mexico. Outside of this enclosed, competitive sector, most of the country still suffered from chronic poverty and lack of opportunities.

At the same time, the industrialization of northern Mexico was not enough to curb the flow of undocumented immigrants to the U.S., whose numbers kept rising together with that of authorized migrants. Meanwhile, U.S. residents of Mexican origin (both regulated and undocumented) became more diverse, as the wives and children of male workers joined them in the U.S. While an important number of them continued to work on farms, many others moved to cities to work in industries, services and construction.

In response to growing undocumented immigration, U.S. President Ronald Reagan (1981–89) signed a new bipartisan immigration law in 1986 that increased penalties for U.S. companies that hired illegal immigrants, made this practice a crime, and dedicated more resources for border and immigration enforcement. The law also regularized the status of over 3 million undocumented immigrants who were already in the U.S., most of whom were of Mexican origin. Further, Reagan extended the benefits of regularization to these immigrants' children by executive action, allowing immigrant families to remain together in the U.S.

The 1986 immigration reform did not, however, expand existing temporary worker programs, just when immigration from Mexico skyrocketed as a result of a prolonged and deep economic crisis in Mexico. Between the 1990s and 2000s, nearly 12 million undocumented immigrants moved to the U.S., more than 70% of them from Mexico. As the issue became more salient to the U.S. political agenda, and U.S. politics more polarized and contentious in general, the chances of passing comprehensive reform of the U.S. broken immigration system became more remote.

NAFTA and lack of immigration reform

In the late 1980s and early 1990s a series of factors contributed to an unprecedented deepening of the Mexico-U.S. bilateral relationship. After decades of stable but distant ties, both sides seemed ready to promote stronger cooperation, especially in the economic arena.

On the Mexican side, the profound economic crisis of the 1980s had convinced PRI leaders of the need to abandon nationalistic economic policies and embrace globalization to boost growth. At the same time, the U.S. had emerged victorious from the Cold War and was confident in the power of market forces to lift living standards at home and abroad. It was said that when U.S. President George H.W. Bush (1989–93) reached out to offer American help to alleviate Mexico's crisis, his counterpart Carlos Salinas de Gortari (1988–94) proposed discussions on a broad and ambitious trade deal between both nations.

In 1988 the U.S. and Canada signed a Free Trade Agreement (FTA), and Mexico soon asked to start negotiations with Washington for a similar deal. For the U.S., an FTA with Mexico was a way to boost the competitiveness of its own economy by creating regional value chains, by which components of finished goods could be built in Mexico to take advantage of lower wages there. Further, it allowed American companies to expand their investments in Mexico and benefit from the country's new pro-market initiatives. Washington was also confident that more trade and investment from U.S. companies would promote economic development on the Mexican side of the border, containing rising immigration.

This potential trade agreement with Mexico became a central issue on the 1992 presidential campaign trail, with independent candidate Ross Perot denouncing the deal, and pointing to the "giant sucking sound" of U.S. jobs moving to Mexico. Despite significant opposition to the potential loss of jobs (Perot obtained 19% of the popular vote in the elections, a high mark for an independent), bilateral negotiations moved forward in the last few months under President Bush, who worried that President-elect Bill Clinton might delay the agreement under pressure from labor unions. In December 1992, the U.S., Mexico and Canada signed NAFTA, which came into effect on the first day of 1994, forging the largest trading bloc in the world.

The agreement had immediate effects: U.S.-Mexico trade doubled in just a few years, from nearly $100 billion in 1994 to more than $200 billion in 1998. Thousands of American, Mexican and foreign industries settled in Mexico's northern states in order to build products and components for U.S. consumers and factories: The number of maquiladoras skyrocketed. Further, American retail and financial companies vastly expanded their operations in Mexico, deepening the interconnection between both economies.

President Clinton (1993–2001) combined the "carrot" of NAFTA with the "stick" of stricter immigration policies, more resources for border security, and the erection of the first permanent barriers along some portions of the southern border to prevent Mexican migrants from entering the U.S. illegally. This hardline immigration policy reflected changing political attitudes in Washington: The Republican Party turned its back on the compromises Reagan had reached on immigration, decrying regularization of undocumented immigrants as "amnesty."

Another display of the increasingly cooperative relations between both nations came shortly after the signing of NAFTA. In 1995, Mexico was on the verge of an economic meltdown as the peso crashed and the country found it hard to repay its ballooning foreign debt. Worried about a ripple effect if Mexico defaulted, and a potential upsurge in immigration toward the U.S. if the Mexican economy collapsed, the Clinton administration took immediate action to assist its neighbor. Bypassing a dubious Congress, the U.S. government hastily put together a $50 billion rescue package with the International Monetary Fund (IMF) and the Group of Seven (G7), of which the U.S. Treasury provided $20 billion in short-term loans. Clinton's effective and timely intervention helped stabilize the Mexican economy and reinforced economic interdependence between both countries. In 1997, Mexico repaid the U.S. with interest (and three years ahead of schedule).

Coming into office after being governor of Texas, a border state, President George W. Bush (2001–09) wanted to build on the progress made by his immediate predecessors and set Mexico as a U.S. foreign policy priority early in his administration. For example, he chose to visit Mexico on his first foreign trip as president, ending a tradition of previous presidents to visit Canada first. While hosting Mexican President Vicente Fox (2000–06) (the first non-PRI president since the 1930s) in the White House on September 5, 2001, Bush proclaimed that "the U.S. has no more important relationship in the world than the one we have with Mexico." Shortly before, Mexico's foreign minister, Jorge Castañeda, had announced that the Mexican government

Photo at left: demonstration against NAFTA in Austin, Texas, on November 13, 1993. (ROBERT DAEMMRICH/SYGMA/GETTY IMAGES). *Photo at right: Bill Clinton makes a speech supporting NAFTA to the Washington Chamber of Commerce, November 1, 1993.* (JEFFREY MARKOWITZ/SYGMA/GETTY IMAGES)

was going for "the whole enchilada," meaning a comprehensive immigration agreement that regularized the status of millions of Mexicans living in the U.S. and provided more opportunities for legal immigration for Mexicans who were doing jobs Americans were not willing to take.

That optimism, however, dissipated after terrorist attacks on September 11, as Washington's attention turned to the global war on terrorism and military interventions in Afghanistan and then Iraq. Despite Fox's pro-market and centrist policies, he continued Mexico's long tradition of displaying an autonomous and independent foreign policy, which sometimes put it at odds with the Bush administration. In 2002, for instance, Mexico announced its withdrawal from the Rio Pact, a regional mutual defense agreement created in 1947. The Fox administration believed the treaty had become "obsolete" and outdated as other, non-military security threats had gained prominence. The diplomatic spat between Mexico and the U.S. became more acute in 2003, when Mexico voted against the invasion of Iraq at the United Nations Security Council. The Bush administration had pressured Mexico to vote in favor and expressed its disappointment.

Despite these tensions, President George W. Bush urged his party to support a comprehensive reform of the U.S. immigration system, one that would expand opportunities for temporary workers and provide a path toward regularization for the millions of undocumented immigrants already in the U.S. The administration also proposed the Development, Relief, and Education for Alien Minors (DREAM) Act, a bill that would have granted a residence permit to children who were brought into the U.S. undocumented but who had grown up and gone to school in the U.S. However, because of Washington's increasingly partisan and obstructionist environment, Bush's immigration initiatives failed to pass.

Despite the benefits of integration, NAFTA became a contentious issue in both the U.S. and Mexico. In the U.S., organized labor and environmental groups denounced American companies that were relocating their production to Mexico to take advantage of lower wages and less strict environmental regulations south of the border. All American auto manufacturers, for instance, built factories in Mexico to supply the U.S. market, accentuating the decline of manufacturing jobs in the U.S. These critics pointed to the evolution of the U.S.-Mexico trade balance: in 1993 the U.S. had a $1.7 billion goods surplus, which had turned into a $71 billion goods deficit by 2017.

But NAFTA was also criticized in Mexico. It did not bring its promised benefits to the Mexican economy as a whole, instead perpetuating the highly unequal maquiladora system, which proved advantageous to only a few as trade grew with the U.S., while the vast majority of Mexicans continued to suffer. While trade with the U.S. boomed and the Mexican economy grew, this growth was not enough to make a significant improvement in the country's extremely high poverty and inequality rates, especially in the impoverished southern areas of the country. In addition, NAFTA closely linked Mexico's economic performance with that of the U.S., deepening the country's dependence on its powerful northern neighbor.

At least part of the criticism against NAFTA on both sides of the border was due to misunderstandings about the goals of the agreement. Eager to convince their respective populations of the benefits of the deal, the U.S. and Mexican governments oversold its implications and raised unrealistic expectations. In an increasingly globalized world, NAFTA was merely an instrument to boost trade integration between the U.S. and Mexico (which it did), not a magical recipe for development, and especially not a solution for the issue of illegal immigration.

Further, NAFTA was signed just as

China was becoming a manufacturing powerhouse that competed against both American and Mexican industries. This became more salient in 2001, when China entered the World Trade Organization (WTO). The influx of relatively cheap Chinese industrial goods dislocated U.S.-Mexico trade and accelerated the decrease in U.S. manufacturing jobs.

Political blockage under Obama

After a decade of close economic interrelation between both economies, the 2008 crisis in the U.S. had major repercussions in Mexico. For instance, in 2009 U.S. gross domestic product (GDP) fell by 2.5%, but Mexico's dropped by 6.6%, illustrating the adage "when the U.S. sneezes, Mexico catches a cold." In Mexico, critics of NAFTA pointed out that higher dependency on the U.S. economy had tied Mexico to the economic cycle of its northern neighbor and failed to generate the wealth and high-quality jobs that had been promised.

In addition to economic output, one of the most significant impacts of the crisis was a change in immigration patterns: Given the lack of employment opportunities in the U.S., the number of Mexicans who wanted to move north fell sharply. In fact, since 2009 more people of Mexican origin have left than entered the U.S. The number of arrests of people trying to enter the U.S. illegally on the southern border—another measure of immigration flows—also declined after the financial crisis.

From early on in his presidency (2009–17), Barack Obama wanted to pass a comprehensive immigration reform package that would provide a path to regularization for the millions of undocumented immigrants in the U.S., and their children. Critics chastised Obama for not pushing for an overhaul of the U.S. immigration system while his party had a majority in both houses of Congress, but the issue was politically explosive and took a back seat to more pressing issues, including healthcare reform and steering the U.S. economy out of a potential depression.

After the Democrats lost control of the House in 2010, Obama sought to reach a deal with congressional Republicans, who were staunchly against anything that would resemble "amnesty for illegal immigrants." To secure the favor of Republican moderates, Obama ordered a strict implementation of U.S. immigration rules, which led to a rise in deportations. In 2010 and 2011, arrests by U.S. Immigration and Customs Enforcement (ICE) reached a peak of more than 300,000 annually.

Despite this hardline stance on undocumented immigration, Obama failed to gain support in Congress for immigration reform. Meanwhile, immigrant rights groups labelled Obama "the deporter in chief," criticizing him for a strict policy of deportations that separated families across the border. At the same time, millions of young people of Mexican origin who had moved to the U.S. as children faced the risk of being deported, despite barely knowing Mexico and identifying as Americans in all but documentation. To tackle this challenge and bypass congressional obstruction, in 2012 Obama implemented some of the provisions included in the failed Bush-era DREAM Act by an executive order known as Deferred Action for Childhood Arrivals (DACA), which provided protection for more than 5 million people. Despite not providing a pathway to citizenship, DACA was strongly opposed by anti-immigration groups within the Republican Party, and was challenged repeatedly in U.S. courts, weakening its effects.

Under Obama, the political debate in the U.S. regarding immigration became even more virulent, as Republicans accused the president of rewarding undocumented immigration through DACA and other measures that favored the reunification of families. In 2010, the Republican-controlled Arizona legislature passed SB 1070, a measure that authorized local law enforcement agents to determine the immigration status of an

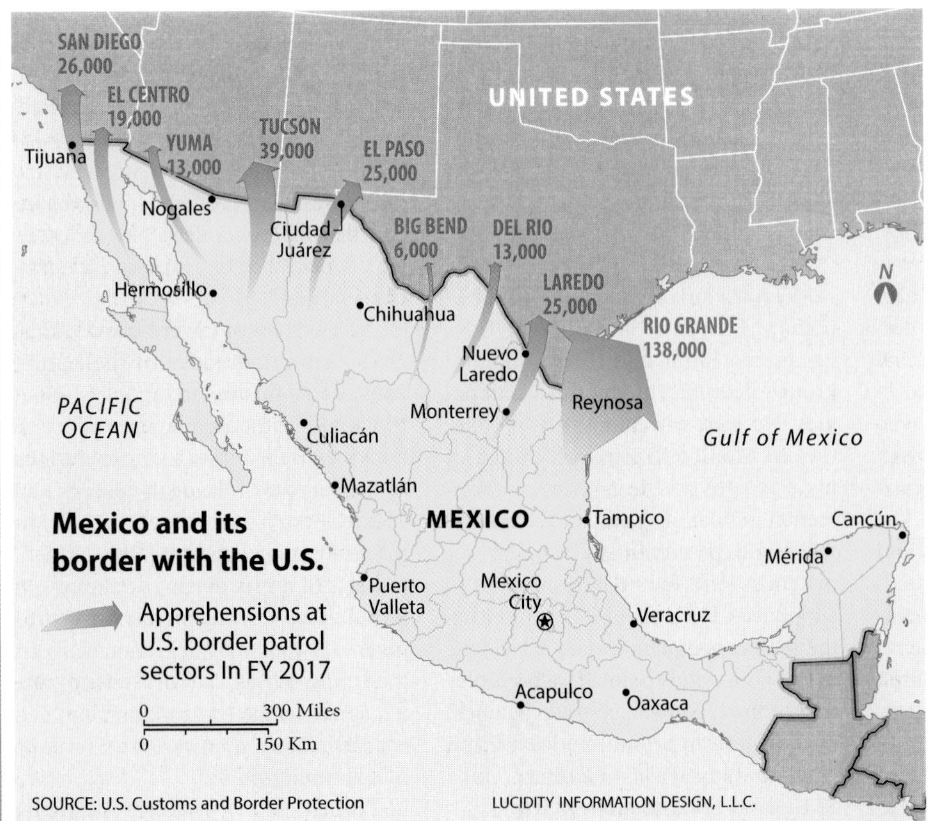

Mexico and its border with the U.S.

individual based on "reasonable suspicion" of them being an "illegal alien." Immigrant rights groups denounced this as an attempt to legalize racial profiling and to terrorize immigrants, and the Obama administration sued to have the act repealed as unconstitutional. The U.S. Supreme Court struck down some of its most contentious provisions in 2012, but by then many U.S. states had enacted hardline measures against undocumented immigrants inspired by the Arizona model. Mexico expressed its concern over these restrictive policies and offered legal counseling from its network of consulates in U.S. border towns and cities.

The U.S.-Mexico relationship was soon tested by a new immigration crisis, this time coming from Central America. Starting in the early 2000s, a growing number of people from Central America's Northern Triangle (Guatemala, Honduras and El Salvador) crossed Mexico's southern border and traversed the country on their way to the U.S., which they hoped to enter illegally. Many of the tens of thousands that took this perilous trail reached the U.S.-Mexico border in a railway known as "The Beast" (an old and slow train that connects Mexico's south and north) or in groups of migrants known as caravans. Most were victims of organized crime groups and human traffickers along the way. In 2014, growing immigration from Central America turned into a major crisis as thousands of unaccompanied minors began reaching the U.S. through its southern border. Some were sent by their families, knowing that U.S. laws do not allow for minors to be deported alone. Others were trying to join their parents, who were already in the U.S. The images of children detained in cage-like government facilities shocked many in the U.S. and posed a serious political challenge for the Obama administration.

In response to this crisis, the U.S. government adopted a two-pronged strategy. The first part was a long-term program to tackle the structural causes that led Central Americans to migrate in the first place. The main instrument of this effort was the Alliance for Prosperity, a development assistance package under which the U.S. would invest $2.6 billion in the Northern Triangle countries between 2015 and 2018. The rationale behind the Alliance, led by then-Vice President Joe Biden, was that punitive measures alone would be ineffective to stop illegal immigration from Central America if the root causes of the problem (poverty, lack of opportunities, drug-related violence) were not addressed, and if government structures in Honduras, El Salvador and Guatemala were not made more accountable and transparent.

Mexico had a central role in the second part of the U.S. strategy to curb immigration from Central America. Starting in 2014, the U.S. offered technical and financial assistance to strengthen Mexico's immigration enforcement efforts on its southern border. Mexican security forces set up more checkpoints and devoted more agents to its crackdown on immigration from Central America, under its U.S.-backed Southern Border Plan. Hundreds of thousands were deported to Guatemala. While this initiative reduced the number of Central Americans reaching the U.S., Mexican security forces have been accused of using excessive force and of committing human rights violations against immigrants. Human rights activists accused the government of Mexican President Enrique Peña Nieto (2012–18) of "doing the U.S.' dirty work" by ruthlessly stopping central American immigrants on its southern border.

A binational war on drugs

In addition to immigration and trade, security cooperation is the final core issue of the U.S.-Mexico relationship. As in other topics, in recent times Mexico and the U.S. have pragmatically come together to deal with a common problem, that of organized criminal groups that challenge the Mexican government and pour drugs onto the U.S. market. For decades, Mexico-based drug organizations have had a symbiotic relationship with the U.S.: First, because the growing consumption of drugs by U.S. citizens fuels demand for the cocaine and heroin that come through Mexico and, second, because Mexican cartels fight the Mexican state largely with guns smuggled (or legally purchased) in the U.S.

A Mexican soldier guards the site where Mexican authorities destroyed confiscated drugs on April 29, 1997 in Matamoros at the border with the U.S. Some 9,871 kilos (21,716 pounds) of cocaine and 3,897 kilos (8,573 pounds) of marijuana were burned. (OMAR TORRES/AFP/GETTY IMAGES)

The importance of anti-drug efforts for the bilateral relationship increased in the 1970s, when President Richard Nixon (1969–74) launched his "war on drugs" as a response to rising consumption in the U.S. In addition to cracking down on drug consumers and sellers within the U.S. through punitive policies and high mandatory minimums, under this "war" the U.S. drastically increased collaboration with the countries from where the drugs came, including Mexico. In the 70s, Mexican criminal organizations controlled the production and smuggling of marijuana for the U.S. market. In 1973, Nixon created the Drug Enforcement Administration (DEA), which would become a key instrument of U.S. support for anti-drug efforts in Latin America. Despite some change in the rhetoric surrounding U.S. anti-drug policy, all of Nixon's successors (both Republican and Democrat) continued his punitive approach.

By the 1980s, Mexican drug traffickers were partnering with Colombian cartels to smuggle Colombian cocaine into the U.S., taking advantage of the networks, contacts and infrastructure on

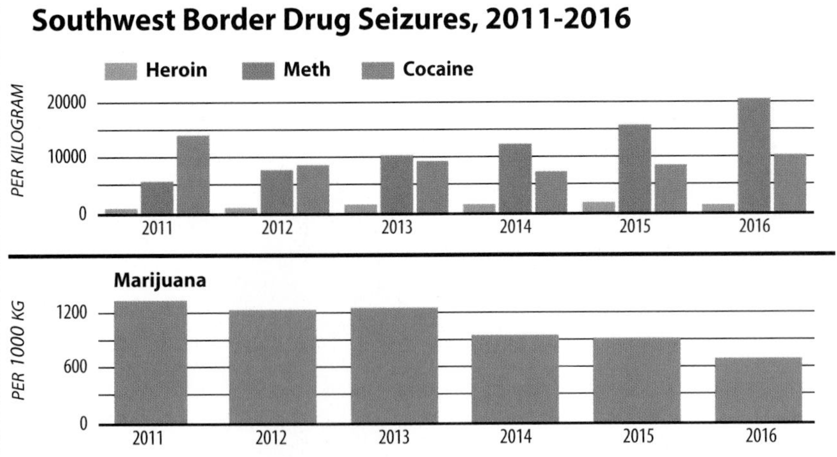

SOURCE: U.S. Department of Homeland Security LUCIDITY INFORMATION DESIGN, L.L.C.

both sides of the border that Mexican criminals had developed for decades to traffic marijuana. This symbiotic relationship between Colombian cartels (which produced the cocaine) and Mexican criminal groups (which smuggled it into the U.S.) became very profitable for both sides. As U.S. anti-drug efforts intensified at home and abroad, trafficking the cocaine into the U.S. became riskier, and therefore even more profitable for Mexican smugglers.

In 1985, the rising power of Mexican drug cartels led to a major diplomatic crisis with the U.S., when henchmen of a Mexican drug lord kidnapped DEA agent Enrique "Kiki" Camarena, who was working undercover against drug-trafficking networks in the Mexican city of Guadalajara. The Reagan administration demanded that the Mexican government find Camarena and nearly shut down the border to exert maximum pressure. One month later, the body of Camarena was found: He had been tortured and murdered. His assassination marked a new phase in U.S. involvement in Mexico's fight against drug cartels: With more assistance and pressure from Washington, Mexico's security forces chased down and dismembered the Guadalajara Cartel, which was behind the death of the DEA agent. But other groups, with even more violent tactics, arose in its wake.

During the 1990s Mexico gained increased importance for the U.S. in its battle against drug trafficking. First, because the Medellín and Cali cartels—the two largest drug organizations in Colombia—were defeated after a long fight with the Colombian state, which had the firm support of the U.S., expressed in financial assistance, military and security technology, and the deployment of more DEA agents. From that moment on, Mexican drug-trafficking organizations took on a larger, more significant role in the cocaine trade, as they became the most powerful side in new partnerships with smaller Colombian producers (including the Revolutionary Armed Forces of Colombia guerrillas, FARC, who fought the Colombian government from 1964 to 2017).

Secondly, Mexican criminal groups became wealthier and more powerful because they established a near monopoly over the smuggling of a highly addictive drug that was surging in the U.S. market: heroin. Unlike cocaine, for which Mexican groups depended on Colombian producers, heroin is made out of poppy, and can be produced in Mexico. The greater role in cocaine trafficking, and the dramatic rise in U.S. consumption of heroin, transformed Mexico's loose networks of drug traffickers into mighty cartels that would grow strong enough to challenge the Mexican state over the control of territories throughout the country. With their expanded resources, Mexican "capos" (as cartel leaders are known) strengthened their influence over Mexico's underfunded security forces and corruption-prone government agencies, on the national and local levels.

In 2006, recently elected Mexican President Felipe Calderón (2006–12) launched an outright offensive against drug cartels, which by then were seen as posing an existential threat to the viability of the Mexican state. In some areas of the country, including border cities such as Ciudad Juárez and Tijuana, criminal organizations operated almost unchecked, unleashing violence against rival groups, independent journalists, civil society activists and public officials who dared to challenge criminal interests. Since most police forces in Mexico were corrupt and had been penetrated by organized crime, Calderón deployed the country's armed forces to lead this new war on drugs.

The U.S. government expressed its immediate and full support for Calderon's offensive. In 2007–08, the Bush administration presented, and the U.S. Congress approved, the Mérida Initiative, a $1.6 billion assistance package to strengthen Mexico's security forces and provide them with the training and equipment they needed to fight the drug cartels. Under this new plan, anti-drug cooperation between the U.S. and Mexico reached unprecedented levels. Both countries shared intelligence on major drug smuggling groups, U.S. drones surveilled the binational border area, and U.S. security agencies set up bases on Mexican soil. Another aspect of the Mérida Initiative, focused on strengthening Mexico's judicial system and other institutions, received less attention from both governments.

The deployment of Mexico's armed forces together with U.S. support and intelligence led to the capture or death of some of the most prominent drug kingpins in the country. Local citizen security initiatives based on prevention and building trust between citizens and security forces contributed to a sharp decrease in murder rates in Ciudad Juárez (formerly known as Mexico's murder capital) and other areas. However, this progress was short-lived. As the Mexican army and navy eliminated capos, the major drug cartels fragmented into smaller and more violent groups, which competed among themselves for declining cartels' territory and drug-smuggling routes into the U.S. For every head of a cartel that Mexico was able to kill or capture, many more appeared.

The arrival of Barack Obama to the presidency brought a renewed emphasis on "shared responsibility" between the U.S. and Mexico on the drug issue, especially by then-Secretary of State Hillary Clinton (2009–13). After all, it was American demand for drugs that was fueling violence in Mexico. Further, because of U.S. lax gun regulations, most of the cartels were able to purchase weapons in the U.S. and smuggle them into Mexico to support their fight against security forces. In emphasizing the need to acknowledge the role of the U.S., and strengthening health-oriented strategies to reduce drug demand, however, Obama was building on what had begun under the Clinton and George W. Bush administrations.

At the same time, despite some broad (and largely failed) efforts to pass criminal justice reform in the U.S. Congress, Obama maintained the essence of Bush's anti-drug policies, including the Mérida Initiative. Meanwhile, violence in Mexico skyrocketed, despite the attempts of President Enrique Peña Nieto, who took office in 2012 promising to put an end to Calderón's war on drug-trafficking. As Mexico was incapable of reforming its underfunded and corrupt security forces, and as smaller drug organizations unleashed unprecedented violence on Mexican communities, the government was forced to continue the use of the armed forces for internal security. The military, however, created more problems, as accusations of massive human rights violations began to emerge throughout Mexico. Since 2006, there have been countless reports of kidnappings, disappearances and acts of torture committed by Mexico's armed and security forces in the name of the war on drugs.

The most tragic indication of this human rights crisis came in September 2014, when 43 students disappeared in the state of Guerrero. Federal security forces and municipal officials were believed to be behind the murder of the missing students, as indicated by independent investigations. The Mexican government was accused of covering up the incident. The Obama administration expressed its frustration with such abuses, and held up millions in Mérida assistance, citing a violation of the program's human rights clauses. These funds, however, represented a small portion of the millions of dollars the U.S. spent in anti-drug efforts in Mexico: Washington had little alternative but to continue working with the Mexican authorities and security forces, despite their many shortcomings.

Relatives and friends of 43 students of the Raul Isidro Burgos rural school who disappeared on September 26, 2014, in the city of Iguala, demonstrate to demand justice in front of the Basilica of Our Lady of Guadalupe in Mexico City on December 26, 2016. The students, from a rural teachers college in the southern state of Guerrero, disappeared after they were attacked by local police in Iguala. (ALFREDO ESTRELLA/AFP/GETTY IMAGES)

The results of the U.S.-backed war on drugs in Mexico are abysmal. As of 2017, the fight against drug cartels has left 200,000 dead and 30,000 missing. That year, 29,000 people were murdered, a historic record. In fact, five of the ten most dangerous cities in the world are in Mexico. Meanwhile, the Mérida Initiative has been completely ineffective in curbing drug consumption in the U.S.: Heroin production tripled between 2013 and 2016, and deaths by heroin overdose in the U.S. surged by 328% between 2010 and 2015, according to the DEA.

A new political era? Trump and López Obrador

Despite significant problems, the bilateral relationship was expected to continue its path toward deeper cooperation and pragmatism after Obama left office. After a long history of distrust, Mexico and the U.S. seemed to have reached a new level of collaboration and mutual understanding, and a clear commitment from both sides to work together in solving common problems. These hopes, however, were completely upended by the political emergence of Donald Trump, who made attacking the bilateral relationship one of the key features of his successful run for the presidency in 2016. Mexico had a central role in two of Trump's most important campaign issues: a protectionist stance on trade and a restrictive view on immigration.

First, Trump blamed Mexico for the decay of the U.S. manufacturing sector, which was in fact well underway before the signing of the agreement, and probably more related to competition from China and other Asian countries, in addition to technological change. Nonetheless, and returning to some of the arguments Ross Perot used in the

U.S. President Donald Trump speaks during an event with families who have lost relatives to crimes caused by illegal immigrants, at the Eisenhower Executive Office Building in Washington, D.C., on June 22, 2018. (JOSHUA ROBERTS/BLOOMBERG/GETTY IMAGES)

early 1990s, Trump accused Mexico of taking advantage of the U.S. and taking U.S. jobs through NAFTA. In Trump's zero-sum perception of trade, all deficits are bad and all surpluses good, disregarding the existence of value chains between Mexico and the U.S. and the benefits trade with Mexico brought for U.S. consumers.

The second issue on which Trump attacked Mexico was immigration, which, as previously discussed, had long been an important topic for the Republican Party. But even if the GOP had been talking about deportations and blocking attempts to regularize the millions of undocumented immigrants already in the U.S., Trump's anti-immigration rhetoric reached unprecedented levels of virulence and xenophobia. During the very first speech of his presidential campaign, Trump disparaged Mexico and used insupportable terms to refer to Mexican immigrants: "They're bringing drugs. They're bringing crime. They're rapists. And some, I assume, are good people." Further, in that same speech, Trump presented one of the most famous and improbable promises of his presidential campaign: to build a massive wall along the entire border between the U.S. and Mexico, which Trump said would be paid for by Mexico, in order to stop immigrants and drugs from entering the U.S.

Trump's attacks on Mexico had clear racist overtones and were detached from reality, but proved instrumental for his electoral win. In particular, his unfounded allegations on trade provided key votes in formerly Democratic-leaning areas of the U.S. rustbelt in the states of Pennsylvania, Michigan and Ohio (which Trump carried against Democratic opponent Hillary Clinton), and his anti-immigration stance proved popular among Republican conservatives. In other words, Trump tapped into anti-Mexican sentiments within U.S. society that remained despite closer bilateral cooperation in the past few decades.

If Trump's campaign rhetoric had generated disgust among Mexicans, his electoral victory dealt a massive blow to the U.S.-Mexico relationship. Polls indicate that the image of the U.S. in Mexico collapsed immediately under President Trump, from 66% to 30% positive, and confidence in the U.S. president in Mexico fell from 49% under Obama to only 5% under Trump. Meanwhile, 94% of Mexicans rejected Trump's border wall.

Meanwhile, Mexico also underwent a significant political shift, with the election in July 2018 of Andrés Manuel López Obrador (or AMLO, as he is known) as president. When he takes office on December 1, López Obrador will become Mexico's first leftist president in generations, as well as the first one to come from outside the two traditional parties (the previously hegemonic PRI and the conservative PAN of former presidents Fox and Calderón). AMLO's historic win reflected Mexican's dissatisfaction with the country's high levels of violence and human rights violations under the U.S.-backed war on drugs. It also expressed their indignation regarding high levels of poverty and inequality, and preva-

COURTESY CAGLE CARTOONS

lent corruption in the federal and local governments.

Despite López Obrador's nationalistic rhetoric, during the campaign he was cautious regarding relations with the U.S. and promised to negotiate with Trump with pragmatism in defense of Mexican interests. The new Mexican president also declared he would be open to discussions with Washington regarding immigration and trade. Trump seemed pleased with AMLO's win, and both leaders highlighted their similarities as nationalistic outsiders who had defeated their respective country's political establishments.

Shortly after López Obrador's electoral victory, the outgoing administration of Enrique Peña Nieto reached a painstaking deal with the U.S. to replace NAFTA, which Canada joined weeks later. The new agreement, called USMCA, includes some of Trump's demands of higher North American content on automobiles exported from Mexico (seeking to prevent Chinese manufactures from entering regional supply chains) and established that a certain percentage of bilateral trade needed to come from areas with high minimum wages, seeking to reduce unfair competition from Mexico. Although it does not fundamentally change the nature of U.S-Mexico trade, the new agreement is a .political victory for Trump, and might reduce bilateral tensions. Nonetheless, the U.S.-Mexico relationship is far from being back to its previous levels of mutual trust and deep cooperation. Regardless of the results of the trade negotiation, Trump's virulent rhetoric against Mexico and Mexicans has caused long-lasting damage to bilateral ties, which will take years to repair. Further, there are still many ways in which AMLO and Trump could clash in the near future, including the former's promise to end the war on drugs, focus on pacification, and legalize most drugs to reduce explosive violence rates in his country.

In addition, Trump might have postponed the implementation of his most outrageous promises on immigration (including the border wall), but his remarks on the issue continue to be full of racist overtones. In recent times he has also switched the target of his anger over trade from Mexico to Canada. But Trump will return to his previous incendiary positions regarding ties with Mexico if he thinks that might be electorally advantageous. For instance, the U.S. president continues to use crimes committed by undocumented immigrants in the U.S. as political fodder, despite evidence showing no relation between illegal immigration and crime rates.

A Mexican climbs the metal wall that divides the border between Mexico and the U.S. to cross illegally into Sunland Park,New Mexico, from Ciudad Juárez, Mexico, on April 6, 2018. (HERIKA MARTINEZ/AFP/GETTY IMAGES)

With a U.S. president who came into office on the back of a wave of manipulative accusations and resentment against Mexico, and a Mexican president who won a huge mandate to upend business as usual and defend his country's interests, the bilateral relationship has entered uncharted territory. In the recent past, Mexico and the U.S. had been able to overcome a history of mutual distrust and dramatically deepen their cooperation in order to address common problems, including drug-trafficking and illegal immigration. Further, under NAFTA both countries have integrated their economies and, despite ongoing challenges, generated millions of new jobs and business opportunities: At least six million U.S. jobs depend on trade with Mexico.

The pragmatic and coolheaded way in which Mexico has reacted to the emergence of Trump is encouraging. Far from imitating Trump's violent rhetoric, Mexican leaders (both from the outgoing Peña Nieto administration and the new government led by López Obrador) have continued to negotiate with the Trump administration, avoiding a crisis that might cost both countries dearly in economic, security and social terms. There is much the U.S. and Mexico could gain if bilateral cooperation continues to deepen. Millions of U.S. citizens have roots in Mexico. And despite such inflamed rhetoric and controversy, 75% of Americans believe that immigration is good for the country.

A U.S. policy toward Mexico that is based on racial stereotypes and political manipulation of reality can cause a lot of damage to what remains the U.S.'s most important bilateral relationship. Any disruption in trade, immigration or security cooperation will have long-lasting effects, and be detrimental to the interests of both countries. The U.S. and Mexico will remain profoundly interrelated, regardless of current disputes, and the leaders of both countries must find ways to work together toward common goals.

discussion questions

1. In the past year, Donald Trump has implemented policies and greatly altered the United States' relationship with Mexico. In what ways do you anticipate the U.S.-Mexico relationship will change when President Andrés Manuel López Obrador takes office in 2018?

2. From the Bracero program to now, several programs have related the U.S. and Mexico. What about these historical programs has contributed to the nature of the U.S.-Mexico relationship today?

3. President Trump recently renegotiated the North American Free Trade Agreement, NAFTA. How will this impact the U.S. and Mexico economically? Will it contribute to any political issues in the future?

4. How do President Trump and President Obama differ on their handling of the U.S.-Mexico connection? What are the strengths and weaknesses of each of their approaches to this relationship?

5. Immigration is portrayed in the media as the center issue of the U.S. and Mexico relationship. Do you agree with this portrayal? Why or why not? What other issues impact the two countries?

6. How has the war on drugs affected the United States and Mexico? Why has it not remedied the issues of drug consumption in the U.S. and corruption in Mexico? How can this initiative become successful?

suggested readings

Bagley, Bruce M. Drug **Trafficking, Organized Crime, and Violence in the Americas Today**. 464 pp. Gainesville, FL: University Press of Florida, 2017. Leading experts in the fields of public health, political science and national security analyze how U.S. policies have affected the internal dynamics of Mexico, Colombia, Bolivia, Peru, Brazil, Argentina, Central America and the Caribbean islands.

Bender, Steven W. **How the West Was Juan: Reimagining the U.S./Mexico Border**. 182 pp. San Diego, CA: San Diego State University Press, 2017. *How the West Was Juan* demarcates a new territory for the physical, psychological, moral, and spiritual borders of the U.S., as well as deconstructing the inaccuracy of traditional history books.

Correa-Cabrera, Guadalupe. **Los Zetas, Inc.: Criminal Corporations, Energy, and Civil War in Mexico**. 400 pp. Austin, TX: University of Texas Press, 2017. Correa-Cabrera identifies the beneficiaries of the war between the Zetas and the Mexican state.

Cantù, Francisco. **The Line Becomes a River: Dispatches from the Border**. 256 pp. New York, NY: Riverhead Books, 2018. Francisco Cantù tells the story of his time served as an agent for the U.S. Border Patrol in the deserts of Arizona, New Mexico and Texas from 2008 to 2012.

Selee, Andrew. **Vanishing Frontiers: The Forces Driving Mexico and the United States Together**. 336 pp. New York, NY: PublicAffairs, 2018. Through portraits, Selee looks at this emerging Mexico, showing how it increasingly influences daily life in the U.S. in surprising ways.

Don't forget: Ballots start on page 103!

To access web links to these readings, as well as links to additional, shorter readings and suggested web sites, GO TO www.greatdecisions.org and click on the topic under Resources, on the right-hand side of the page.

The state of the State Department and American diplomacy

by Nicholas Burns

People arrive at the State Department before the American Foreign Service Association (AFSA) Memorial Plaque Ceremony for Steven Farley, at the U.S. State Department, May 6, 2016, in Washington, DC. Steven Farley, a State Department employee, died on June 4, 2008, when an improvised explosive device detonated prior to a meeting between American officials and members of the Sadr City District Council in Iraq. Housed in the diplomatic lobby of the State Department, the memorial wall plaques honor diplomats who have given their lives in the line of duty. (DREW ANGERER/GETTY IMAGES)

The U.S. State Department serves a critical role of the nation. Its men and women in the Foreign and Civil Service are on the front lines for the U.S. in over 277 embassies and consulates abroad. They assist American citizens in distress, interview all foreigners seeking to enter the U.S. as visitors, immigrants and refugees. They help American companies to succeed overseas and represent the U.S. in global conferences and negotiations on every international issue of concern to the country from climate change to drug trafficking to nuclear proliferation and the fight against HIV/AIDs.

As they represent the most powerful nation on earth, what American diplomats do and say overseas matters to the rest of the world. They work arm and arm with the U.S. military, lead negotiations to end wars and to achieve peace and are often the ultimate arbiters in ongoing disputes between Israelis and Palestinians, Indians and Pakistanis, Greeks and Turks. U.S. diplomats are highly trained, multilingual and have years of experience living and working abroad for their country.

Despite its central role in global politics, however, the State Department is experiencing one of the most serious

AMBASSADOR (RET.) NICHOLAS BURNS *is Goodman Professor of the Practice of Diplomacy and International Politics at Harvard's Kennedy School of Government. He served in the U.S. Foreign Service including as Under Secretary of State for Political Affairs and Ambassador to NATO and to Greece.*

crises in its long, 229-year service to the country. Its principal challenge is in its relationship with President Donald Trump. While some recent American presidents, such as Richard Nixon, often kept State at arms length, most—George H.W. Bush, Bill Clinton, George W. Bush and Barack Obama come to mind— have taken advantage of the expertise and unique global reach of the Foreign Service.

As Trump enters his third year in office, he is presiding over one of the most difficult relationships an American president has ever had with the State Department. During the first two years of his Presidency, Trump has effectively sidelined the State Department's career diplomats by seeking to cut the budget by one third, failing to promote senior officers, leaving a historically high number of senior positions unfilled and diminishing morale to historically low levels. He has also practiced an often go-it-alone foreign policy that has alienated many of America's traditional friends and allies and been overly accommodating with many of its most dangerous adversaries such as Vladimir Putin's Russia.

Trump has been right to commit time and attention to the U.S. military given its current focus on defeating ISIS, stabilizing Iraq, Syria and Afghanistan and balancing growing Russian power in Eastern Europe and a newly assertive China in the Indo-Pacific. He succeeded in securing sizeable funding for the Pentagon. He has also appointed an unusually high number of military officers to senior positions in the cabinet and White House staff. He has not given diplomacy and diplomats, however, anything close to similar attention or priority.

As the U.S. faces a multiplicity of complex national security challenges in the year ahead, Americans need to reflect on the reality that the military is stretched thin and is not the right instrument for many of the challenges the country faces from climate change, the threats of pandemics and the rise of anti-democratic populism in Europe. While the military will continue to be the primary vehicle to defend the U.S. from foreign threats, the U.S. also needs a strong, fully funded and capable State Department to take the lead on many global challenges and to advance the ball on the more positive opportunities for the American people in the next decade.

The State Department, however, has been in a state of crisis since the start of the Trump Administration. It is poorly funded and in need of both revival and reform to strengthen its capacity to carry out its vital work in the international arena. It also needs far greater attention, support and leadership from the president if it is to succeed fully in the years ahead.

The Trump era in American diplomacy

During President Trump's first two years in office, he has signaled very little interest in the State Department and in diplomacy itself. From the start, the president and his Office of Management and Budget tried to downsize and sideline the State Department. In both 2017 and 2018, the president advocated a 30% budget cut in funding for the State Department that, if enacted, would have been devastating to its operational capacity and morale.

At the same time, Trump's first Secretary of State, Rex Tillerson, initiated a restructuring of the State Department and a hiring freeze that, if they had been sustained, would have led to the radical downsizing of the Foreign and Civil Service officer corps. To make matters worse, the Administration was extremely slow in naming people to senior positions in the State Department and Ambassadorial appointments overseas. Many career officers felt sidelined and unappreciated by the new team.

The Administration's policy decisions from the start contributed to the crisis. Trump contested the consensus among all post-World War Two (WWII) presidents of both parties that the U.S. should lead the liberal international order and by giving priority attention to the web of alliances and international organizations that enhance U.S. power and global stability. He set out, in fact, to reverse seven decades of American policy in four key areas:

- First, he became a leading critic of the close Transatlantic ties that all prior presidents have supported since WWII. Trump has been acutely critical of NATO and failed, on his first visit to NATO Headquarters in Brussels, even to reaffirm the Article 5 mutual defense clause in the 1949 NATO treaty that is the Alliance's key commitment among its 29 members. He has characterized the European Union as a "foe" and strategic competitor of the U.S. As a result, the U.S. has the most strained relationship with Europe and Canada since well before WWII.
- Second, Trump has sought to dismantle the multilateral trade system that had helped the global economy to grow and millions all over the world to make the leap from poverty to the middle class in recent decades. He said no to the proposed Trans-Pacific Partnership (TPP) with 11 countries of the Americas and Asia representing 40% of global GDP. TPP was designed in part as a major strategic move by President Obama to expand the collective leverage of these countries over a Chinese government guilty of predatory trade practices that have harmed our workers and economies. Trump ended the NAFTA agreement with Canada and Mexico while commencing near simultaneous trade wars with both of them, the European Union, China, Japan and South Korea. While the Administration ended up negotiating a new agreement with Canada and Mexico, the damage had been done to American credibility on trade.

! Before you read, download the companion **Glossary** that includes definitions, a guide to acronyms and abbreviations used in the article, and other material. Go to **www.greatdecisions.org** and select a topic in the Resources section on the right-hand side of the page.

■ Third, he altered America's post-war consensus that the U.S. should keep its doors open to legal immigration and refugee admittance. Indeed, at the very start of his time in office, Trump enacted a ban on travel from specific Muslim-majority nations. That led to a rare protest by more than 1,000 Foreign Service Officers. At a time of the greatest refugee crisis since World War Two (there are over 65 million refugees and internally displaced people in the world today), Trump has slashed refugee admittance since Obama's last year in office. This reverses the U.S. decades-long policy of sharing responsibility with other wealthy countries to accept refugees from war zones and to maintain a steady flow of legal immigrants that many believe strengthen America's economic future.

■ Fourth, Trump has not been a vocal, public champion of democracy in Europe where it is threatened by the rise of anti-democratic populist movements across the continent. On the contrary, he has been an often-caustic critic of leaders in some of America's closest allied countries—Germany's Angela Merkel, France's Emmanuel Macron, Britain's Theresa May and Canada's Justin Trudeau. In contrast, Trump has embraced openly anti-democratic leaders in Hungary, Poland and Italy and been outwardly complimentary and even fawning to Kim Jung Un, Vladimir Putin and Xi Jinping. American presidents since Franklin Roosevelt have been considered, and have seen themselves, as leaders of the West. Trump has abdicated that role to the detriment of America's credibility in Europe and beyond.

(From L to R) Canadian Prime Minister Justin Trudeau, Morocco's Prince Moulay Hassan, Moroccan King Mohammed VI, U.S. First Lady Melania Trump, U.S. President Donald Trump, German Chancellor Angela Merkel, French President Emmanuel Macron and his wife Brigitte Macron, Russian President Vladimir Putin and Australian Governor-General Peter Cosgrove attend a ceremony at the Arc de Triomphe in Paris on November 11, 2018, as part of commemorations marking the 100th anniversary of the November 11, 1918, armistice, ending World War I. (LUDOVIC MARIN/AFP/GETTY IMAGES)

Trump has also led the U.S. out of a number of international agreements and organizations including the Paris Climate Change Agreement, the Iran Nuclear Deal, the International Organization of Migration, UNESCO and others.

These abrupt and significant policy changes combined, with the threat of draconian budget cuts and lack of presidential respect for the Foreign Service, to produce a true crisis of leadership and morale inside the State Department. Several of the most senior officers in the Department were fired in Trump's first few tumultuous months in office. Others resigned in opposition to the more isolationist policies of the president. Hiring of new junior officers fell by two thirds in Trump's first year

U.S. President Donald Trump (L) chats with Russia's President Vladimir Putin as they attend the APEC Economic Leaders' Meeting, part of the Asia-Pacific Economic Cooperation (APEC) leaders' summit in the central Vietnamese city of Danang on November 11, 2017. (MIKHAIL KLIMENTYEV/SPUTNIK/AFP/GETTY IMAGES)

North Korea's leader Kim Jong Un (R) walks with U.S. President Donald Trump during a break in talks at their historic summit in Singapore on June 12, 2018. The two became the first sitting U.S. and North Korean leaders to meet and negotiate to end a decades-old nuclear stand-off. (ANTHONY WALLACE/AFP/GETTY IMAGES)

in office. A hiring freeze was imposed across the Department. A historically high number of senior officers resigned or retired earlier than expected. By the end of 2018, according to the American Foreign Service Association (AFSA), over 60 ambassadorships were still vacant, including to Saudi Arabia and Turkey during the Khashoggi crisis, Australia and Singapore, South Africa, Jordan, Egypt and Pakistan.

This unprecedented crisis—produced by the Trump team's mishandling of the State Department, the vacant positions, low morale and the president's own seeming disinterest in diplomacy—will continue into 2019 and may last for the entirety of the Trump presidency. The president has placed himself at the center of the storm. When questioned in November 2017 about the vacant ambassadorial positions, he told Fox News, "I'm the only one who matters, because when it comes to it, that's what the policy is going to be." That Trump statement made crystal clear his disregard for the State Department and its career diplomats.

Tillerson's one-year tenure as Secretary of State was marked by controversy, an Administration attempt to gut the State Department budget and the ill-fated reform efforts. He appeared to many in the Department to be isolated from the rank and file. Working mainly with a small group of aides, he did not consult as closely with the career diplomats as previous Secretaries had done in the management of the daily diplomacy of the U.S. He did not offer himself as a champion of a diplomatic service that felt beleaguered and unappreciated by the president and his team.

Tillerson's successor, Mike Pompeo, has tried hard to rescue a badly damaged Foreign Service and State Department. He lifted Tillerson's ill-advised hiring freeze, appointed senior Foreign Service Officers such as Ambassador David Hale to be Under Secretary of State for Political Affairs and the well-regarded Senior Foreign Service Ambassador Mike McKinley as Chief of Staff. Pompeo has been a consistent public advocate for the Department. Morale seems to have improved. Many career professionals see in Pompeo a West Point graduate who served in the military and as CIA Director and who thus understands the federal workforce.

How effectively Pompeo can protect the State Department budget in 2019–20, however, will be a major factor in his legacy as Secretary of State as the White House and Office of Management and Budget (OMB) may attempt again in 2019 to slash the State Department budget.

The long-term budgetary stakes are high for the future of the State Department. As AFSA has made clear recently, the 2019 budget battle will determine, more than any other factor, the immediate future of the Foreign Service and the State Department during the Trump era.

As AFSA reported in late 2018, the State Department's budget is not at

Secretary of State John Kerry testifies during a Senate Foreign Relations Committee hearing, on Capitol Hill February 23, 2016 in Washington, DC. The committee is hearing testimony from Secretary Kerry on President Obama's FY2017 State Department budget request. (MARK WILSON/GETTY IMAGES)

all secure. While Congress has set the State Department budget at $55.9 billion (compared to over $700 billion for the Department of Defense) it charges there has been "a dramatic decline in spending on core diplomatic capability over the last decade—from one dollar in 2008 to just 76 cents in 2016." By core diplomatic funding, AFSA points to "funding for political, economic and public diplomacy" activities—the central work of American embassies and consulates overseas. AFSA believes Trump's proposed budget cuts would reduce that figure to 69 cents.

And, while the U.S. spends less on diplomats, China is expanding its own spending on its growing (second in the world to the U.S. in numbers of embassies and consulates) diplomatic corps.

The silver lining is this dire situation for the State Department has been Republican and Democratic leaders of the Congress. In both 2017 and 2018, the Congress opposed the Trump budget cuts for the State Department and restored most of the funding. Indeed, when I testified in spring 2017 before the House Foreign Affairs Committee in defense of spending on diplomacy, I expected to be challenged by members of the president's party. Instead, I was surprised and impressed that the clear majority of members from both parties believed a one-third budget cut was unwarranted.

CIA Director Mike Pompeo speaks at a Senate Select Committee on Intelligence hearing on worldwide threats, Tuesday, February 13, 2018, in Washington, DC. (ANDREW HARNIK/AP PHOTO)

As the new Congress will face this same budget battle in 2019, it would do well to reflect on the long history of the Department and its central role in our government today. As the world's preeminent global power, the U.S. needs a first-rate diplomatic corps. Its history and mission make the case that the U.S. cannot hope to have a successful foreign policy without an adequately funded State Department at center stage.

The State Department's place in American history

The State Department's history is intertwined with that of the U.S. itself. It was the first of the cabinet agencies to be created in 1789 after the adoption of the Constitution. For that reason, the secretary of state is fourth in line to the presidency and the senior member of the cabinet. The Secretary of State is also the official custodian of the Great Seal of the U.S. for confirmation of official appointments and official business. The Great Seal, in fact, is kept on the first floor of the modern State Department in "Foggy Bottom" in Washington, DC.

Many of the founding fathers served as secretary, including Thomas Jefferson (the first to hold the office), John Marshall, James Madison and John Quincy Adams. They helped the first presidents to set the initial foreign policy vision of the young republic. In those days, being secretary of state was a stepping stone to the presidency itself as Jefferson, Madison, Monroe and John Quincy Adams all made the leap to the highest office.

As a country born in revolution against a colonial power, the young U.S. saw its interests very differently than European countries across the Atlantic. Jefferson thought of America as an "Empire of Liberty" rather than a country that should seek to emulate the empires of the world. Madison helped Jefferson to negotiate the Louisiana Purchase that came close to doubling the size of the country.

These early secretaries of state were focused as much on the building of the new nation at home as on international developments beyond American shores. And some of them were decidedly anti-interventionist.

Adams said famously of America in a July 4, 1821, speech, "Wherever the

CORNELIUS TIEBOUT, ENGRAVER FROM PAINTING BY REMBRANDT PEALE: THOMAS JEFFERSON, PRESIDENT OF THE UNITED STATES. [PHILADELPHIA: PUBLISHED BY A. DAY] PHOTOGRAPH/LIBRARY OF CONGRESS, ITEM, 96522974

Dr. Henry Kissinger (L), U.S. Presidential National Security Adviser, shakes hands with Chinese Premier Zhou Enlai of the People's Republic of China at their meeting at Government Guest House in Peking (Beijing), China, July 9, 1971. (AP PHOTO)

standard of freedom and independence has been or shall be unfurled, there will her heart, her benedictions and her prayers be. But she goes not abroad in search of monsters to destroy. She is the well-wisher to the freedom and independence of all. She is the champion and vindicator only of her own."

President James Monroe's celebrated 1823 doctrine warned European powers to end their colonial expansion in the western hemisphere.

Through the coming decades, American diplomats helped the new country to expand in North America under the banner of Manifest Destiny and to begin to compete with the world powers of the day. President James K. Polk's victory in the Mexican War led to the negotiation of the 1848 Treaty of Guadalupe Hidalgo and the 1853 Gadsden Purchase that gave the U.S. Texas, California and much of the modern southwest. Lincoln's Secretary, William Henry Seward, purchased Alaska from Russia.

In the first decade of the 20th century, President Teddy Roosevelt's Secretary of State, John Hay, helped to vault the U.S. into the ranks of the great powers. It was Roosevelt, in fact, who negotiated the 1905 Treaty of Portsmouth that ended the war between Russia and Japan. That diplomatic effort made Roosevelt the first American recipient of the Nobel Peace Prize.

As the U.S. became more powerful in global affairs, its diplomatic influence increased immeasurably. Woodrow Wilson and his Secretary of State Robert Lansing took center stage in negotiating the end of World War One and the creation of a new global order at the Versailles Conference in 1919.

After the allied victory in WWII, Secretary George Marshall authored one of the most important and consequential initiatives in American history—the Marshall Plan that helped to rebuild Europe after the Second World War. Secretary Dean Acheson was the inspiration behind the creation of NATO in 1949. Secretary Henry Kissinger led the historic opening to China in 1972 and Secretary James A. Baker III negotiated the unification of Germany and the peaceful end to the Cold War in 1990–91.

In recent decades, some of our most talented public servants have led the men and women of the State Department—George Shultz, Warren Christopher, Madeleine Albright, Colin Powell, Condoleezza Rice, Hillary Clinton and John Kerry among them.

As American power and influence have grown in the world, its wisest leaders have understood the call to U.S. global leadership requires a well-supported and fully engaged State Department.

The mission and value of the State Department

As the president and Congress debate the future of the State Department and American diplomacy in the year ahead, they might also reflect on its mission and value to Americans in the 21st century.

The State Department serves as the principal cabinet agency that represents the American government and people in nearly every country of the world. Diplomacy is one of the most important instruments Americans have to defend their country and advance its many political, security, cultural and economic interests in a complex world.

Consider some of the State Department's primary missions:

- American diplomats provide a full range of services for Americans living and traveling outside the U.S. from issuing passports to registering births of American citizens, to providing notary services, to bailing Americans out of jail, registering weddings as well as deaths;
- They also help American businesses to secure investment and trade opportunities overseas. The Commerce Department's Foreign Commercial Service and American ambassadors and economic officers work closely with American businesses large and small to make sure they have a level playing field in overseas markets and the full support of the government;
- More than 277 U.S. embassies and consulates conduct official relations

with foreign governments and international organizations on every issue under the sun from the promotion of democracy and human rights to nuclear arms limitation, weapons sales to friends and allies, climate and environmental issues, the struggle against crime and drug cartels, global health policy including the threat of pandemics and many other issues. The writ of American diplomacy encompasses all the threats that endanger the nation and all the opportunities to seek prosperity, stability, justice and peace in this century.

■ Career foreign service officers who staff American embassies and consulates negotiate treaties and agreements and help to resolve conflicts and end wars when necessary. In recent decades, American diplomats helped U.S. presidents negotiate the historic Egypt-Israel Peace Agreement in 1979, the Dayton Accords that ended the brutal was in Bosnia in 1995, nuclear arms limitation agreements with the USSR and Russia, the U.S.-India civil nuclear agreement and the nuclear deal with Iran.

In the year ahead, American diplomats will lead the talks with North Korea to end its nuclear weapons program. They will be responsible for negotiating an end to the bloody wars in Syria and Yemen. They will monitor human rights crises in Myanmar, western China, the Central African Republic and in Central America. They will represent the U.S, at the United Nations and in war zones from Afghanistan to Iraq and beyond.

The State Department is a relatively small government agency compared to the Pentagon or the Department of Homeland Security. The Foreign Service is comprised of roughly 8,000 women and men who serve around the world and at the Department in Washington. It is an elite service. Officers must pass a rigorous and competitive written examination, a series of oral interviews and a security clearance.

A typical senior foreign service officer is multilingual, has served in American embassies in multiple countries as a political, economic, public diplomacy, consular or management officer. He or she has to be able to work effectively in Washington in the policy battles inside each Administration as well as overseas in widely varying foreign cultures. As an officer corps, they are some of the finest experts in the U.S. on the major countries, regions, languages and cultures of the world.

As is the case with all federal civil servants, State Department career officials must also be nonpartisan. They enter the workforce with the understanding that they will serve presidents and secretaries of state of both parties over the course of a career. Their obligation and commitment is not to enter into partisan politics but to give equal effort and dedication to each president elected by the American people.

As is the case with all U.S. government employees, career foreign service officers take an oath not to the president (as foreign diplomats often do to their sovereign) but to the Constitution.

One of the most important contributions career diplomats make to the country is their nonpartisan service. They provide the permanent expertise and experience in foreign policy as well as continuity for each president. Officers are accustomed to serving across party lines. In my own career, I worked from 1990 to January 1993 at the National Security Council (NSC) in the White House as Director of Soviet Affairs for President George H.W. Bush. When President Clinton was sworn into office on January 20, 1993, I was asked to stay on for two additional years in the same office at the NSC to work for him. This was not at all unusual but part of the pattern for career officers.

In sum, while the U.S. relies on its superb military to protect Americans from foreign aggression, it also relies on the State Department and Foreign Service to protect the country from those same threats and to represent it internationally as the strongest and most active power in the world today.

U.S. Secretary of State Madeleine Albright points to a globe during her testimony February 10, 1998, to members of the Senate Foreign Relations Committee on Capitol Hill in Washington, DC. Albright testified about the State Department budget and other issues.
(TIM SLOAN/AFP/GETTY IMAGES)

Challenges ahead

As President Trump and his successors look out at the world, they would do well to think that the State Department may be as important to our future as the military has been over the past 18 years since 9/11.

Al Qaeda's attacks on New York and the Pentagon ushered in an unusual phase in American foreign policy where the priority swung to the major wars in Afghanistan and Iraq and the military's smaller counter-insurgency campaigns in Syria, the Horn of Africa, West Africa, the Philippines and other parts of the Middle East and Asia. During this period, the military took on an outsized role in American foreign policy and in how Americans thought about defending the country in a new and dangerous era.

Since 9/11, the primary strategic priority of the U.S. has been to defeat the terrorist threat to the country. That made the military the major instrument of American power. The U.S. came out swinging after the attacks of September 11, 2001. The Bush and Obama Administrations gave first emphasis to the huge increase in military spending, the trillions of dollars spent in Iraq and Afghanistan alone and the deployment of hundreds of thousands of American troops to over 100 countries in the world.

The Trump Administration has made a major and welcome shift in American policy since 2017. It now lists the challenge of dealing with authoritarian governments in Russia and China as the most important U.S. security priority rather than terrorism. We are slowly but surely entering a new and more traditional phase in U.S. global policy of focusing on maintaining strategic positions in Europe and Asia to preserve the power of our country and that of our allies.

This major change alters the mission of the U.S. military to be able to contain Putin in Eastern Europe and balance China's rising power in the Indo-Pacific.

It will also alter the role and mission of the State Department and American diplomacy. By necessity, diplomacy will play a more central role in the next ten years than it did in the past decade. The U.S. will need to rebuild its alliances in NATO and with its East Asian allies. It will need to construct coalitions of countries to take on the major transnational challenges from climate change to drug and crime cartels to global public health and protecting the U.S. economy and government from cyber aggression.

The U.S. will likely remain the strongest global power for the next several decades. No other country has the same combination of economic weight and innovation, political influence, global military power and cultural influence. In absolute terms, it is difficult to imagine China or any other country surpassing the U.S. as the world's preeminent power. But, in relative terms, the gap between the U.S., and other powers—China, India, Russia, the European Union—is narrowing. The U.S. will not always be able to get its way by threatening or using force. It will need to rely more on its wits than in past decades. That means elevating diplomacy to a first-order priority.

The first thing is to start rebuilding the State Department and Foreign Service. After all, most national security experts understand that combining diplomatic and military strength in a cohesive strategy will give the U.S. the greatest chance to succeed in the world today.

After 9/11, the U.S. led with a military-first strategy. Going forward, the country will more often than not need to adopt a diplomacy-first strategy when facing a tough international crisis. A good general rule is to first exhaust diplomatic efforts to end a war or to resolve a dispute with a powerful adversary. It is only when it is clear that diplomacy cannot work that presidents should consider resorting to the military.

To accomplish this transformation in American policy, it stands to reason the U.S. will need a strong, well-funded State Department and Foreign Service. The U.S. will need to recruit, train and maintain a group of men and women to represent the country overseas, to protect American citizens in distress, to help U.S. companies compete for foreign contracts, to build the coalitions that will power American and American influence in the decades ahead. That is the case for a new commitment to America's diplomats as they lead the country forward in an increasingly challenging international arena.

discussion questions

1. What is the role of the State Department and diplomacy in American foreign policy? What are the benefits to the U.S.?

2. What has been the Trump Administration's attitude toward diplomacy and America's diplomats? Why did the Trump Administration seek to reduce the State Department budget by one third? What would have been the consequences if it had succeeded?

3. As the U.S. focus on terrorism gives way to a return to great power rivalry with China and Russia, what kind of diplomatic assets will the U.S. need around the world to be effective?

4. Is the U.S, entering an era when it needs a stronger focus on diplomacy to go along with its emphasis on military power since 9/11?

5. Among the most important U.S. challenges will be how to combat the great transnational threats that confront every nation—climate change, drug and crime cartels, cyber threats, global health and other challenges. How difficult will it be to create coalitions of countries to take on these challenges?

6. We also have many positive opportunities in the world today from continuing the historic reduction of poverty to advances in global health to the rise of women in business and government. How can the U.S. use its diplomatic power to push these advances forward and to make the world more stable, just and peaceful?

suggested readings

Daalder, Ivo H. and Lindsay, James M. **The Empty Throne: America's Abdication of Global Leadership**. 256 pp. New York, NY: Public Affairs, 2018. An inside portrait of the greatest lurch in U.S. foreign policy since the decision to retreat back into Fortress America after World War I.

Kagan, Robert. **The Jungle Grows Back: America and Our Imperiled World**. 192 pp. New York, NY: Alfred A. Knopf, 2018. An argument for America's role as an enforcer of peace and order throughout the world—and what is likely to happen if we withdraw and focus our attention inward.

Burns, Nicholas and Crocker, Ryan C. "Dismantling the Foreign Service." **The New York Times**, November 27, 2017. Two experienced diplomats detail the slow unraveling of American diplomacy and the Foreign Service, and urge Congress to act.

Farrow, Ronan. **War on Peace: The End of Diplomacy and the Decline of American Influence.** 392 pp. New York, NY: W.W. Norton & Company, 2018. Drawing on newly unearthed documents, and richly informed by rare interviews with warlords, whistle-blowers, and policymakers—including every living former secretary of state from Henry Kissinger to Hillary Clinton to Rex Tillerson—War on Peace makes a powerful case for an endangered profession. Diplomacy, Farrow argues, has declined after decades of political cowardice, shortsightedness, and outright malice—but it may just offer America a way out of a world at war.

Huddleston, Vicki. **Our Woman in Havana: A Diplomat's Chronicle of America's Long Struggle with Castro's Cuba.** 304 pp. New York, NY: Overlook Press, 2018. This book chronicles the past several decades of U.S.-Cuba relations from the bird's-eye view of State Department veteran and longtime Cuba hand Vicki Huddleston, the U.S.'s top diplomat in Havana under Presidents Clinton and George W. Bush.

Steil, Benn. **The Marshall Plan: Dawn of the Cold War.** 624 pp. New York, NY: Simon and Schuster, 2018. Provides critical context into understanding today's international landscape. Drawing on new material from American, Russian, German and other European archives, Steil's account will add to understanding of the Marshall Plan and the birth of the Cold War.

Eicher, Peter D. **Raising the Flag: America's First Envoys in Faraway Lands.** 416 pp. Lincoln, NE: Potomac Books, 2018. From the American Revolution to the Civil War, Eicher profiles the characters who influenced the formative period of American diplomacy and the first steps the U.S. took as a world power. The book illuminates how American ideas, values, and power helped shape the modern world.

Don't forget: Ballots start on page 103!

To access web links to these readings, as well as links to additional, shorter readings and suggested web sites,

GO TO www.greatdecisions.org

and click on the topic under Resources, on the right-hand side of the page.

Global Discussion Questions

No decision in foreign policy is made in a vacuum, and the repercussions of any single decision have far-reaching effects across the range of strategic interests on the U.S. policy agenda. This GREAT DECISIONS feature is intended to facilitate the discussion of this year's topics in a global context, to discuss the linkages between the topics and to encourage consideration of the broader impact of decision-making.

1. Consider "Nuclear negotiations" in the context of "Cyber Conflicts." As shown in both articles, both nuclear weapons and cyber-attacks could be devastating for target countries. How are these two systems of attack related? What steps can the United States take to protect itself against both of these threats?

2. Consider "U.S. and Mexico" in the context of "U.S. and China." The United States has been reworking economic ties with Mexico (the end of NAFTA), while progressing a trade war with China. How can the United States balance its changing economic ties with both countries? How will both of these transitions affect the global economy?

3. Consider "Migration" in the context of "The Rise of Populism." Anti-migration sentiments in Europe have contributed to the rise of populism in the EU. Are the two necessarily correlated? Is it possible to have high migration without populism pervading government? What are the specific issues that tie the two together?

4. Consider "Nuclear negotiations" in the context of "Middle East." Middle Eastern countries, such as Iraq and Iran, have been at the center of the nuclear debate in the past. Is the Middle East still a pressing nuclear concern for the United States? Why or why not? How do the nuclear arsenals of Israel and Pakistan affect your answer?

5. Consider "Cyber conflicts" in the context of "U.S. and China." The United States has discovered that China has breached U.S. cyber security. How does this affect the United States' relationship with China, specifically economically? What steps can be taken to preserve good relations with China while protecting against cyber breaches?

6. Consider "State of the State Department" in the context of "U.S. and Mexico." How has the current administration handled foreign policy issues with Mexico? What are the State Department's priorities when dealing with Mexico? How will Mexico's new administration fair with the State Department?

7. Consider "State of the State Department" in the context of "Cyber Conflicts." What steps has the State Department taken to protect against cyber conflicts? How has the administration dealt with issues of cyber security both within the United States and in the world?

8. Consider "Migration" in the context of "U.S. and Mexico." Both Europe and the United States have dealt with migration. What similarities are there between Europe's response to migration and the United States' response since 2015? How has migration impacted politics in the two regions?

9. Consider "The Rise of Populism" in the context of "State of the State Department." How has the rise of populism in Europe affected the United States and its relationship with Europe? How has the State Department reacted to populism in Europe?

10. Consider "The Middle East" in the context of "Migration." Many of the migrants and refugees discussed in the "Migration" article come from the Middle East. What interests does Europe have in the Middle East? How has migration changed the relationship between the EU and the Middle East in general?

For glossaries, additional readings and more, visit

www.GreatDecisions.org

INDEX TO GREAT DECISIONS TOPICS
2008–2018

About the balloting process...

Dear Great Decisions Participants,

As you may already know, my name is Dr. Lauren Prather and I have been working with the Foreign Policy Association (FPA) for the last five years on the National Opinion Ballot (NOB). A version of this letter has appeared in previous briefing books, so I'm only writing a quick hello this year.

My research is primarily focused on international relations. I am a faculty member at the School of Global Policy and Strategy at the University of California, San Diego (UCSD) and have research projects on a range of public opinion topics, from foreign aid to climate change to national security issues. I also teach a class on public opinion and foreign policy for my university.

One of the key difficulties in my research is that the public is often uniformed or misinformed about the topics. This is where you come in! The Great Decisions participants continue to be some of the most informed Americans about foreign policy issues, and the NOB is the perfect opportunity to voice those opinions.

The NOB is also one of the only public opinion surveys in the United States that attempts to gather the opinions of the educated public. Thus, it has great value to researchers and policymakers alike. Some of the questions in which researchers are interested include the following:

- Are the opinions of the educated public significantly different from those of the average American?
- How does public opinion about foreign policy change over time?
- How does public opinion on one foreign policy issue relate to public opinion on other foreign policy issues? For example, are people who support U.S. government policies to mitigate climate change more or less willing to support drilling in the Arctic?
- How do different segments of the population, men or women, liberals or conservatives, view foreign policy choices?

In order to answer the types of questions researchers are interested in, such as how do people's opinions change over time, the NOB needs to have certain attributes. We need to have a way to organize the ballots by participant across all topics. That way, we know, for example, how participant #47 responded to the question about climate change mitigation and how he or she responded to the question about drilling, even if those were in different topics in the NOB. Your random ID number is the **only thing** connected to your responses and **never** your e-mail address. In fact, as a researcher, I must receive the approval of my Institutional Review Board by demonstrating that your data will be protected at all times, and that your responses will be both confidential and anonymous.

If you have any questions or comments, I am always happy to respond via e-mail at LPrather@ucsd.edu. To learn more about my research and teaching, you can visit my website at www.laurenprather.org.

Thank you again to everyone who has participated in the NOB over the years. I have learned a tremendous amount about your foreign policy views and it has greatly informed my own research. In the future, I hope to communicate to the scholarly world and policy communities how the educated American public thinks about foreign policy.

Sincerely,
Lauren Prather

2019 National Opinion Ballot

First, we'd like to ask you for some information about your participation in the Great Decisions program. If you are not currently a Great Decisions program member, please skip to the "background" section.

How long have you participated in the Great Decisions program (i.e., attended one or more discussion sessions)?

- ❑ This is the first year I have participated
- ❑ I participated in one previous year
- ❑ I participated in more than one previous year

How did you learn about the Great Decisions Program?

- ❑ Word of mouth
- ❑ Local library
- ❑ Foreign Policy Association website
- ❑ Promotional brochure
- ❑ Other organization ___________________

Where does your Great Decisions group meet?

- ❑ Private home
- ❑ Library
- ❑ Community center
- ❑ Learning in retirement
- ❑ Other ___________________

How many hours, on average, do you spend reading one Great Decisions chapter?

- ❑ Less than 1 hour
- ❑ 1–2 hours
- ❑ 3–4 hours
- ❑ More than 4 hours

Would you say you have or have not changed your opinion in a fairly significant way as a result of taking part in the Great Decisions program?

- ❑ Have
- ❑ Have not
- ❑ Not sure

Background Section: Next, we'd like to ask you some information about your background.

How strongly do you agree or disagree with the following statement? Although the media often reports about national and international events and developments, this news is seldom as interesting as the things that happen directly in our own community and neighborhood.

- ❑ Agree strongly
- ❑ Agree somewhat
- ❑ Neither agree nor disagree
- ❑ Disagree somewhat
- ❑ Disagree strongly

Generally speaking, how interested are you in politics?

- ❑ Very much interested
- ❑ Somewhat interested
- ❑ Not too interested
- ❑ Not interested at all

Do you think it is best for the future of the United States if the U.S. takes an active role in world affairs or stays out of world affairs?

- ❑ Takes an active role in world affairs
- ❑ Stays out of world affairs

How often are you asked for your opinion on foreign policy?

- ❑ Often
- ❑ Sometimes
- ❑ Never

Have you been abroad during the last two years?

- ❑ Yes
- ❑ No

Do you know, or are you learning, a foreign language?

- ❑ Yes
- ❑ No

Enter your answers online at www.fpa.org/ballot

Do you have any close friends or family that live in other countries?

- ❑ Yes
- ❑ No

Do you donate to any charities that help the poor in other countries?

- ❑ Yes
- ❑ No

Generally speaking, do you usually think of yourself as a Republican, a Democrat, an Independent or something else?

- ❑ Republican
- ❑ Democrat
- ❑ Independent
- ❑ Other ____________________

With which gender do you most identify?

- ❑ Male
- ❑ Female
- ❑ Transgender male
- ❑ Transgender female
- ❑ Gender variant/non-conforming
- ❑ Other ____________________
- ❑ Prefer not to answer

What race do you consider yourself?

- ❑ White/Caucasian
- ❑ Black/African American
- ❑ Hispanic/Latino
- ❑ Asian American
- ❑ Native American
- ❑ Other ____________________
- ❑ Prefer not to answer

Were you born in the United States or another country?

- ❑ United States
- ❑ Another country

Are you a citizen of the United States, another country, or are you a citizen of both the United States and another country?

- ❑ United States
- ❑ Another country
- ❑ United States and another country

How important is religion in your life?

- ❑ Very important
- ❑ Somewhat important
- ❑ Not too important
- ❑ Not at all important

What is your age? ____________

Are you currently employed?

- ❑ Full-time employee
- ❑ Part-time employee
- ❑ Self-employed
- ❑ Unemployed
- ❑ Retired
- ❑ Student
- ❑ Homemaker

What are the first three digits of your zip code? (This will allow us to do a state-by-state breakdown of results.)

____________ ____________ ____________

Can you give us an estimate of your household income in 2018 before taxes?

- ❑ Below $30,000
- ❑ $30,000–$50,000
- ❑ $50,000–$75,000
- ❑ $75,000–$100,000
- ❑ $100,000–$150,000
- ❑ Over $150,000
- ❑ Not sure
- ❑ Prefer not to say

What is the highest level of education you have completed?

- ❑ Did not graduate from high school
- ❑ High school graduate
- ❑ Some college, but no degree (yet)
- ❑ 2-year college degree
- ❑ 4-year college degree
- ❑ Some postgraduate work, but no degree (yet)
- ❑ Post-graduate degree (MA, MBA, MD, JD, PhD, etc.)

Now we would like to ask you some ballot questions from previous years:

1. From 2007's "International migration in a gloablizing economy": Do you think its a contradictions to support the free movement of goods and services that characterize globalization, on the one hand, and to limit hte free movement of wokers,on the other hand?

- ❑ Yes
- ❑ No

2. From 2012's "Mexico: transborder crime and governence": Who should lead the efforts to combat drug cartels and criminality in North and Central America?

- ❑ U.S. alone
- ❑ Mexico alone
- ❑ U.S. and Mexico
- ❑ Central American Nations
- ❑ Mexico and Central American Nations

3. From 2013's "Turkey's challenges": How likely or not do you think it is that Turkey will join the European Union?

- ❑ Very likely
- ❑ Somewhat likely
- ❑ Not too likely
- ❑ Not likely at all

4. From 2012's "Promoting democracy": In your opinion, which method of promoting democracy is the most appropriate unilateral U.S. strategy?

- ❑ Diplomacy
- ❑ Sanctions (includes conditional aid)
- ❑ Democracy assistance in the form of funding, training, organizing, etc.
- ❑ Military force

5. From 2011's "Cybersecurity": Which of the following is the most compelling argument for cyberspace governance?

- ❑ The proliferation of internationalized cybercrime
- ❑ The incidence of "political" cyber-attacks (e.g. pro-nationalist hackers)
- ❑ The impact of cyber activity on foreign and military policy
- ❑ The possibility of a cyber "arms race" in the near future
- ❑ Other

6. From 2010's "China looka at the world: the world looks at China": Given the rising strength and power of China in the international system, what do you expect a future China to look like? (Select one option)

- ❑ Replacing the U.S. as the hegemon in a unipolar world order.
- ❑ Taking on the role the USSR had during the cold war as a major rival to the U.S. in a bipolar world.
- ❑ Becoming one of the "poles" in a multipolar world order
- ❑ Domestic issues in China will prevent it from assuming a larger global role.

7. From 2013's "Trade": People debate whether the U.S. government should increase restrictions on imports, keep restrictions on imports at current levels or decrease restrictions on imports. What do you think the U.S. government should do?

- ❑ Increase restrictions on imports
- ❑ Keep restrictions on imports at current levels
- ❑ Decrease restrictions on imports

8. From 2002's "Alone or together: the U.S. and the world": Overall, have organizations such as the World Bank, the International Monetary Fund and the World Trade Organization done more good than harm for poor nations?

- ❑ More good
- ❑ More harm
- ❑ Both equally

9. From 2015's "Sectarianism in the Middle East": In terms of the political situation in the Middle East, which is the most important?

- ❑ Democratic governments, even if there is less stability
- ❑ Stable governments, even if there is less democracy

10. From 2009's "The global financial crisis and its effects": Which of the following statements best describes the future U.S. role in the world?

- ❑ The U.S. will remain the dominant power for the next 10 years
- ❑ The U.S. will remain the dominant power for the foreseeable future
- ❑ The U.S. is no longer the dominant global power

11. From 2007's "U.S.-China economic relations": In terms of the U.S., do you see China's surging economy as:

- ❑ A threat, taking jobs from the U.S.
- ❑ A boon, providing cheap goods to the U.S.
- ❑ Both

12. From 2007's "Russia and 'Putinism'": Considering the following, do you believe that, as a matter of policy, the U.S. should:

12.1 Actively seek a closer and more stable relationship with Russia?

- ❑ Yes
- ❑ No

12.2 Attempt to have friendly relations with the former Russian republics but avoid meddling in Moscow's 'sphere of influence'?

- ❑ Yes
- ❑ No

12.3 Make strong efforts to establish close ties to those former Russian republics that could be most use to the U.S. for security reasons or to promote stable access to fossil fuels for the U.S. and its European allies?

- ❑ Yes
- ❑ No

13. From 2014's "Syria's Refugee Crisis": In general, do you support or oppose Western countries sending arms and military supplies to anti-government groups in Syria?

- ❑ Support strongly
- ❑ Support somewhat
- ❑ Oppose somewhat
- ❑ Oppose strongly
- ❑ Not sure

Topic 1. Refugees and Global Migration

1. Have you engaged in any of the following activities related to the "Refugees and Global Migration?" topic? Mark all that you have done or mark none of the above.

- ❑ Read the article on global migration in the 2019 Great Decisions briefing book
- ❑ Discussed the article on global migration with a Great Decisions discussion group
- ❑ Discussed the article on global migration with friends and family
- ❑ Followed news related to global migration
- ❑ Taken a class in which you learned about issues related to global migration
- ❑ Have or had a job related to global migration
- ❑ None of the above

2. How interested would you say you are in issues related to global migration?

- ❑ Very interested
- ❑ Somewhat interested
- ❑ Not too interested
- ❑ Not at all interested

3. To what extent do you think migrants, especially refugees and asylum-seekers, pose a threat to the host country's security?

- ❑ Major threat
- ❑ Minor threat
- ❑ No threat

4a. Do you think global migration has a positive, negative, or neutral effect on the culture of the host country?

- ❑ Positive
- ❑ Negative
- ❑ Neutral

4b. Do you think global migration has a positive, negative, or neutral effect on the economy of the host country?

- ❑ Positive
- ❑ Negative
- ❑ Neutral

4c. Do you think global migration has a positive, negative, or neutral effect on the security of the host country?

- ❑ Positive
- ❑ Negative
- ❑ Neutral

5. Do countries like Germany and the United States with the resourcees to take in migrants like refugees and asylum-seekers have a resposibility to do so?

- ❑ Yes, countries with resources have a responsibility to take in refugees and asylum-seekers.
- ❑ No, countries with resources do not have responsibility to take in refugees and asylum seekers.

6a. Do you believe there should be a limit on how many global migrants can settle in the United States per year?

- ❑ Yes, migration should be limited
- ❑ No, migration should not be limited.

6b. In general, do you believe all countries should limit on how many global migrants can settle in their country per year?

- ❑ Yes, migration should be limited
- ❑ No, migration should not be limited.

7. Do you believe that migration is a global "crisis"?

- ❑ Yes
- ❑ No

8. To what extent do you think it is important to consider what country or region migrants are coming from when approving their stay in new countries?

- ❑ Very important
- ❑ Somewhat important
- ❑ Not too important
- ❑ Not important at all

9. Do you think the U.S. has a responsibility to accept refugees from Syria into the country, or do you think the U.S. does not have a responsibility to do this?

- ❑ The U.S. has a responsibility to accept refugees from Syria
- ❑ The U.S. does not have a responsibility to accept refugees from Syria

10. President Trump initiated a travel ban for people from seven countries including Iran, Iraw, Syria, and Yemen. The ban also includes restrictions on refugees until enhanced vetting procedures are put in place. Do you think a ban on travel from these seven countries is necessary as a safeguard against terrorism until enhanced vetting procedures can be put into place, is unnecessary because it goes against American principles and travel can become more secure as vetting procedures are improved, or, do you not know enough about this issue to have an opinion at this time?

- ❑ The travel ban is necessary
- ❑ The travel ban is unnecessary
- ❑ Not sure

11. Would you like to share any other thoughts with us about global migration? If so, please use the space below.

. . . .

. . . .

. . . .

. . . .

Topic 2. The Middle East: Regional Disorder

1. Have you engaged in any of the following activities related to the "The Middle East: Regional Disorder" topic? Mark all that you have done or mark none of the above.

- ❑ Read the article on the Middle East in the 2019 Great Decisions briefing book
- ❑ Discussed the article on the Middle East with a Great Decisions discussion group
- ❑ Discussed the article on the Middle East with friends and family
- ❑ Followed news related to the Middle East
- ❑ Taken a class in which you learned about issues related to the Middle East
- ❑ Have or had a job related to the Middle East
- ❑ Traveled to the Middle East
- ❑ None of the above

2. How interested would you say you are in issues related to the Middle East?

- ❑ Very interested
- ❑ Somewhat interested
- ❑ Not too interested
- ❑ Not at all interested

3. After reading this article, which of these four do you think is the key issue faced by countries in the Middle East?

- ❑ Relations with neighbors
- ❑ Global Relations
- ❑ Terrorism
- ❑ War

4. Consider the following, do you believe that, as a matter of policy, the U.S. should...

4.1. Actively seek to benefit ourselves and our allies in the Middle East?

- ❑ Yes
- ❑ No

4.2. Serve as an outside party to help settle disputes between countries in the Middle East?

- ❑ Yes
- ❑ No

4.3. Have no role or influence in the Middle East at all?

- ❑ Very effective
- ❑ Somewhat effective
- ❑ Not too effective
- ❑ Not effective at all

5. Since the "Arab Spring" in 2011, in your opinion has the Middle East,

- ❑ Become More Democratic
- ❑ Become Less Democratic
- ❑ About the same as it was

6. After reading the article, what is your opinion on how the role of the U.S. has affected the Middle East?

- ❑ Positive
- ❑ Negative
- ❑ Mixed
- ❑ Neither

7. To what extent do you agree with the Trump Administration's decision to move the U.S. embassy to Jerusalem?

- ❑ Strongly agree
- ❑ Somewhat agree
- ❑ Somewhat disagree
- ❑ Strongly disagree

8. To what extent do you agree that the United States should continue selling weapons to Saudi Arabia?

- ❑ Strongly agree
- ❑ Somewhat agree
- ❑ Somewhat disagree
- ❑ Strongly disagree

9. To what extent do you agree that the United States should pressure Saudi Arabia to end the war in Yemen?

- ❑ Strongly agree
- ❑ Somewhat agree
- ❑ Somewhat disagree
- ❑ Strongly disagree

10. To what extent do you favor or oppose moving the U.S. Embassy in Israel from Tel Aviv to Jerusalem?

- ❑ Strongly favor
- ❑ Somewhat favor
- ❑ Somewhat oppose
- ❑ Strongly oppose

11. Would you like to share any other thoughts with us about the Middle East? If so, please use the space below.

. . . .

. . . .

. . . .

Topic 3. Nuclear negotiations: Back to the Future?

1. Have you engaged in any of the following activities related to the "Nuclear Negotiations: Back to the Future?" topic? Mark all that you have done or mark none of the above.

- ❑ Read the article on nuclear negotiations in the 2019 Great Decisions briefing book
- ❑ Discussed the article on nuclear negotiations with a Great Decisions discussion group
- ❑ Discussed the article on nuclear negotiations with friends and family
- ❑ Followed news related to nuclear negotiations
- ❑ Taken a class in which you learned about issues related to nuclear negotiations
- ❑ Have or had a job related to nuclear negotiations
- ❑ None of the above

2. How interested would you say you are in issues related to nuclear negotiations?

- ❑ Very interested
- ❑ Somewhat interested
- ❑ Not too interested
- ❑ Not at all interested

3a. To what extent do you think North Korea's nuclear program poses a threat to the United States?

- ❑ Major threat
- ❑ Minor threat
- ❑ No threat

3b. To what extent do you think North Korea's nuclear program poses a threat to the world?

- ❑ Major threat
- ❑ Minor threat
- ❑ No threat

4. How satisfied have you been with the way the United States interacts diplomatically with North Korea?

- ❑ Very satisfied
- ❑ Somewhat satisfied
- ❑ Somewhat dissatisfied
- ❑ Very dissatisfied

5. Do you think there is a possibility of nuclear war in the near future?

- ❑ Yes
- ❑ No
- ❑ Unsure

6. How confident do you feel in the United States' diplomatic ability to negotiate nuclear power and weapons with other countries?

- ❑ Very confident
- ❑ Somewhat confident
- ❑ Not too confident
- ❑ Not confident at all

7. Do you think current nuclear negotiation issues may lead to a new cold war with Russia?

- ❑ Yes
- ❑ No
- ❑ Maybe

8. In your opinion, is the development of nuclear weapons by other countries always a negative or malicious action?

- ❑ Yes
- ❑ No
- ❑ Maybe

9. At the summit on June 12 between President Trump and North Korean leader Kim Jong-Un and subsequent negotiations, do you think North Korea has agreed to give up its nuclear weapons?

- ❑ Yes
- ❑ No

10. Overall, do you think that the United States gained more from the summit, North Korea gained more, or do you think both countries gained about the same amount from the summit?

- ❑ The United States gained more from the summit
- ❑ North Korea gained more from the summit
- ❑ Both countries gained about the same from the summit

11. Do you think it is more important to avoid war with North Korea, or do you think it is more important to take away North Korea's nuclear weapons?

- ❑ More important to avoid war with North Korea
- ❑ More important to take away North Korea's nuclear weapons

12. Would you like to share any other thoughts with us about nuclear negotiations? If so, please use the space below.

. . . .

. . . .

Topic 4. The Rise of Populism in Europe

1. Have you engaged in any of the following activities related to the "The Rise of Populism in Europe" topic? Mark all that you have done or mark none of the above.

- ❑ Read the article on populism in Europe in the 2018 Great Decisions briefing book
- ❑ Discussed the article on populism in Europe with a Great Decisions discussion group
- ❑ Discussed the article on populism in Europe with friends and family
- ❑ Followed news related to populism in Europe
- ❑ Taken a class in which you learned about issues related to populism in Europe
- ❑ Have or had a job related to populism in Europe
- ❑ Traveled to Europe
- ❑ None of the above

2. How interested would you say you are in issues related to populism in Europe?

- ❑ Very interested
- ❑ Somewhat interested
- ❑ Not too interested
- ❑ Not at all interested

3. Are you concerned that populism is a threat to the European Union?

- ❑ Very concerned
- ❑ Somewhat concerned
- ❑ Not too concerned
- ❑ Not concerned at all

4. Do you think that populism in the European Union is a threat to the United States?

- ❑ Major threat
- ❑ Minor threat
- ❑ No threat

5. Do you think the rise of populism in Europe leads to higher incidences of terrorism in the European Union?

- ❑ Absolutely
- ❑ Somewhat
- ❑ Unsure
- ❑ Not likely
- ❑ Not at all

6. How likely do you think it is that populism will become a dominant ideology in political parties across the European Union?

- ❑ Very likely
- ❑ Somewhat likely
- ❑ Not too likely
- ❑ Not likely at all

7. How likely do you think it is that a wave of populism will spread to the United States?

- ❑ Very likely
- ❑ Somewhat likely
- ❑ Not too likely
- ❑ Not likely at all

8. How likely do you think it is that a wave of populism will spread across the world?

- ❑ Very likely
- ❑ Somewhat likely
- ❑ Not too likely
- ❑ Not likely at all

9. Question: How likely are you to agree or disagree with the following statement: It is very important to have been born in the U.S. to truly be "one of us"?

- ❑ Favorable
- ❑ Unfavorable

9. Would you like to share any other thoughts with us about populism in Europe? If so, please use the space below.

. . . .

. . . .

Topic 5. Decoding U.S.-China Trade

1. Have you engaged in any of the following activities related to the "Decoding U.S.-China Trade" topic? Mark all that you have done or mark none of the above.

- ❑ Read the article on the U.S. and China in the 2019 Great Decisions briefing book
- ❑ Discussed the article on the U.S. and China with a Great Decisions discussion group
- ❑ Discussed the article on the U.S. and China with friends and family
- ❑ Followed news related to the U.S. and China
- ❑ Taken a class in which you learned about issues related to the U.S. and China
- ❑ Have or had a job related to the U.S. and China
- ❑ Traveled to China
- ❑ None of the above

2. How interested would you say you are in issues related to the U.S. and China?

- ❑ Very interested
- ❑ Somewhat interested
- ❑ Not too interested
- ❑ Not at all interested

3. On September 17, 2018, President Donald Trump announced tariffs on $200 billion worth of Chinese imports, totaling $250 billion worth of tariffs on Chinese products. To what extent do you agree with President Donald Trump's decision to impose tariffs on Chinese imports?

- ❑ Very much agree
- ❑ Somewhat agree
- ❑ Neither agree nor disagree
- ❑ Somewhat disagree
- ❑ Very much disagree

4. Do you think President Trump's tariffs on Chinese imports will protect U.S. jobs?

- ❑ Yes, it will protect U.S. jobs
- ❑ It might protect some U.S. jobs
- ❑ Unsure
- ❑ It might not protect some U.S. jobs
- ❑ It will not protect any U.S. jobs

5. How do you think tariffs between the United States and China impact the global economy?

- ❑ Greatly improve the global economy
- ❑ Somewhat improve the global economy
- ❑ No effect
- ❑ Somewhat weaken the global economy
- ❑ Greatly weaken the global economy

6. How do you think tariffs between the United States and China will impact the United States' economy?

- ❑ Greatly improve the global economy
- ❑ Somewhat improve the global economy
- ❑ No effect
- ❑ Somewhat weaken the global economy
- ❑ Greatly weaken the global economy

7a. Do you think that tariffs between the United States and China could escalate into a trade war?

- ❑ Yes
- ❑ No
- ❑ Maybe

7c. To what extent would you personally affected by a trade war, either through the prices you pay or the business you work for, or would you probably not be affectedy?

- ❑ Positively affected
- ❑ Negatively affected
- ❑ Probably not affected

8. To what extent do you think the recent tariffs between the U.S. and China will affect consumers in the United States?

- ❑ Primarily positively
- ❑ Somewhat positively
- ❑ Somewhat negatively
- ❑ Primarily negatively

9. To what extent do you support or oppose raising tariffs on products imported from China if the tariffs resulted in China raising tariffs on American products

- ❑ Strongly support
- ❑ Somewhat support
- ❑ Somewhat oppose
- ❑ Strongly oppose

10. Would you like to share any other thoughts with us about the U.S. and China? If so, please use the space below.

. . . .

. . . .

. . . .

. . . .

Topic 6. Cyber Conflict and Geopolitics

1. Have you engaged in any of the following activities related to the "Cyber Conflicts and Geopolitics" topic? Mark all that you have done or mark none of the above.

- ❑ Read the article on cybersecurity in the 2019 Great Decisions briefing book
- ❑ Discussed the article on cybersecurity with a Great Decisions discussion group
- ❑ Discussed the article on cybersecurity with friends and family
- ❑ Followed news related to cybersecurity
- ❑ Taken a class in which you learned about issues related to cybersecurity
- ❑ Have or had a job related to cybersecurity
- ❑ None of the above

2. How interested would you say you are in issues related to cybersecurity?

- ❑ Very interested
- ❑ Somewhat interested
- ❑ Not too interested
- ❑ Not at all interested

3. How effective do you think each of the following approaches is to achieving the foreign policy goals of the United States?

- ❑ Strongly agree
- ❑ Somewhat agree
- ❑ Neither agree nor disagree
- ❑ Somewhat disagree
- ❑ Strongly disagree

4. Which area do you think is under the most immediate threat of cyber conflicts?

- ❑ International communications
- ❑ U.S. government communications
- ❑ U.S. elections
- ❑ The U.S. economy

5. In your opinion, what actions should the United States take first to protect itself against cyber conflicts?

- ❑ Push to create international cybersecurity laws
- ❑ Develop stronger <u>defensive</u> mechanisms against cyber-attacks
- ❑ Develop stronger <u>offensive</u> mechanisms to launch cyber-attacks against others
- ❑ Nothing, the United States is adequately protected against cyber threats

6. Do you agree that the government's computer systems and satellite communications, especially in space, should be treated the same as physical territory?

- ❑ Strongly agree
- ❑ Somewhat agree
- ❑ Somewhat disagree
- ❑ Strongly disagree

7. To what extent do you agree with the following statement: The United States is especially at risk for cyber-attacks.

- ❑ Strongly agree
- ❑ Somewhat agree
- ❑ Somewhat disagree
- ❑ Strongly disagree

8. How worried are you that a cyber-attack on US government computers could have a negative impact on you, such as tampering with your Social Security or tax records – very worried, somewhat worried, not too worried, or not at all worried?

- ❑ Very worried
- ❑ Somewhat worried
- ❑ Not too worried
- ❑ Not at all worried

9. Would you like to share any other thoughts with us about U.S. global engagement and the military? If so, please use the space below.

. . . .

. . . .

. . . .

. . . .

Topic 7. The United States and Mexico: Partnership Tested

1. Have you engaged in any of the following activities related to the "The United States and Mexico: Partnership Tested" topic? Mark all that you have done or mark none of the above.

- ❑ Read the article on the U.S. and Mexico in the 2019 Great Decisions briefing book
- ❑ Discussed the article on the U.S. and Mexico with a Great Decisions discussion group
- ❑ Discussed the article on the U.S. and Mexico with friends
  and family
- ❑ Followed news related to the U.S. and Mexico
- ❑ Taken a class in which you learned about issues related to the U.S. and Mexico
- ❑ Have or had a job related to the U.S. and Mexico
- ❑ Traveled to Mexico
- ❑ None of the above

2. How interested would you say you are in issues related to the U.S. and Mexico?

- ❑ Very interested
- ❑ Somewhat interested
- ❑ Not too interested
- ❑ Not at all interested

3. After reading the article, do you think U.S. and Mexico relations have changed for the better, for the worse, or stayed the same?

- ❑ Changed for the better
- ❑ Stayed the same
- ❑ Changed for the worse

4. Do you think Mexico's most recently elected president Andrès Manuel López Obrador and U.S. President Donald Trump's relationship will improve or weaken the two countries' relationship?

- ❑ Improve greatly
- ❑ Improve somewhat
- ❑ Stay the same
- ❑ Weaken somewhat
- ❑ Weaken greatly

5. Do you think President Donald Trump considers Mexico to be a friend or an enemy of the United States?

- ❑ Friend
- ❑ Enemy
- ❑ Not sure

6a. To what extent do you approve or disapprove of the way the United States has been handling the war on drugs?

- ❑ Strongly approve
- ❑ Somewhat approve
- ❑ Neither approve nor disapprove
- ❑ Somewhat disapprove
- ❑ Strongly disapprove

6b. To what extent do you approve or disapprove of the way the United States has been handling immigration?

- ❑ Strongly approve
- ❑ Somewhat approve
- ❑ Neither approve nor disapprove
- ❑ Somewhat disapprove
- ❑ Strongly disapprove

6c. To what extent do you approve or disapprove of the way the United States has been handling border control?

- ❑ Strongly approve
- ❑ Somewhat approve
- ❑ Neither approve nor disapprove
- ❑ Somewhat disapprove
- ❑ Strongly disapprove

7. Generally, do you think American foreign policy has a positive effect on South Africa or a negative effect, or does American foreign policy have no effect on South Africa?

- ❑ Positive effect
- ❑ Negative effect
- ❑ No effect

8. With regards to the relationship between the U.S. and Mexico, which of the following do you think is the biggest issue testing the relationship? (Choose only one)

- ❑ Mass Migration from Central America
- ❑ Drug Cartels
- ❑ Terrorism and Organized Crime
- ❑ NAFTA and Trade
- ❑ Other (Please specify)

9. Recently NAFTA was renegotiated and the new trade deal is called the USMCA. Do you think the USMCA will have a positive impact on the U.S. economy, a negative impact on the U.S. economy, or not much of an impact on the U.S. economy?

- ❑ Positive impact on the U.S. economy
- ❑ Negative impact on the U.S. economy
- ❑ Not much of an impact on the U.S. economy

10. In October 2018, President Trump announced he would send 15,000 U.S. troops to the Mexico border to prevent a migrant caravan from entering the United States. To what extent did you support this decision?

- ❑ Strongly support
- ❑ Somewhat support
- ❑ Neither support nor oppose
- ❑ Somewhat oppose
- ❑ Strongly oppose

11. To what extent do you support or oppose building a wall along the border with Mexico?

- ❑ Strongly support
- ❑ Somewhat support
- ❑ Somewhat oppose
- ❑ Strongly oppose

12. Would you like to share any other thoughts with us about the U.S. and Mexico? If so, please use the space below.

. . . .

. . . .

. . . .

. . . .

. . . .

Topic 8. State of the State Department and Diplomacy

1. Have you engaged in any of the following activities related to the "State of the State Department and Diplomacy" topic? Mark all that you have done or mark none of the above.

- ❑ Read the article on the State Department and diplomacy in the 2019 Great Decisions briefing book
- ❑ Discussed the article on the State Department and diplomacy with a Great Decisions discussion group
- ❑ Discussed the article on the State Department and diplomacy with friends and family
- ❑ Followed news related to the State Department and diplomacy
- ❑ Taken a class in which you learned about issues related to the State Department and diplomacy
- ❑ Have or had a job related to the State Department and diplomacy
- ❑ None of the above

2. How interested would you say you are in issues related to the State Department and diplomacy?

- ❑ Very interested
- ❑ Somewhat interested
- ❑ Not too interested
- ❑ Not at all interested

3. How satisfied have you been with the foreign diplomacy of the State Department?

- ❑ Very satisfied
- ❑ Somewhat satisfied
- ❑ Not too satisfied
- ❑ Not at all satisfied

4. To what extent do you think the State Department's reputation has been affected on the world stage since the 2016 election of Donald Trump?

- ❑ Positively affected
- ❑ Not affected
- ❑ Negatively affected

5. In your opinion, how important is the role of the State Department in foreign policy decision making?

- ❑ Very important
- ❑ Somewhat important
- ❑ Not too important
- ❑ Not important at all

6. To what extent do you agree or disagree that federal departments, like the State Department, have grown too big to be effective?

- ❑ Strongly agree
- ❑ Somewhat agree
- ❑ Neither agree or disagree
- ❑ Somewhat disagree
- ❑ Strongly disagree

7. If you were making up the budget for the federal government this year, would you increase spending, decrease spending or keep spending the same for the State Department and American embassies?

- ❑ Increase spending
- ❑ Decrease spending
- ❑ Keep spending the same

8. Please select which of the following statements comes closer to your opinion:

- ❑ The best way to ensure peace is through military strength
- ❑ Good diplomacy is the best way to ensure peace

9. Would you like to share any other thoughts with us about the State Department and diplomacy? If so, please use the space below.

. . . .

. . . .

. . . .

. . . .

. . . .

. . . .

Become a Member

For nearly a century, members of the Association have played key roles in government, think tanks, academia and the private sector.

Make a Donation

Your support helps the Foreign Policy Association's programs dedicated to global affairs education.

As an active participant in the FPA's Great Decisions program, we encourage you to join the community today's foreign policy thought leaders.

Member—$250

Benefits:

- Free admission to all Associate events (includes member's family)
- Discounted admission for all other guests to Associate events
- Complimentary **Great Decisions** briefing book
- Complimentary issue of FPA's annual ***National Opinion Ballot Report***

Visit us online at

www.fpa.org/membership

Make a fully tax-deductible contribution to FPA's Annual Fund 2019.

To contribute to the Annual Fund 2019, visit us online at **www.fpa.org** or call the Membership Department at

(800) 628-5754 ext. 333

The generosity of donors who contribute $500 or more is acknowledged in FPA's *Annual Report.*

All financial contributions are tax-deductible to the fullest extent of the law under section 501 (c)(3) of the IRS code.

FPA also offers membership at the Sponsor Member and Patron Member levels. To learn more, visit us online at www.fpa.org/membership or call (800) 628-5754 ext. 333.

Return this form by mail to: Foreign Policy Association, 470 Park Avenue South, New York, N.Y. 10016. *Or fax to:* (212) 481-9275.

ORDER ONLINE: WWW.GREATDECISIONS.ORG

OR CALL (800) 477-5836

FOR MEMBERSHIP: WWW.FPA.ORG/MEMBERSHIP

❑ *MR.* ❑ *MRS.* ❑ *MS.* ❑ *DR.* ❑ *PROF.*

NAME ____________________

ADDRESS ____________________

____________________ **APT/FLOOR** ________

CITY ____________ **STATE** ________ **ZIP** ________

TEL ____________________

E-MAIL ____________________

❑ *AMEX* ❑ *VISA* ❑ *MC* ❑ *DISCOVER*

❑ *CHECK (ENCLOSED)*

CHECKS SHOULD BE PAYABLE TO FOREIGN POLICY ASSOCIATION.

CARD NO.

SIGNATURE OF CARDHOLDER

EXP. DATE (MM/YY)

PRODUCT	QTY	PRICE	COST
GREAT DECISIONS 2019 Briefing Book (FPA31691)		$32	
SPECIAL OFFER TEN PACK SPECIAL GREAT DECISIONS 2019 (FPA31688) *Includes 10% discount		$288	
GREAT DECISIONS TELEVISION SERIES GD ON DVD 2019 (FPA31682)		$40	
GREAT DECISIONS 2019 TEACHER'S PACKET (1 Briefing Book, 1 Teacher's Guide and 1 DVD (FPA 31684) E-MAIL: (REQUIRED) ____		$70	
GREAT DECISIONS CLASSROOM-PACKET (1 Teacher's Packet & 30 Briefing Books (FPA31685) E-MAIL: (REQUIRED) ____		$725	
MEMBERSHIP		$250	
ANNUAL FUND 2019 (ANY AMOUNT)			

SUBTOTAL	$
*plus S & H**	$
TOTAL	$

**For details and shipping charges, call FPA's Sales Department at* (800) 477-5836.

Orders mailed to FPA without the shipping charge will be held.